Essential law for information professionals

Paul Pedley

Published by
Facet Publishing
7 Ridgmount Street
London WC1E 7AE

Facet Publishing (formerly Library Association Publishing) is wholly owned by CILIP: the Chartered Institute of Library and Information Professionals.

First published 2003

British Library Cataloguing in Publication Data
A catalogue record for this book is available from the British Library.

ISBN 1-85604-440-8

Typeset in Aldine 401 and Humanist 521 by Facet Publishing.
Printed and made in Great Britain by MPG Books Ltd, Bodmin, Cornwall.

Dedication

This book is dedicated to the memory of Justin Arundale. During what was then The Library Association's Members' Day 2001, Justin approached me about jointly authoring a book on essential law for information professionals, and so this was very much his idea. Tragically Justin died on 12 September 2002. I would very much like to record my thanks to him for his help, advice and encouragement in the early stages of working on the book; and I missed the opportunity that we would otherwise have had of being able to continue that exchange of ideas and thoughts about a topic that both of us had found to be so interesting.

Acknowledgements

The author would like to express his gratitude to Charles Oppenheim of Loughborough University and Chris O'Hare of London Metropolitan University, as well as Jennifer McMartin of MacRoberts solicitors, who all read the text and offered comments and feedback.

Disclaimer

Paul Pedley is not a lawyer and is not able to give legal advice. The contents of this book are intended to raise awareness of key legal issues affecting information professionals, but the book does not constitute legal advice and should not be relied upon in that way.

Contents

List of figures and tables

Freedom of information

Breach of confidence and privacy

Contracts and licensing agreements

Internet and electronic commerce law

Disability discrimination

Table of statutes, etc.

Acts of Parliament

International treaties and conventions

European directives

European regulations

Table of cases

Abbreviations

ALCS	Authors Licensing and Collecting Society
ASA	Advertising Standards Authority
BBC	British Broadcasting Corporation
CAP	Committee of Advertising Practice
CAUCE	Coalition Against Unsolicited Commercial Email
CCTV	Closed Circuit Television
CDPA	Copyright Designs and Patents Act 1988
CILIP	Chartered Institute of Library and Information Professionals
CIPD	Chartered Institute of Personnel and Development
CIQM	Centre for Information Quality Management
CLA	Copyright Licensing Agency
CMA	Computer Misuse Act
CMLR	Common Market Law Reports
CPU	Central Processing Unit
DACS	Design Artists Copyright Society
DDA	Disability Discrimination Act 1995
DPA	Data Protection Act 1998
DSA	Direct Selling Association
EBLIDA	European Bureau of Library, Information and Documentation Associations
EBLR	European Business Law Review
ECDR	European Copyright & Design Reports
ECJ	European Court of Justice
ECMS	Electronic Copyright Management Systems
ECR	European Court Reports
ECUP	European Copyright Users Platform
EEA	European Economic Area
EIIA	European Information Industry Association
EIPR	European Intellectual Property Review
EIR	Environmental Information Regulations
EIRENE	European Information Researchers Network
ERO	Electoral Registration Officer
EU	European Union
EuroCAUCE	European Coalition Against Unsolicited Commercial Email
FAQs	Frequently Asked Questions

FOIA	Freedom of Information Act 2000
FOI(S)A	Freedom of Information (Scotland) Act 2002
FSR	Fleet Street Reports
GATS	General Agreement on Trade in Services
GATT	General Agreement on Tariffs and Trade
GCHQ	Government Communications Headquarters
HEO	Higher Education Officer
HMSO	Her Majesty's Stationery Office
ICANN	Internet Corporation for Assigned Names and Numbers
ICOLC	International Coalition of Library Consortia
ICSTIS	Independent Committee for the Supervision of Standards of Telephone Information Service
IFLA	International Federation of Library Associations
IPR	Intellectual Property Rights
ISP	Internet Service Provider
ITC	Independent Television Commission
JISC	Joint Information Systems Committee
LACA	Libraries and Archives Copyright Alliance
LCD	Lord Chancellor's Department
MSP	Member of the Scottish Parliament
NESLI	National Electronic Site Licence Initiative
NHS	National Health Service
NLA	Newspaper Licensing Society
OECD	Organization for Economic Co-operation and Development
OFT	Office of Fair Trading
OPAC	Online Public Access Catalogue
PA	Publishers Association
PII	Professional Indemnity Insurance
PLS	Publishers Licensing Society
PRO	Public Records Office
RIPA	Regulation of Investigatory Powers Act 2000
RPC	Reports of Patent Cases
RUSA	Reference and User Services Association
SCIP	Society of Competitive Intelligence Professionals
SENDA	Special Educational Needs and Disability Act
SIS	Secret Intelligence Service
SMS	Short Message Service
SPO	Statutory Publications Office

TLR	Times Law Reports
TRIPS	Trade Related Aspects of Intellectual Property
UCC	Universal Copyright Convention
UKOLUG	UK Online User Group
UNESCO	United Nations Educational, Scientific and Cultural Organization
VAT	Value Added Tax
VDU	Visual Display Unit
WIPO	World Intellectual Property Organization
WTO	World Trade Organization

1 General law and background

1.1 Introduction

This chapter provides a brief introduction to the United Kingdom's legal system (1.2), contrasting the common law system (1.2.1), which operates in England and Wales, with the civil law system (1.2.2), which is used in most of continental Europe. It then gives a brief overview of the civil and criminal courts (1.3). Sources of law are briefly outlined (1.4), including both primary sources – statutory material and law reports (1.4.2) – and secondary sources. There is an explanation of how laws are made, following the stages through which a government bill goes before it becomes law (1.4.1). There is also a brief listing of key websites for legal information.

The chapter looks at the law of the European Union (1.5), and then concludes with a brief outline of key legal concepts – what is meant by criminal law (1.6.1), civil law (1.6.2), the law of tort (delict in Scotland) (1.6.3) and the law of contract (1.6.4).

1.2 Legal system

The United Kingdom consists of three distinct jurisdictions, each with its own court system and legal profession: England and Wales, Scotland, and Northern Ireland.

The UK joined the European Economic Community (now the European Union) in 1973, which means that we are required to incorporate European legislation into UK law, and to recognize the jurisdiction of the European Court of Justice in matters of EU law.

When the Labour Party came to power in 1997, they embarked on a number of constitutional reforms. These included a programme of devolved government. We now have a separate Scottish Parliament and Welsh Assembly. Northern Ireland already had its own Assembly

The Scottish Parliament legislates in areas of domestic policy. But matters best dealt with at UK level remain reserved to the UK parliament and government. These include defence, foreign affairs, economic and fiscal policy, social security, employment law, and aspects of transport and energy policy.

The Welsh Assembly has powers to legislate in domestic areas, but this excludes foreign affairs and defence, taxation, overall economic policy, social security and broadcasting. They are only able to pass subordinate legislation – Statutory Instruments – not Acts.

The UK is a signatory of the European Convention on Human Rights[1] and this was incorporated into UK law by the Human Rights Act 1998.

There is no written constitution as such in the UK. The constitutional law of the UK consists of statute law and case law. In addition there are international treaties and conventions to which the UK is a signatory which have binding force.

There are two basic systems of law: the common law system, which is used in England and Wales; and the civil law system, which is used by most of continental Europe and parts of Latin America. The legal systems of England, Wales and Northern Ireland are very similar. Scotland has a hybrid system of civil and common law.

1.2.1   Common law system

English law is called common law because it aims to be the same, whichever court made the decision. It began soon after the Norman Conquest of 1066, when the King and court travelled around the country hearing grievances. The common law system is based on the principle of deciding cases by reference to previous judicial decisions (known as 'precedent'), rather than to written statutes drafted by legislative bodies. For example, the basic concepts of contract law are found in precedent. A body of English law has evolved from the 12th century onwards.

Reported cases present specific problems out of which a point of law is extracted. Formulation of the law is bottom-up from a specific event to a general principle. Judicial decisions accumulate around a particular kind of dispute and general rules or precedents emerge. These precedents are binding on other courts at the same or a lower level in the hierarchy. The same decision must result from another situation in which the material or relevant facts are the same. The law evolves by means of opinion changing as to which facts are relevant; and by novel situations arising.

1.2.2   Civil law system

The civil law system is used by most of continental Europe and parts of Latin America. The law is all written down in statutes in a very logical and organized (codified) way across all the subject areas. In such systems, precedent is not normally recognized as a source of law, although it can be used as a supplementary source. This results in a top-down system of a codified law book, which is based upon broad principles and then broken into legal topics similar to those of the common law countries.

In the civil law system, case law is illustrative, as the court relies more on commentaries from professors and judges published in books and journal articles. The civil law system – which is based on ancient Roman law – arose from many countries being given the Napoleonic code when occupied during the Napoleonic era. Since then national laws have diverged, but remain basically similar.

1.3   Court system

England and Wales, Scotland and Northern Ireland have their own hierarchy of courts, although they are all divided into two sections – criminal and civil.

1.3.1   England and Wales

The lowest criminal courts are the Magistrates Courts, which deal with minor offences. More serious cases are heard in the Crown Court in front of a judge and jury. The Crown Court also hears cases appealed from the Magistrates Courts on factual points. Cases can be appealed on points of law to the High Court (Queen's Bench Division). Appeals against conviction and sentence go to the Court of Appeal (Criminal Division).

Civil cases at first instance are heard in the County Courts for minor claims. More serious cases are dealt with by the High Court, which is divided into three divisions: Queen's Bench, Family and Chancery. Cases may be appealed to the Court of Appeal (Civil Division). The House of Lords is currently the supreme court of appeal, although in June 2003 the Prime Minister announced that a new Supreme Court would be created to replace the existing system of Law Lords operating as a committee of the House of Lords.

Procedure in the civil courts is now governed by the Civil Procedure Rules, which took effect in April 1999, after the Woolf Report 'Access to Justice', which instigated the most wide-ranging changes to civil litigation since the turn of the 20th century. These were developed from a number of overriding objectives: the Rules sought to change the adversarial nature of litigation and to introduce a fairer, faster and cheaper system of civil justice in which the courts exercised more control over the proceedings. Previous rules regarding civil litigation conduct (the Rules of the Supreme Court, known as 'The White Book' and the County Court Rules, known as the 'Green Book') were almost completely replaced by the Civil Procedure Rules, which were an entirely new regime for dealing with civil disputes.

1.3.2   Scotland

There are three levels of court procedure in criminal matters in Scotland. The lowest criminal courts are the District Courts, which are presided over by justices of peace and in some cases stipendiary magistrates. These courts deal with minor offences such as breach of the peace and shoplifting, and their powers to sentence are limited.

Next are the Sheriff Courts, which deal with minor offences (where a sheriff presides), while more serious offences, except murder and rape, are dealt with by a sheriff sitting with a jury. A sheriff sitting alone has limited sentencing powers in comparison to a sheriff sitting with a jury.

The most serious offences in Scotland are heard by the High Court of Justiciary. This is also the final appeal court for all criminal matters in Scotland. The principal forms of civil procedure in Scotland are small claims, summary cause and ordinary procedure in the Sheriff Court, and Court of Session procedure.

Small claims is intended to be simple and cheap and is for all claims under £750. Summary cause is for sums between £750 and £1,500. Ordinary cause procedure and Court of Session procedure are more formal with full written pleadings.

The Outer House of the Court of Session can hear most types of civil case. The Inner House of the Court of Session is generally the court of appeal from the Outer House, sheriffs and certain tribunals. Thereafter appeals in civil cases can be made to the House of Lords. The system of Law Lords operating as a committee of the House of Lords is being replaced by a new Supreme Court.

1.3.3   Northern Ireland

The highest court in Northern Ireland is the Supreme Court of Judicature, which consists of the Court of Appeal, the High Court and the Crown Court. There are then the lower courts: the county courts with criminal and civil jurisdiction, and the magistrates courts. Cases which start in either the Crown Court or the High Court can be appealed to the Court of Appeal in Belfast; and, where leave is given, to the House of Lords. Cases which start in either the county courts or the magistrates courts can only be appealed as far as the Court of Appeal in Belfast; and unlike the equivalent in England and Wales, this is not split into a Civil Division and a Criminal Division.

1.3.4   Tribunals

In addition to the courts there are also a number of specialized tribunals, which hear appeals on decisions made by various public bodies and government departments. Tribunals cover areas such as employment, immigration, social security, tax and land. Three tribunals relate to areas of law covered in this book. The Information Tribunal considers appeals arising from decisions and notices issued by the Information Commissioner under powers granted by the Data Protection Act 1998, the Telecommunications (Data Protection and Privacy) Regulations 1999 [2] and the Freedom of Information Act 2000. It was previously called the Data Protection Tribunal, until its name changed as a result of the Freedom of Information Act 2000.

The Regulation of Investigatory Powers Act 2000 (RIPA) provides for an independent tribunal made up of senior members of the legal profession and appointed by the Queen. The role of the Investigatory Powers Tribunal is to consider all complaints against the Intelligence Services (security service, SIS and GCHQ), and those against law enforcement agencies and public authorities in respect of powers granted by RIPA; and to consider proceedings brought under Section 7 of the Human Rights Act 1998 against the Intelligence Services and law enforcement agencies in respect of these powers.

The other tribunal covered in this book is the Copyright Tribunal (see 2.6).

In March 2003 the government announced[3] a major shake up to create a unified tribunals service in the light of Sir Andrew Leggatt's 'Review of tribunals: one service, one system'.[4] A White Paper was to be published during the course of 2003 outlining the changes which intended to increase accessibility to tribunals, raise customer service standards and improve administration.

1.4   Sources of law

Statutory legislation and case law are the primary sources of law, with text-books, journal articles, encyclopaedias, indices and digests making up a body of secondary sources.

Legislation in the UK can apply to the country as a whole; or, bearing in mind the impact of devolved government, there can also be Scottish legislation, Welsh legislation, and Northern Irish legislation.

United Kingdom primary legislation consists of public and general acts; and local and personal acts – such as ones which are of specific and limited nature – for example, the Land at Palace Avenue, Kensington (Acquisition of Freehold) Act 2002. Acts of parliament typically have a section just before any schedules which is headed 'short title, commencement, extent' and which outlines the short title by which the Act is known; the arrangements for the coming into force of the Act; and whether the Act applies to particular countries.

1.4.1   Progress of UK government legislation

UK government bills can start in either the House of Commons or the House of Lords, although bills whose main purpose is taxation or expenditure start in the House of Commons. Some bills may have been preceded by a consultation document (Green Paper) and/or by a statement of policy (White Paper), although this is optional.

Bills are drafted by lawyers in the Parliamentary Counsel Office, which is part of the Cabinet Office. The daily Order Paper contains a Notice of Presentation of the Bill and this is the first reading of the Bill. The Minister or a government whip then names a day for the Bill's second reading. The Bill is then allocated a Bill number and is printed by The Stationery Office – for example, Legal Deposit Libraries Bill [HC] Bill 26 of Session 2002/03. The text of Bills can also be found on the internet.[5] Explanatory notes are published to accompany the Bill. These normally include a summary of the main purpose of the Bill and a commentary on individual clauses and schedules – for example, Legal Deposit Libraries Bill Explanatory Notes [HC] Bill 26-EN of Session 2002/03.

The second reading debate is announced by the Leader of the House in a Business Statement. The second reading is the time for the House to consider the principles of the Bill. The debate on second reading is printed in

Hansard.[6] After the second reading, the Bill has its Committee stage. This would normally take place in a Standing Committee, but it may be taken in a committee of the whole House or a Special Standing Committee depending on the nature of the Bill.

The next stage is the consideration or report stage. The House can make further amendments to the Bill at that stage, but does not consider the clauses and schedules to which no amendments have been tabled. The final Commons stage of the Bill is the third reading. This enables the House to take an overview of the Bill as amended in committee. No amendments can be made at this stage. Once it has passed its third reading in the Commons, the Bill is then sent to the House of Lords.

The legislative process in the House of Lords is broadly similar to that in the House of Commons. However, there are a few important differences:

1 After the second reading, bills are usually submitted to a committee of the whole House.
2 There is no guillotine, and debate on amendments is unrestricted.
3 Amendments can be made at the third reading as well as at committee and consideration stage.

The House of Lords and House of Commons must finally agree a text of each Bill. In practice, in order for this to happen a Bill can travel backwards and forwards between the two houses several times. If the Lords have not amended a Commons Bill, they must inform the Commons of that fact.

Once the text of a Bill has been approved by both houses, the Bill is then submitted for Royal Assent. Some Acts come into force immediately on Royal Assent, whilst others can be brought into force on a date or dates stated in the Act, or on a date or dates appointed by the Minister by means of commencement orders which can activate either all or part of the Act; or the Act could come into force through a combination of these.

The House of Commons Weekly Information Bulletin can be used in order to monitor the progress of Bills through parliament.

Statutory Instruments are regulations made under the authority of an Act of Parliament. They often provide the detail required for the application of the Statute such as what forms to fill in, the level of fees to be paid or provisions for the commencement of an Act (i.e. when it comes into force).

1.4.2   Law reports

Cases in the courts are reported in numerous series of law reports. Until 1865 in England case reporting was undertaken by private court reporters, and the resultant publications are known as the nominate reports, because they are usually known by the name of the reporter. These have been gathered together in a collection called the English Reports. In 1865 the reporting of cases was systematized by the Incorporated Council of Law Reporting, which started publishing series of reports organized according to the court, collectively known as The Law Reports. These are recognized as being the most authoritative in the hierarchy of reports.

The main series of law reports in England and Wales are:

- The Law Reports 1865– (which is in four separate series: Chancery Division (Ch.), Appeal Cases (AC), Family Division (Fam.), Queen's Bench (QB))
- Weekly Law Reports 1954–
- All England Law Reports 1936– .

In Scotland, the most authoritative reports are produced by a non-profit making body, the Scottish Council of Law Reporting, but most reporting is undertaken by commercial publishing companies.

The main reports are the Session Cases and these commenced in their present form in 1907. Previously, like the English Law Reports, the reports were known by the names of the editor and were collectively referred to as the nominate reports.

The other common reports are:

- Scots Law Times
- Scottish Civil Law Reports 1987–
- Scottish Criminal Case Reports 1981–
- Greens Weekly Digest 1986– .

In Northern Ireland the official law reports are the Northern Ireland Law Reports. There are also the Northern Ireland Judgments Bulletin, the Irish Reports and the Irish Law Times Reports.

In addition, there are many specialized reports covering different areas of law. The most comprehensive list of citations in the UK is Donald Raistrick's *Index to Legal Citations and Abbreviations*.[7]

The starting point for research on English law is Halsbury's Laws of England, and in Scotland it is Stair's Institutions of the Law of Scotland. When using sources of legal information it is vital to make sure that the books, journal articles or web pages you use are up to date, or that at the very least you are aware of the changes that have taken place since they were written. Bear in mind that the law is changing rapidly in the areas covered by this book. The free web-based sources are not normally annotated, amended or hyperlinked, so it is necessary to use commercial subscription services in order to get the most up-to-date information.

There are a number of guides to law libraries and legal research. These include:

Clinch, P. (2000) *Legal Information: what it is and where to find it*, Europa Publications.

Clinch, P. (2001) *Using a Law Library: a student's guide to legal research skills*, 2nd edn, Blackstone Press.

Holborn, G. (2001) *Butterworths Legal Research Guide*, 2nd edn, Butterworths.

Holmes, N. and Venables, D. (1999) *Researching the Legal Web*, 2nd edn, Butterworths.

McKie, S. (1993) *Legal Research: how to find and understand the law*, Cavendish Publishing.

Pester, D. (2003) *Finding Legal Information: a guide to print and electronic resources*, Chandos Publishing.

Thomas, P. A. and Knowles, J. (2001) *Dane & Thomas: how to use a law library*, 4th edn, Sweet & Maxwell.

1.4.3 Websites

1.4.3.1 Parliamentary websites

United Kingdom Parliament www.parliament.uk
Northern Ireland Assembly www.ni-assembly.gov.uk
National Assembly for Wales www.assembly.wales.gov.uk
Scottish Parliament www.scottish.parliament.uk
Tynwald (Parliament of the Isle of Man) www.tynwald.org.im/

1.4.3.2   Government, legislation and law reports

UK Online www.ukonline.gov.uk is a portal to the websites of central government.

HMSO website www.hmso.gov.uk has the texts of statutes and statutory instruments.

TSO (The Stationery Office) www.tso.co.uk is an online index to TSO publications.

Government News Network www.gnn.gov.uk contains press releases of central government departments.

Parliament website for bills www.parliament.uk/bills/bills.cfm.

POLIS (Parliamentary Online Indexing Service) www.polis.parliament.uk contains parliamentary debates.

BAILII (British and Irish Legal Information Institute) www.bailii.org

House of Lords Judicial Office www.parliament.the-stationery-office. co.uk/pa/ld/ldjudinf.htm

Court Service www.courtservice.gov.uk

Scottish Court Service www.scotscourts.gov.uk

Northern Ireland Court Service www.courtsni.gov.uk/

1.4.3.3   Legal information portals

Legal Resources in the UK and Ireland (Delia Venables) www.venables.co.uk/
Sarah Carter's LawLinks http://library.kent.ac.uk/library/lawlinks/

The Statutory Publications Office, an office within the Lord Chancellor's Department (LCD), is producing a Statute Law Database of United Kingdom legislation. The Lord Chancellor's Department is being replaced by the Department for Constitutional Affairs, which will incorporate most of the responsibilities of the former LCD. The database under development currently contains the text of all Acts that were in force on 1 February 1991, and all Acts and printed Statutory Instruments passed since then. It also contains local legislation, both primary and printed secondary. The main task of the SPO editorial team is to apply the effects of amending legislation to primary legislation. The key feature of the central database being maintained by the SPO is that it will provide a historical view of primary legislation for any specific day from the base date of 1 February 1991 and any prospective legislation. However, the database is not yet publicly available, although it has been in the offing for a long time.

1.5   European Union

The European Communities Act 1972 gives European Community legislation 'direct effect' in the United Kingdom.

European law consists of four main strands:

1 *Treaties* are referred to as the 'primary' legislation of the Community as they form the constitution and give the structure of institutions and extent of powers.

   The principles of European law derive from the 1957 Treaty of Rome, but this has been amended by a number of other treaties such as the Maastricht Treaty and the Treaty of Amsterdam.

2 *Regulations* are the principal means by which the Community legislates. They are binding in their entirety. They are directly applicable and do not need to be transposed into national law by the respective member states in order for them to take effect. An example of a regulation would be Regulation (EC) No 1049/2001 regarding public access to European Parliament, Council and Commission documents.

3 *Directives* are the main form of substantive law. They are formulated by the European Commission, where they are subject to extensive consultation and are thereafter passed by a combination of the Parliament and the Council of Ministers. Directives only state the effects to be achieved and many directives leave the practical application to national discretion, so one needs to be aware of the non-harmonized details. Directives only take effect when enacted into national laws, which usually takes several years, although generally a period of implementation is prescribed by each directive.

   Taking the copyright directive 2001/29/EC as an example: the directive was published in the Official Journal on 22 June 2001 and Article 13 of the directive states that 'member states shall bring into force the laws, regulations and administrative provisions necessary to comply with this directive before 22 December 2002.' In fact, the European Commission was keen for the copyright directive to come into force at roughly the same time as the electronic commerce directive, and they therefore said that the time for implementation was 18 months rather than two years.

   With the copyright directive, article 5 on exceptions and limitations is an example of harmonized and non-harmonized details within a directive. Article 5 has one compulsory exception, but then provides for a series of optional exceptions from which member states can choose the ones that they wish to implement. Where there is a compulsory exception, the law is harmonized throughout the European Union; whereas the remaining exceptions are optional and therefore the law is not harmonized because there is scope for each member state to select a different mix of exceptions to implement within their own countries.

The member states of the European Union are Austria, Belgium, Denmark, Finland, France, Germany, Greece, Ireland, Italy, Luxembourg, Netherlands, Portugal, Spain, Sweden and the United Kingdom. In December 2002 the EU agreed to expand to 25 countries by allowing membership for Cyprus, Czech Republic, Estonia, Hungary, Latvia, Lithuania, Malta, Poland, Slovakia and Slovenia.

4 *Decisions* are from the Commission or the Council of Ministers, not from the European Court of Justice. These are generally of restricted application and importance. Normally these are addressed to member states.

1.6   Legal concepts/terminology
1.6.1   Criminal law

A crime is defined as an offence where the state acts against the individual to defend a collective interest. The punishments are fines, probation, community service (which are seen as alternatives to custody) or a prison sentence. Criminal law is the branch of law which defines crimes and fixes punishments for them. Also included in criminal law are rules and procedures for preventing and investigating crimes and prosecuting criminals, as well as the regulations governing the constitution of courts, the conduct of trials, the organization of police forces and the administration of penal institutions. In general, the criminal law of most modern societies classifies crimes as: offences against the safety of the society; offences against the administration of justice; offences against the public welfare; offences against property; and offences threatening the lives or safety of people.

1.6.2   Civil law

Civil law deals with disputes between individuals or organizations. The state's role is simply to provide the means by which they can be resolved. This is a different meaning to the civil law system used in most of continental

Europe. Punishment usually consists of either damages or restitution – injunction/interdict.

1.6.3 Tort (England, Wales, Northern Ireland) / Delict (Scotland)

When a contract (1.6.4) cannot apply, third-party agreements called torts might apply. These encompass mainly obligations and duties of care. These duties of care are owed to those foreseeably affected by one's actions, balanced by a concern not to extend this to remote and generalized effects. A standard test of reasonableness has to be applied, whereby you must take reasonable care to avoid all acts and omissions which you can reasonably foresee would be likely to injure your neighbour.

Torts are essentially civil wrongs that provide individuals with a cause of action for damages in respect of the breach of a legal duty. They include negligence, and as far as information professionals are concerned, professional negligence covers things like the accuracy of information; and they would also include defamation. In deciding whether an information professional's actions were negligent, they would be judged against the actions of their fellow professionals. (Chapter 8 deals in more detail with professional negligence as it relates to information professionals.)

Basically, rights in tort are civil rights of action which are available for the recovery of unliquidated damages by persons who have sustained injury or loss from acts or statements or omissions of others in breach of duty or contravention of a right imposed or conferred by law, rather than by contract. Damage includes economic as well as physical damage.

1.6.4 Contract law

A contract, in law, is an agreement that creates an obligation binding upon the parties involved. It is a promise or set of promises which the law will enforce. To constitute a valid contract, there must be two or more separate and definite parties to the contract. There must be an offer, acceptance, intention to create legal relations (and capacity to do so) and consideration (although consideration is not required in Scotland) supporting those promises. There has to be a mutual exchange of promises for a contract to arise.

In general, contracts may be either oral or written. Certain classes of contracts, however, in order to be enforceable, must be written and signed. These include contracts involving the sale and transfer of real estate, and contracts to guarantee or answer for the miscarriage, debt or default of another person.

In England, Wales and Northern Ireland, the Supply of Goods and Services Act 1982 implies terms into a contract, such as implying that the service must be carried out with reasonable care and skill. Customers in Scotland continue to rely on their common law rights. This Act is particularly relevant to information professionals. However, please note that the parties can agree that the implied rights should not apply to the provision of the service but any exclusion or restriction shall be subject to the terms of the Unfair Contract Terms Act 1977.

Under the Unfair Contract Terms Act 1977 a person cannot exclude or restrict his liability for the death or personal injury resulting from negligence. He can exclude or restrict liability for other loss or damage resulting from negligence only if the exclusion clauses satisfy a test of reasonableness. It would be for the party seeking to impose a contract term to demonstrate to the court that it was reasonable, should they be challenged.

The Unfair Terms in Consumer Contracts Regulations 1999[8] provide that a term which has not been individually negotiated in a consumer contract is unfair if, contrary to the requirement of good faith, it causes a significant imbalance in the rights and obligations of the parties to the detriment of the consumer.

Chapter 9 considers contracts and licensing in more detail, especially as they relate to the work of information professionals, such as contracts for searching online databases or having access to proprietary information.

1.7   Summary

In this chapter we have looked at the different types of legal system – the common law system and the civil law system, and also the court system. The chapter outlined primary and secondary sources of law (1.4), and the importance of ensuring that the information used is totally up to date. As the United Kingdom is a member of the European Union, the chapter also looked at the role of EU law (1.5), and finally concluded with a brief outline of key legal concepts: criminal law (1.6.1), civil law (1.6.2), the law of tort/delict (1.6.3) and the law of contract (1.6.4)).

It is important to recognize that where legal matters are concerned, there are very few clearly right or wrong answers, hence the reason for many issues having to be resolved in court. Dealing with legal issues is often a matter of risk management. Bearing in mind that it isn't always clear whether something is considered to be legal, how can organizations and individuals minimize the risk of legal action being taken out against them?

Throughout the United Kingdom, the law is uniform in many respects. The laws of England and Wales and Northern Ireland are particularly close, while there are a number of differences with the law of Scotland. This book is based upon the laws of the United Kingdom, and whilst it will be of interest to information professionals working in other parts of the world, the reader should bear in mind that it is written from a UK perspective.

The next chapter deals with the topic of copyright law – an area that is extremely complex, and one which information professionals have to grapple with almost every day.

Notes and references

1   Available at www.hri.org/docs/ECHR50.html#C.SecI
2   Telecommunications (Data Protection and Privacy) Regulations 1999: SI 1999/2093
3   LCD press notice 106/03 of 11 March 2003: 'Government announces modernised tribunal service in the greatest shake-up for forty years.'
4   Available at www.tribunals-review.org.uk
5   Available at www.parliament.the-stationery-office.co.uk/pa/pabills.htm
6   Available at www.parliament.uk/hansard/hansard.cfm
7   Raistrick, D. (1994) *Index to Legal Citations and Abbreviations*, 2nd edn, Bowker Saur.
8   SI 1999/2083

2 Copyright

Author's note (regarding implementation of the copyright directive)

The UK government, along with all EU member states, was obliged to implement copyright directive 2001/29/EC 'on the harmonization of certain aspects of copyright and related rights in the information society' within their national laws by 22 December 2002. The UK did not meet this deadline, and at the time of writing [July 2003] the long-awaited Statutory Instrument had not been published. Indeed, the Patent Office were unable to confirm the title that the Statutory Instrument would use. The UK implementing measure is referred to a number of times in the text of the book, and because of a lack of SI number or title, the convention used is 'SI 2003/xxxx'. The comments on the Statutory Instrument are therefore largely based on the information given in the consultation paper issued by the Patent Office on 7 August 2002. For the precise wording of the legislation, readers should check the text of the statutory instrument once it has been published.

2.1 Introduction

Information professionals have a duty to foster the fullest possible access to information for their users whilst also respecting the intellectual property protections afforded to people for their creativity and innovation. This chapter outlines the general principles of copyright law (2.2). It then considers the legal and regulatory environment within which we operate (2.4), which includes international treaties and conventions, European directives, and UK statute law. These are supplemented by case law, which can help to clarify particular points of law. The exceptions or permitted acts are considered (2.5), in particular fair dealing and library privilege. It is necessary to consider licensing where people wish to copy beyond the extents and purposes that are set out in statute law, and the chapter looks at the licences available through the Copyright Licensing Agency, Newspaper Licensing Agency, Design Artists Copyright Society, Ordnance Survey and HMSO (2.6). The application of copyright law in the electronic environment is considered (2.7), including how copyright applies to the internet, the question of deep linking, and the licensing of electronic resources. The implications of the database regulations are outlined (2.7.2), and how they impact upon not only electronic databases, but also hard-copy ones such as reference directories. Finally, a number of ethical and professional issues are considered (2.8), including the conflict stemming from the need to provide access to information whilst recognizing the need to protect copyright.

2.2   General principles

Copyright is the right to prevent the copying of work which has been created by intellectual effort. It protects information and ideas where these have been reduced into the form of a 'work'. Copyright is augmented by 'database right' – a *sui generis*[1] right to prevent extraction and re-utilization of all or a substantial part of a database.

Copyright subsists in

- original literary, dramatic, musical or artistic works
- sound recordings, films or broadcasts
- the typographical arrangement of published editions.

It is said that copyright 'subsists' rather than 'exists' because copyright cannot exist by itself but only within the work which has been created (see also Figure 2.1).

Books
Articles
Photographs
Films and videos
Sound recordings
Artistic works
Musical works
Computer programs
Databases
Typographical arrangements

Fig. 2.1   *What is protected by copyright?*

Article 27 of the Universal Declaration of Human Rights[2] says:

> (1) Everyone has the right freely to participate in the cultural life of the community, to enjoy the arts and to share in scientific advancement and its benefits.
>
> (2) Everyone has the right to the protection of the moral and material interests resulting from any scientific, literary or artistic production of which he is the author.

There are clearly tensions between the need to give authors protection for their work and the need to allow people access to material for the betterment of society, to promote education, science and scholarship. That is why the monopoly rights that the law confers on the owners of copyright have a number of built-in safeguards. These include a number of exceptions to copyright such as fair dealing (see 2.5.1) and limiting the term that copyright lasts before works enter the public domain.

Copyright is automatic. It is not necessary to go through a registration process before copyright can be claimed. Legal deposit[3] is not a pre-requisite for claiming copyright. One myth is that if there is no copyright symbol on a work then it is not protected by copyright. Whilst it is true that the copyright symbol © is not necessary for a work to have copyright protection, it is, however, advisable to put a copyright notice on a work that you create as a reminder to those who make use of that work of your rights. You could use the copyright notice to tell potential users the precise level of copying that you are willing to permit. For example:

> You are allowed to redistribute this newsletter in its entirety, on a non-commercial basis. This includes making it available (in full and as published) on your corporate intranet. However, individual sections may not be copied and/or distributed without the prior written agreement of the publishers.

In general, the author of a work is the first owner of any copyright in it. However, where the work is made by an employee in the course of their employment, the employer is the first owner of any copyright in the work subject to any express written agreement to the contrary. This only applies to employees, not to contractors, so the mere fact that a work has been commissioned and paid for does not give the ownership of the copyright to the commissioning party. It is important, therefore, to ensure that appropriate mechanisms are in place to deal with the ownership of the rights in content. For example, an organization may wish to publish information on a website. That information may come from a number of sources such as external developers, consultants and internal employees. The organization in question will therefore need to be sure that it secures assignments of rights from any third parties, and they should also be certain that any employees created the content during the course of their employment. It is all too often the case in practice that assignments are not obtained, which can cause problems if the organization wishes to sell, copy or license any of the copyright. It is therefore of the utmost importance that organizations regularly audit their rights to ascertain any ownership difficulties.

2.3 Economic and moral rights

Copyright owners have a number of exclusive rights to their works. The 'economic' rights[4] that a copyright owner has are the rights to:

- copy the work (which includes storing the work electronically)
- issue copies of the work to the public
- rent or lend the work to the public
- perform, show or play the work in public
- communicate the work to the public
- make an adaptation or translation of the work.

If anyone other than the copyright owner does any of these activities without permission or licence, unless it is under one of the statutory exceptions, that would be a primary infringement of the copyright.

There are also some acts which could be said to be secondary infringements (ss22–6):

- importing an infringing copy
- possessing or dealing with an infringing copy
- providing the means for making infringing copies
- permitting the use of premises for infringing performance
- providing apparatus for infringing performance.

Copyright owners also have a number of moral rights. These include:

* the right of paternity
* the right of integrity
* the right to object to false attribution.

The right of paternity is the right of the author to be identified as such. This right of attribution or paternity is not infringed unless the author has asserted their right to be identified as the author of the work. That is why you will often find a statement at the beginning of a book along the lines of 'Joe Bloggs asserts his right to be identified as the author of this work in accordance with the terms of the Copyright, Designs and Patents Act 1988 (CDPA).'

The right of integrity is the right of the author to prevent or object to derogatory treatment of their work. The right to object to false attribution is the right of persons not to have literary, dramatic or musical works falsely attributed to them.

2.4   Legislative framework

The legislative and regulatory framework for UK copyright consists of four key components. These are:

* international treaties and conventions to which the UK is a signatory
* European directives which the UK as a member state of the EU is obliged to implement
* UK legislation in the form of Acts of Parliament and Statutory Instruments
* supplementary case law.

2.4.1   Berne Copyright Convention

The main copyright convention is the Berne Copyright Convention for the protection of literary and artistic works, to which most countries are signed up. The original agreement was drawn up in 1886 and since then there have been a number of revisions, the most recent revision dating from 1979. Under the convention authors are entitled to some basic rights of protection for their intellectual output. Berne also recognizes the need for people to have access to protected works, and so it allows exceptions and limitations to the exclusive rights (see Figure 2.2), although these must pass a three-step test (see Figure 2.3).

• translation	(article 8)
• reproduction	(article 9)
• public performance	(article 11)
• communication to the public	(article 11)
• recording of musical works	
• broadcasting	(article 11)
• cinematic adaptations	(article 14)
• adaptations, arrangements and other alterations	(article 12)
• moral rights	(article 6)

Fig. 2.2   *Exclusive rights set out in the Berne convention (as amended in Paris, 1971)*

1	that the exception only applies in special (defined) cases
2	provided that such reproduction does not conflict with the normal exploitation of the work
3	and does not unreasonably prejudice the legitimate interests of the author

Fig. 2.3   *Berne three-step test*

The Berne convention is based upon three principles:

1 Reciprocal protection – among Berne Union members, each state must protect the works of others to the same level as in their own countries, provided the term accorded is not longer than that for its own works.
2 Minimum standards for duration and scope of rights – author's life plus 50 years or, for anonymous works, 50 years after making available to the public.
3 Automatic protection, with no registration.

The UK is a signatory to the Berne Convention.

2.4.2   Universal Copyright Convention

The Universal Copyright Convention (UCC) was agreed at a 1952 UNESCO conference in Geneva. The main features of the convention are that:

1 Works of a given country must carry a copyright notice to secure protection in other UCC countries – it was this convention that established the copyright symbol ©.

2 Foreign works must be treated as though they are national works – the 'national treatment' principle.

3 A minimum term of protection of life plus 25 years.

4 The author's translation rights may be subjected to compulsory licensing.

The two conventions are not mutually exclusive, and the UK is also a member of the Universal Copyright Convention.

2.4.3   TRIPS

The World Trade Organization (WTO) signed an agreement in 1994 which had an annex known as TRIPS[5] – Trade Related Aspects of Intellectual Property. This is designed to ensure that intellectual property rights do not themselves become barriers to legitimate trade.

The three main features of the agreement are:

- the minimum standards of protection to be provided by each member on:
  — the subject-matter to be provided
  — the rights to be conferred
  — permissible exceptions to those rights
  — the minimum duration of protection
- the production of general principles applicable to all intellectual property rights (IPR) enforcement procedures in order that rights holders can effectively enforce their rights
- the agreement that disputes between WTO members about TRIPS obligations will be subject to the WTO's dispute settlement procedures.

The TRIPS agreement is often described as one of the three 'pillars' of the WTO, alongside the agreements on trade in goods (GATT) and trade in services (GATS).

There is a TRIPS council comprising all WTO members which is responsible for monitoring the operation of the agreement and how members comply with their obligations to it. The UK is a signatory of TRIPS.

2.4.4   WIPO Copyright Treaty

The World Intellectual Property Organization (WIPO) is a United Nations body which is responsible for administering many of the international conventions on intellectual property. In December 1996 around 100 countries adopted the WIPO Copyright Treaty and the WIPO Performances and Phonograms Treaty. The WIPO Copyright Treaty of 1996 introduced a new right of communication to the public, and it also gave legal protection and legal remedies against circumvention of technological measures, in order to prevent unauthorized access to works. The European directive on the harmonization of certain aspects of copyright and related rights [2001/29/EC] implemented the 1996 WIPO treaties in the European Union.

2.4.5   European directives on copyright matters

Changes to UK copyright law are increasingly often the result of developments at a European level. The aim of the European Commission is to harmonize copyright laws in the member states in order to achieve a level playing field for copyright protection across national borders. This will allow the Single Market to become a reality for new products and services containing intellectual property. There have been a number of European directives on copyright over the past decade or so:

2.4.5.1   On the legal protection of computer programs [91/250/EEC]

Computer programs are protected as literary works, which gives them the full protection of the Berne Copyright Convention. The term 'computer programs' includes preparatory design work leading to the development of a computer program provided that the nature of the preparatory work is such that a computer program can result from it at a later stage.

2.4.5.2   On rental and lending right [92/100/EEC]

Authors and performers have an exclusive right to authorize or prohibit rental and lending of their works. 'Rental' means making available for use for a limited period of time and for direct or indirect economic or commercial advantage. 'Lending' means making available for use for a limited period of time and *not* for direct or indirect economic or commercial advantage.

2.4.5.3   Harmonizing the term of copyright protection [93/98/EEC]

This extended the term of protection for copyright literary, dramatic, musical and artistic works and films from 50 to 70 years after the year of the death of the author; and gave a new right – publication right – to works in which copyright had expired and which had not previously been published

2.4.5.4   On the legal protection of databases [96/9/EEC]

This introduced the new form of *sui generis* property protection for databases to prevent unfair extraction and re-utilization of their contents.

2.4.5.5   On the harmonization of certain aspects of copyright and related rights [2001/29/EC]

This enabled the EU and its member states to ratify the provisions of the two 1996 WIPO treaties – the Copyright Treaty and the Performers and Producers of Phonograms Treaty – and updated the law to incorporate new technology, including internet practices.

2.4.5.6   On the resale right for the benefit of the author of an original work of art (droit de suite) [2001/84/EC]

Provides an artist with a right to receive a royalty based on the price obtained for any resale of an original work of art, subsequent to the first transfer by the artist. The right does not apply, however, to resales between individuals acting in their private capacity, without the participation of an art market professional; and to resales by persons acting in their private capacity to museums which are not for profit and are open to the public.

2.4.6   UK legislation

The principal UK copyright legislation is the Copyright, Designs and Patents Act 1988 (CDPA), which came into force on 1 August 1989. The CDPA 1988 has been amended on a number of occasions – by the Broadcasting Acts of 1990 and 1996, the Copyright, etc. and Trade Marks (Offences and Enforcement) Act 2002, the Copyright (Visually Impaired Persons) Act 2002 (not yet brought into force at the time of writing – July 2003) – and by secondary legislation (Statutory Instruments) which interpret and modify it:

- SI 1992/3233 – The Copyright (Computer Programs) Regulations 1992
- SI 1995/3297 – The Duration of Copyright and Rights in Performances Regulations 1995
- SI 1996/2967 – The Copyright and Related Rights Regulations 1996

- SI 1997/3032 – The Copyright and Rights in Databases Regulations 1997
- SI 2000/1175 – The Conditional Access (Unauthorised Decoders) Regulations 2000
- SI 2003/xxxx implementing directive 2001/29/EC.

All of these Statutory Instruments implement European Union directives.

The Patent Office is responsible for developing and carrying out UK policy on all aspects of intellectual property. They develop UK law on intellectual property, and promote UK interests in international efforts to harmonize and simplify intellectual property law. The Intellectual Property and Innovation Directorate of the Patent Office deals with policy on copyright, rights in performances and design right.

2.4.7 Supplementary case law

No matter how well a piece of legislation is drafted, there will always be 'grey' areas of interpretation or situations requiring further clarification about how the law applies to a particular set of circumstances, so the fourth component in the regulatory and legislative regime for copyright is that of case law. Under the English common law tradition, case law plays a key role.

If the reader wants to find out more about case law relating to copyright, there isn't one handy place where all copyright case law can be found. One problem is that in many situations legal disputes might never reach court; or even where they do, the parties might reach an out-of-court settlement, which would mean that no legal precedent is set. There are, however, a number of specialized series of law reports in the intellectual property field. These include:

- Fleet Street Reports (FSR) [Sweet & Maxwell]
- European Copyright and Design Reports (ECDR) [Sweet & Maxwell].

Matters relating to EU law are adjudicated by the European Court of Justice (ECJ) and the Court of First Instance, and these are published in the Common Market Law Reports (CMLR) [Sweet & Maxwell] and the official Report of Cases brought before the ECJ, which are commonly known as European Court Reports (ECR). A number of the broadsheets publish law reports such as *The Times*, *The Independent*, and *The Daily Telegraph*.

Other useful sources of information on copyright case law include the journal *European Intellectual Property Review* (EIPR) [Sweet & Maxwell], a book entitled *Cases and Materials on Intellectual Property*[6] and commercial online information systems such as Westlaw, Lexis, and Lawtel.

2.5   Acts permitted in relation to copyright works

Chapter III of the CDPA covers acts permitted in relation to copyright works, otherwise known as exceptions. All of the UK's copyright exceptions have to conform to directive 2001/29/EC on the harmonization of certain aspects of copyright and related rights in the information society. Article 5(5) of the directive states that 'the exceptions and limitations . . . shall only be applied in certain special cases which do not conflict with a normal exploitation of the work or other subject matter and do not unreasonably prejudice the legitimate interests of the author.' This is based on the Berne three-step test (see Figure 2.3).

The Patent Office took the view that they would not introduce the test as such into UK law as a general constraint on exceptions, but that they would continue with the existing practice in the CDPA of using the test as a standard in framing exceptions to rights. In other words, all exceptions to copyright must first pass the Berne three-step test before they can be considered for possible inclusion in statute law, but there is no need for the wording of the three-step test to appear before each exception in the legislation.

The main copyright exceptions of interest to librarians have been fair dealing for research and private study and library privilege. Both of these have had their scope narrowed by SI 2003/xxxx. This statutory instrument implements directive 2001/29/EC in UK law and it narrows both the exception of fair dealing for the purposes of research or private study and library privilege, so that they now relate only to copying undertaken for non-commercial purposes.

2.5.1   Fair dealing

Fair dealing is effectively a 'defence' against accusations of infringement rather than a licence to copy (see Figure 2.4). Following the implementation of directive 2001/29/EC into UK law through SI 2003/xxxx, Section 29(1) of the CDPA says that 'Fair dealing with a literary, dramatic, musical or artistic work for the purposes of research for a non-commercial purpose does not infringe any copyright in the work provided that it is accompanied by a sufficient acknowledgement', while section 29(1C) says that 'Fair dealing with a literary, dramatic, musical or artistic work for the purposes of private study does not infringe any copyright in the work.'

The problem is that the CDPA does not define what is meant by the phrase 'fair dealing'. It is therefore left for the courts to decide on a case-by-case basis whether or not a particular instance of copying was fair – a point made by Lord Denning in Hubbard v. Vosper [1972] 2 QB 84 CA, which pre-dates the CDPA.

1	Fair dealing has not been defined by statute.
2	It must fit into one of the following three categories:
	• research for a non-commercial purpose or private study
	• criticism and review
	• reporting current events.
3	In the case of research for a non-commercial purpose or private study, multiple copying would not be fair dealing.
4	Courts are left to decide what constitutes 'fair dealing' on a case-by-case basis.
5	It relates to the quality as well as the quantity of what is being copied.

Fig. 2.4   *What is fair dealing?*

The phrase 'fair dealing' is commonly thought to mean that the copying would not unfairly deprive the copyright owner of income for their intellectual property. Copyright owners earn income not just from sales of the original work, but also from photocopying undertaken under licensing schemes operated by collective licensing societies such as the Copyright Licensing Agency (CLA). This income is a just return for the creative work of the author and the financial investment made by the publisher.

If you rely on the fair dealing exceptions to justify copying activity, then you should minimize the risks of copyright infringement by considering the following points:

1 To be considered 'fair dealing', the copying must fit within one of the following three categories:
   • Research for a non-commercial purpose or private study s29(1)
   • criticism and review s30(1)
   • reporting current events s30(2) (this does not cover photographs).

2 Multiple copying for the purpose of non-commercial research or private study would not be considered to be fair, nor would systematic single copying. Therefore the copying would need to be restricted to making a single copy.

3 Multiple copying for the purposes of criticism and review, or reporting current events is permitted.

4 CILIP recommends that copying under the exception for fair dealing for the purposes of non-commercial research and private study shall be kept within the limits set out in the Library Regulations.[7] The Library Association copyright guide for industrial and commercial libraries[8] says that 'although this has not been tested, it is generally agreed that one complete chapter or a maximum otherwise of 5% of extracts from a published work would be reasonable.'

5 If the copying is likely to have a significant economic impact upon the copyright owner, then it would not be considered to be fair dealing.

6 Ask yourself whether you intend to copy a 'substantial' part. The legislation does not define what is meant by 'substantial', although it is clear from case law that 'substantial' relates not just to quantity but also to quality. For example, if you were to copy a two-page executive summary from a market-research report and that contained the most valuable findings from the report, the rights-owner might argue that the copying was unfair. In a quick guide to copyright and moral rights, the Society of Authors[9] mentions one case where four lines from a 32-line poem were held to amount to a 'substantial part'.

7 What is the purpose of the copying? If the copying is undertaken to support research for a commercial purpose, then fair dealing for research cannot be used as a defence (see Figure 2.5).

1	Copying for a commercial purpose has not been defined by statute.
2	The European Court of Justice has the final say.
3	The test is whether the research is for a commercial purpose, not whether it is done by a commercial body.
4	When deciding whether or not research has a non-commercial purpose, businesses will only need to consider what is known at the time of copying.
5	Some research in a commercial environment could be classed as non-commercial, such as copying to support private study for law exams.

Fig. 2.5   *What constitutes copying for a commercial purpose?*

There are no formal guidelines as to what would count as commercial copying, although there are a number of useful indicators:

1   The British Library has issued a set of frequently asked questions[10] (FAQs) on the changes to UK copyright law which came about through SI 2003/xxxx.
2   Charles Oppenheim set out a number of examples of what he considers would be commercial and what would be non-commercial copying.[11]

The legislation does not provide us with a definition of what is meant by copying 'for a non-commercial purpose' or 'copying for a commercial purpose'. The Intellectual Property and Innovation Directorate at the Patent Office believe that to try and define it would result in less flexibility for librarians and researchers. In any case, it would ultimately be for the ECJ to decide precisely what research for a commercial purpose means. We do, however, have a number of helpful pointers to try and determine what would be copying for a commercial purpose. The test is whether the research is for a commercial purpose, not whether it is done by a commercial body. Research carried out may have no immediate commercial goal but may possibly have an unforeseen commercial application at a later date. The law can not expect you to do more than decide what is the case on the day you ask for the copy. This could be relevant when the commercial purpose is as yet unknown or undefined. If there is no commercial purpose on the day the copy is requested, then it would seem reasonable to sign the copyright declaration form as non-commercial (see Figure 2.8 on page 34), which is required for all copying under the library regulations,[12] but ultimately only the courts and the ECJ can decide. If it is known that research is directly funded by a commercial organization and related to a product or service which will be going into the market, then it is likely to be for a commercial purpose. Some research in a commercial environment could be classed as non-commercial such as copying by an individual for law exams.

Where the copying is undertaken within the scope of the fair dealing provisions, this would normally require acknowledgement. However, section 30(3) does say that 'no acknowledgement is required in connection with the reporting of current events by means of a sound recording, film or broadcast where this would be impossible for reasons of practicality or otherwise.'

Copyright legislation does not set out percentages or numbers of words that can legitimately be copied under the exceptions. The recommended limits set out in Figure 2.6 should therefore be given with a health warning to the effect that they are merely guidance, and a court would make a judgment about what was fair dealing based on the circumstances of each individual case. They are based on the premise that fair-dealing copying for non-commercial research or private study purposes should observe the same limits that are set out in the Library Regulations (SI 1989/1212); the 5% limit for books, 10% limit for short works and the 10% limit for British Standards are all based on guidance from CILIP,[13] and the limits for quotations are based on guidance from the British Copyright Council which has since been withdrawn.

Fair dealing for research for non-commercial purposes and private study only

Books	Up to a maximum of 5% of extracts or one complete chapter
Journals	One article from a single issue of a journal
Short works	CILIP recommends that up to 10% of a work is reasonable for short works provided that the extract does not amount to more than 20 pages
British Standards	10% of a standard

Fair dealing for criticism or review

Quotations	A single extract of up to 400 words or in the case of multiple extracts up to 300 words per extract so long as the total is no more than 800 words

Disclaimer
These copying limits are set out for guidance. It is not possible to give a definitive set of copying limits because a court would come to a judgment based on the specific facts involved in each individual case.

Fig. 2.6   *Guidance on what you are allowed to copy*

2.5.2   The Library Provisions in the CDPA 1988

Sections 38–43 of the CDPA deal with copying by librarians and archivists, and they should be read in conjunction with SI 1989/1212 – The Copyright (Librarians and Archivists) (Copying of Copyright Material) Regulations 1989 – and SI 1996/2967 – The Copyright and Related Rights Regulations 1996.

Library privilege applies to staff who work in 'prescribed libraries' and who carry out photocopying on behalf of their users (see Figure 2.7). Schedule 1 of SI 1989/1212 sets out which libraries are 'prescribed'. These include:

- public libraries
- national libraries
- libraries in educational establishments
- parliamentary and government libraries
- local authority libraries
- libraries whose main purpose is to encourage the study of a wide range of subjects (including libraries outside the UK).

The regulations specifically exclude libraries that are conducted for profit.

1	Library privilege only applies to 'prescribed' (not-for-profit) libraries.
2	It provides an indemnity for librarians copying on behalf of their users so long as the conditions are met.
3	It only applies to copying for non-commercial purposes or private study.
4	Library users must sign a statutory declaration form.
5	It is important to retain the statutory declaration because it is the librarian's indemnity. The minimum period that these should be kept for would be six years plus the current year, taking account of the Limitation Act 1980 [this act does not relate to Scotland, where the Prescription and Limitation (Scotland) Act 1973 applies].
6	Librarians should be cautious about giving out advice to their users on what constitutes copying for a commercial purpose. They must not knowingly be party to advising or telling people how to fill in the declaration or they could be liable for any infringement too.

Fig. 2.7   *Library privilege*

Libraries have special privileges to copy:

- for their readers (ss38–9)
- for other libraries (s41):
  — any library in the UK can supply a copy of an item, but only 'prescribed libraries' can receive copies
- for preservation (s42) under the following conditions:
  — the work is in the permanent collection for reference or lending only to other libraries and archives
  — the copy made will only be used for these purposes
  — where it is not reasonably practicable to purchase a copy of the item
- for replacement (s42) of all or part of a work for a prescribed library provided that each of the following conditions as set out in the Library Regulations[14] are met:

— the copy is required to replace an item which has been lost, damaged or destroyed
— the work being replaced was in the permanent collection for reference or lending only to other libraries
— the copy made will be only used for these same purposes
— a copy cannot reasonably be purchased
— the requesting library provides a declaration saying it is a prescribed library and the purposes for which it requires the copy (i.e. if the item has been lost, destroyed or damaged)
— the requesting library pays a sum equivalent to but not exceeding the cost (including a contribution to the general expenses of the library or archive) attributable to its production

and to copy certain unpublished works (s43):

• if the document was deposited before it was published
• if the copyright owner has not prohibited copying
• if the reader pays a sum equivalent to but not exceeding the cost (including a contribution to the general expenses of the library or archive) attributable to their production
• if a statutory declaration is signed, which must state that:
    — the work was not published before it was deposited
    — the copy is for research for a non-commercial purpose or private study and will not be further copied
    — a copy has not previously been supplied.

[The wording of sections 42 and 43 may change once directive 2001/29/EC has been implemented.]

Library privilege covers copying undertaken by library staff on behalf of their users, whether they be local users or interlibrary users. It cannot be claimed by the individual users themselves. Library privilege covers literary, dramatic or musical works, including typographical arrangements and illustrations, but it does not cover artistic works.

Under library privilege, library staff can make one copy of an article from an issue of a periodical; or a reasonable proportion of a non-periodical work provided that a number of conditions are met:

- that the user signs the necessary statutory declaration form
- that the user pays an appropriate sum so that the library is able to recover the costs of production of the photocopy
- that no more than one article from a periodical issue can be copied or a reasonable proportion of any non-periodical work.
- that the librarian is satisfied that the criteria set out in the legislation are met.

The statutory declaration form (see the sample copyright declaration form in Figure 2.8) which library users are required to sign must state:

- that a copy has not previously been supplied (by any librarian)
- that the copies are for research for a non-commercial purpose or private study and will not be further copied
- that they are not aware that anyone with whom they work or study has made, or intends to make, a request for substantially the same material for substantially the same purpose.

The Library Regulations do not require the declaration form to be precisely the same as the one which appears in Schedule 2 to the SI, but that it is 'substantially in accordance' with that form (see Figure 2.8). If the declaration is false the copy is an infringing copy and the reader is responsible.

Whilst it is certainly the case that librarians have previously relied upon the fair dealing and library privilege exceptions as their main justification for copying of copyright works, the CDPA does contain a number of other exceptions. For example, there are exceptions relating to public administration which permit copying for parliamentary and judicial proceedings (s45), Royal Commissions and statutory enquiries (s46), material open to public inspection or on official register (s47), material communicated to the Crown in the course of public business (s48), public records (s49) and acts done under statutory authority (s50).

The business community will experience difficulty trying to fit their copying into any of the current exceptions, and they are advised to look to the copyright licences offered by the collective licensing societies as a solution.

DECLARATION: COPY OF ARTICLE OR PART OF PUBLISHED WORK

To:

The Librarian of..Library

[Address of Library]

Please supply me with a copy of:

* the article in the periodical, the particulars of which are

[ ]

* the part of the published work, the particulars of which are

[ ]

required by me for the purposes of research for a non-commercial purpose or private study

2. I declare that –

(a) I have not previously been supplied with a copy of the same material by you or any other librarian;

(b) I will not use the copy except for research for a non-commercial purpose or private study and will not supply a copy of it to any other person; and

(c) to the best of my knowledge no other person with whom I work or study has made or intends to make, at or about the same time as this request, a request for substantially the same material for substantially the same purpose.

3. I understand that if the declaration is false in a material particular the copy supplied to me by you will be an infringing copy and that I shall be liable for infringement of copyright as if I had made the copy myself.

† Signature ....

Date ....

Name ....

Address ....

....

....

---

* Delete whichever is inappropriate.

† This must be the personal signature of the person making the request. A stamped or typewritten signature, or the signature of an agent, is *not* acceptable.

Fig. 2.8   *Copyright declaration form*

2.6   Licensing

What the law does not allow can often be done with the copyright owner's consent through an appropriate licence. The CDPA allows for the setting-up of collective licensing bodies such as the Copyright Licensing Agency (CLA) or the Newspaper Licensing Agency (NLA). Where there is a dispute between a collecting society and users or groups representing users, these can be referred to the Copyright Tribunal. The decisions of the Copyright Tribunal are appealable to the High Court (or in Scotland to the Court of Session) only on a point of law. Details of Copyright Tribunal cases can be found on the Patent Office website at www.patent.gov.uk/copy/tribunal/index.htm.

2.6.1   Copyright Licensing Agency

The Copyright Licensing Agency (CLA) is one of the UK's largest reproduction rights organizations. It is a not-for-profit company which was established in 1982 by the Publishers Licensing Society (PLS) and the Authors Licensing and Collecting Society (ALCS). The CLA licenses photocopying from magazines, books and journals, and takes action against infringers.

The CLA offers a range of licences, according to the type of organization. The licences available include ones for business, central government, local government, public bodies, universities and schools. There is also a licence available for press cuttings agencies. As required by s136 of the CDPA,[15] licence holders are given an indemnity against liability for infringement provided that the licence terms are complied with.

The CLA regularly publishes a 'list of excluded categories and excluded works', which lists the publishers and/or the individual titles that cannot be copied under the terms of the licence agreement. It also lists a number of other countries whose works are covered by the licence. There are also a number of 'excluded categories' such as printed music, workbooks, work cards or assignment sheets, bibles, liturgical works, orders of service, tests or public examination papers, industrial house journals, photographs and all UK newspapers.

In the third quarter of 2002, CLA introduced a new business licence. The key changes of this licence are that:

* scanned copies can be distributed by e-mail
* there is no limit on the number of photocopies or scanned copies of licensed material which may be made or distributed

- photocopying and scanning of artistic works such as photographs, diagrams and illustrations are now included in the licence
- copies can be made and distributed from copies received from licensed press cuttings agencies and copyright-fee-paid copies from document delivery services.

Whilst copies can be scanned and distributed by e-mail, the standard business licence does not permit these electronic copies to be stored in a central repository available to others in the organization such as a company intranet, a networked computer drive or a shared system such as Lotus Notes. The CLA has been discussing with rights-owners the possibility of offering an enhanced business licence which would cater for those requirements, but it remains to be seen whether this will get sufficient rights-holder support. Under the standard business licence electronic copies can, however, be retained permanently so long as they are housed on a standalone PC or on a non-networked drive.

The licence fee is usually based on a rate per professional employee, and the interpretation of what is meant by a 'professional employee' will differ from sector to sector. In the government sector, for example, this means staff who are at higher executive officer (HEO) level or above.

There is one licence available from the CLA which is not based upon a rate per professional employee, and that is the small business licence which is available for businesses employing up to 50 employees. Businesses employing up to 10 people are charged a fee of £95 per year, and those employing between 11 and 50 employees a fee of £295. The small business licence incorporates the same terms as the business licence.

The CLA exists in order to collect licence fees from organizations wishing to make copies of items and then pass those fees on to authors and publishers. In order for the fee distributions to be fair to authors and publishers, it is necessary to gather information on what material is being copied. It is for this reason that licence holders are required to complete an annual information audit in which they tell the CLA what journals they subscribe to and what books they have purchased in the previous 12 months. Surveys are also undertaken to record what is being copied. The fees are then distributed to authors, publishers, and visual creators and artists, through the ALCS, the PLS and DACS respectively.

2.6.2   Newspaper Licensing Agency

Set up in January 1996, the NLA operates a licensing scheme to collect royalties on behalf of newspaper publishers. The NLA licence covers UK national and regional papers, and a number of foreign titles. There are a number of different types of licence available such as ones for professional practices, schools, public relations agencies, and trade or professional associations.

The NLA licence covers the photocopying on paper of newspaper articles, either on an ad-hoc basis or as part of a press cuttings service. The standard licence permits the copying of a maximum of 250 copies of any one article. It covers paper-to-paper copying only unless you opt to pay for an electronic extension. It is not possible to have an electronic licence in its own right, but only as an extension to the main licence. This permits in-house electronic scanning of cuttings taken from newspapers covered by the NLA for circulation by e-mail or by electronic means such as an intranet. However, the licence only allows these to be retained electronically for up to seven days.

The NLA licence does not cover the copying of photographs, illustrations or advertisements. The copying that is permitted is intended for management information purposes only, and thus it specifically excludes copying for distribution internally to a sales force for use as a sales aid; inclusion in an in-house publication; inclusion in the company's annual report and accounts; or copying for marketing or promotional purposes. Such copying would require the user to obtain permission directly from the newspaper publishers.

2.6.3   Design Artists Copyright Society

Formed in 1983, DACS represents visual creators, artists and photographers. It licenses the use of artistic works such as photographs, sculptures, charts, maps, cartoons and diagrams. DACS also pursues cases of copyright infringement on behalf of its members.

Many artists create their works as a result of a commission, and they might directly administer and control their primary rights, but they may not be able to control their secondary rights. DACS manages this for them through their 'Payback' campaign. Some of the rights that are often collectively licensed and administered include off-air recording right, reprographic right, cable retransmission right, and terrestrial and satellite broadcast rights.

DACS lobbied on behalf of its members for the Artist's Resale Right (*droit de suite*) which was passed in a directive in 2001,[16] under which an artist will get a percentage each time a work is sold after the first sale. The right will come into force for living artists on 1 January 2006. The royalty payment will be payable where the resale involves art dealers or other art market professionals as sellers, buyers or intermediaries. This royalty will not be payable where the resale takes place directly between private individuals or where the resale price is below a certain limit.

2.6.4   Ordnance Survey

The Ordnance Survey provides a licensing system for people to be able to make use of their mapping products such as maps and aerial photographs. There are licences available for education, local authorities, commercial and business, legal procedures and planning permissions. These licences are used by about 13,000 customers ranging from solicitors, shopkeepers and estate agents through to engineers. Under these licences, users pay an annual fee in order to be able to make unlimited copies of paper maps for internal business use or to publish Ordnance Survey mapping externally for display and promotion purposes, so long as this does not result in any direct financial gain from the use of the mapping. It is worth noting that librarians are not entitled to copy artistic works – including maps – under the Library Regulations, although they can undertake a limited amount of copying for non-commercial purposes under fair dealing.

The Ordnance Survey website (www.ordsvy.gov.uk) has a number of useful publications on copyright such as *Copyright 4 – copying our paper maps for business use*, as well as a set of FAQs.

2.6.5   HMSO

In March 1999 the White Paper 'The future management of crown copyright'[17] announced that unrestricted copying and reproduction of certain categories of Crown copyright material would be permitted. Copyright is waived in material such as court forms, legislation and government press notices in order to encourage its widespread use for reference and onward dissemination to all with interests in these areas. Where people wish to use material in which copyright has been waived, HMSO does ask that users ensure that the material is reproduced accurately and not in a misleading context, that the material is correctly acknowledged, and that the source and status of the material is identified. HMSO issues guidance to government departments, agencies and all users of Crown-copyright-protected material in the form of a series of guidance notes which are available on the HMSO website (www.hmso.gov.uk/guides.htm).

In addition to the Crown copyright material for which a waiver applies as set out in the HMSO guidance notes, more material can be copied under a 'click use' licence from HMSO (www.clickanduse.hmso.gov.uk). The main purpose of the 'click use' licence is to provide users with a fast system which lets them re-use a wide range of core government information that is central to the process of government and is subject to Crown copyright protection. The 'click use' licence does not cover computer programs, software, personal identity documents, or value added products or services that have been developed by government; and there are also many departments with government trading fund status whose material is also outside the remit of the 'click use' licence.

In April 2003 the government announced[18] the setting up of an Advisory Panel on Crown Copyright, chaired by Prof. Richard Susskind. The Panel is charged with advising ministers strategically on how to open up opportunities for greater re-use of Government information by the private and voluntary sectors of the economy, and advising the Controller of HMSO about changes and opportunities in the information industry.

In addition to Crown copyright material, HMSO manage parliamentary copyright on behalf of the parliamentary authorities. They provide guidance on the levels of copying of parliamentary material that are permitted through the 'Dear Librarian' letter (see Figure 2.9). This states that people are entitled to make one photocopy of a document in its entirety so long as no more than one copy is made for any one individual and that the copies are not distributed to other individuals or organizations; and they can also make multiple copies of extracts of up to 30% of a work or one complete chapter, whichever is the greater.

2.7 Electronic copyright

Under UK law, copyright material sent over the internet or stored on web servers will generally be protected in the same way as material in other media. So anyone wishing to put copyright material on the internet, or further distribute or download such material that others have placed on the internet, should ensure that they have the permission of the owners of the rights in the material.

The 'Dear Librarian' letter permits users to copy the text from any single title or document in its entirety provided that:

- no more than one photocopy is made for any one individual
- copies are not distributed to other individuals or organizations.

There is an exception for schools and places of higher education, who are allowed to provide a single copy to each student.

The guidelines also permit unlimited photocopies of extracts from any title or document provided that the extracts from any single work do not exceed 30% or one complete chapter or equivalent, whichever is the greater.

The categories of parliamentary material covered by these guidelines include:

- Lords and Commons Official Reports (Hansard)
- House Business Papers, including Journals of both Houses, Lords Minutes, the Vote Bundle, Commons Order Books
- Commons Public Bill Lists
- Statutory Instruments Lists
- Weekly Information Bulletin
- Sessional Information Digest.

For full details see the text of the 'Dear Librarian' letter at www.hmso.gov.uk/liblet.htm.

Fig. 2.9   *Parliamentary material that can be copied under the 'Dear Librarian' letter*

Works which are 'published' in electronic form, such as electronic journals, PDF documents on the internet, CD-ROM or online databases, are protected in the same way as their printed equivalents. Copying in relation to any description of work includes the making of copies which are transient or are incidental to some other use of the work (CDPA s17(6)). This is an issue in the electronic environment, because when you look at a web page, for example, you will have made more than one copy simply by virtue of the way in which the technology works – the copy that you see on the screen as well as the copy that is automatically saved to your web browser's cache. It is for this reason that directive 2001/29/EC has one mandatory exception. Article 5.1 requires member states to provide an exception to the reproduction right for certain temporary acts which are transient or incidental, and so SI 2003/xxxx inserts s31A into the CDPA:

> Copyright in a literary work, other than a computer program or a database, or in a dramatic, musical or artistic work, the typographical arrangement of a published edition, a sound recording or a film, is not infringed by the making of a temporary copy which is transient or incidental, which

is an integral and essential part of a technological process and the sole purpose of which is to enable—

(a) a transmission of the work in a network between third parties by an intermediary; or

(b) a lawful use of the work;

and which has no independent economic significance.

2.7.1   Internet

In a single web page there can be many different copyrights. For example, the textual articles are literary works; the graphics are artistic works; sound files are sound recordings containing musical works; and the HTML coding and metadata are literary works. People wishing to undertake copying of material on the internet which falls outside any of the permitted acts should check to see if there is a copyright notice on the web page. If the copying is not covered in the copyright notice, or if there is no copyright notice on the website, then you should ask for permission by contacting the webmaster. For the avoidance of doubt, there is no implied licence to copy material available on the internet, and material both on websites and in e-mail messages is protected by copyright law.

It is not just a question of copyright that librarians need to consider. They will also need to bear in mind that, under The Copyright Rights in Databases Regulations 1997,[19] many websites will fall under the definition of a database and will have the protection of database right (see section 2.7.2). An important legal case which dealt with database right was that of British Horseracing Board (BHB) v. William Hill.[20] The BHB won a high court challenge against William Hill over the use of pre-race data. BHB argued that internet bookmakers who wished to use information such as runners and riders should pay a copyright fee. The court decided that the defendants had infringed the database right in listings of horses scheduled to run in forthcoming races. It was accepted that there was nothing intellectual or creative in making such lists, but that since considerable investment had gone into the creation of the lists, database right was justified. The case was appealed to the European Court of Justice,[21] and at the time of writing it had still to make its decision on the matter.

The right to communicate a work to the public is a restricted act. It is therefore an infringement of copyright to include all or a substantial part of a copyright work in a broadcast or any kind of on-demand or interactive service. The definition of 'on-demand or interactive service' is wide enough to include any form of website.[22] So, if you publish content in which you do not own the rights onto a website, there are a number of remedies available to the copyright owner of that material. These include damages and an injunction to stop the inclusion of the material on the website. If you published copyright material to a website and knew, or had good reason to know, that you would be infringing copyright in that material, then you would be committing a criminal offence, for which the maximum penalty would be two years in prison and an unlimited fine.

2.7.1.1   Hyperlinking and deep linking

Hyperlinking is an integral part of the way in which the web works, allowing people either to jump from one website to another or to navigate from one page within a site to another page on the same site. There have been quite a number of legal cases which have considered the use of hyperlinks, and in particular deep links, and whether or not these are legitimate.

Deep linking is the practice of linking to a web page at a lower level than the home page. The use of deep links can be problematic for a number of reasons:

1 If the website that you are linking to has banner advertisements which appear on the home page for which the site owner gets an income based upon the number of 'click throughs', then you should avoid linking to a page further down within the site because it could be argued that, by deep linking within the site, you are depriving the site owner of income.

2 By deep linking to a page within a site, you might be said to be encouraging people to go directly to a page when the site owner might want you to see a set of terms and conditions before viewing any pages on their site. Indeed, by getting people to circumvent the page containing terms and conditions of use, you might actually be stopping people from seeing that the site owner has clearly stated in those terms and conditions of use that deep linking is not permitted.

3 Linking may be judged to be an infringement of database right. In Stepstone v. OFiR[23] a German court took the view that Stepstone's website which provided a database of job vacancies, was protected by the database

right, and that OFiR's activities amounted to the repeated and systematic extraction of insubstantial parts of Stepstone's database, which prejudiced Stepstone's legitimate interests.

4 The use of frames technology can also be problematic. With frames it is possible to link from one website to another without users realizing that they have linked through to an external site. This could suggest a false association with the other site.

Since there are technical measures available to webmasters which would prevent people from being able to deep-link to pages within their site, it could be argued that if a site owner wishes to stop people from deep linking, then they should employ the measures that are available to achieve this. However, this could be considered to be unreasonable, because the technical measures referred to can be extremely expensive.

Looking at some of the legal cases that have addressed the question of deep linking, one is led to the conclusion that the law is still uncertain in this particular area. In the author's opinion, however, to respond to this by avoiding the use of links altogether is an overreaction to the perceived risks. I would advise anyone wishing to make use of hyperlinking and deep linking to bear in mind the points outlined in Figure 2.10.

1	Make it clear what is being done and who you are linking to.
2	Avoid using frames technology which could result in you appearing to pass off someone's content as your own.
3	Ideally, the hyperlink should open up in a new page.
4	Use a disclaimer about the content of external sites.
5	Check the terms and conditions for websites that you wish to link to.
6	Do not circumvent anti-linking measures.
7	Link to the home page if that will do.
8	Avoid deep linking that is commercially unfair (i.e. which will lead you to benefit commercially at the expense of the owner of the site you are linking to).
9	Inform the content owners that you wish to link to their site. This is a matter of good netiquette and may lead to them creating a reciprocal link from their website.

Fig. 2.10   *Points to consider when deep linking*

2.7.2   Database regulations

The Copyright and Rights in Databases Regulations[24] came into force on 1 January 1998. They implement council directive 96/9/EC on the legal protection of databases. The regulations introduce a new right – database right – which subsists if there has been a subtantial investment in obtaining, verifying or presenting the contents of the database. In order for a database to qualify additionally for full copyright protection, it must be the author's own intellectual creation by virtue of the selection and arrangement of the contents. The regulations do not consider a 'database' to be limited to electronic information, but rather as any collection of independent works, data or other materials which are arranged in a systematic or methodical way and are individually accessible by electronic or other means. Collections of data such as directories, encyclopaedias, statistical databases, online collections of journals, multimedia collections and many websites would fit this definition of a database.

Fair dealing with a database is permitted so long as the person extracting the material is a lawful user of the database, and as such that person must show that their purpose is illustration for teaching, research or private study and not for any commercial purpose, and that the source is indicated. The regulations state that 'the doing of anything in relation to a database for the purposes of research for a commercial purpose is not fair dealing with the database.' They distinguish clearly between research or private study and research for commercial purposes. This is the first time that such a distinction has been made in UK copyright law, and this principle has been extended in SI 2003/xxxx, which implements directive 2001/29/EC.

Some databases might qualify for both copyright and database right. In the case of copyright the protection would be for 70 years from the end of the year of death of the author if there is one, or the end of the year of first publication if there isn't a personal author. In the case of database right, the period of protection would be for 15 years from its creation or from its being made available to the public if this occurs during the 15-year period. Importantly, any substantial new investment would qualify the database for a new 15-year term of protection. Many 'databases' are maintained continually and this can involve a significant investment. As such, they can end up being protected for an indefinite period.

2.7.3   Licensing of electronic resources

One of the problems with electronic information is that there is a dependence on licences and contracts to permit copying rather than on copyright law, and these licences often differ on key points from one supplier to another. It is for this reason that a number of initiatives have been undertaken to try and come up with a standard licence for electronic resources. These include John Cox Associates,[25] ECUP (European Copyright Users Platform),[26] ICOLC (International Coalition of Library Consortia),[27] and the Joint Information Systems Committee (JISC)/Publishers Association[28] initiative.

With electronic information, if you do not own the copyright in a work and don't have a licence to use the work, there will be a number of key issues to consider. If you post to a website material in which you do not own the rights, then you will be communicating it to the public, and could potentially face a prison sentence of up to two years. Another issue relates to circulating electronic copies to others. If, for example, you send an e-mail to several people which contains a scanned item in which you do not own the rights, you will have undertaken multiple copying. In those circumstances it cannot be said to be covered by the provisions for fair dealing for non-commercial purposes or private study.

2.7.3.1   JISC/PA Guidelines on Fair Dealing in an Electronic Environment

In 1998, JISC and the Publishers Association published a set of *Guidelines for Fair Dealing in an Electronic Environment*.[29] These guidelines were intended specifically for the higher education sector. The main aim of the JISC/Publishers Association working party was to identify any possible areas of agreement between representatives of JISC and the Publishers Association on a practical definition of fair dealing of materials in electronic form, and, if possible, the necessary mechanisms that might be used to provide a workable monitoring system (see Table 2.1). The agreement contains the following definitions:

- *electronic publication*: publication created in electronic format or originally in paper form and converted under copyright law
- *part*: one article from a journal issue, one chapter from a book, or 10% of other works
- *issue*: collection of articles issued at the same time under same issue number.

Table 2.1   *JISC/PA guidelines on fair dealing in an electronic environment*

Acceptable	Not acceptable
Viewing on screen	
Printing to paper – one copy of a part	
Copying to disk – part	Copying to disk – all
Transmission to enable printing – part	Transmission to enable printing – all
Transmission for permanent storage – part	Transmission for permanent storage – all
	Posting on a network or WWW site open to the public
	Copying and transmitting an image, or a set of images, with little or no text associated with them is probably not fair dealing.

2.7.4   Electronic copyright management systems

Electronic copyright management systems (ECMS) can provide a techno-logical solution for rights-owners wishing to ensure that their intellectual prop-erty is not copied or redisseminated in an unauthorized manner. They can provide robust and reliable tamper-proof mechanisms for controlling the usage of copyright material. An electronic copyright management system has two key roles. One relates to tracking and monitoring usage, and therefore deals with the area of security and authentication; and the other concerns payment issues through the licensing of material and charging of royalties.

In principle, all of the copyright exceptions or permitted acts apply to dig-ital information. However, if the rights-owners have made use of technical measures to prevent access to their work(s), such copyright exceptions are practically worthless, because it would be illegal to try and break any copy protection that is in place. SI 2003/xxxx implements the provisions of direc-tive 2001/29/EC into UK law, and this makes it an offence to break through a technical protection measure or to remove or alter information from an elec-tronic copyright management system.

2.7.5   Electronic signatures and copyright declaration forms

Section 7 of the Electronic Communications Act 2000 implemented the provisions of directive 1999/93/EC[30] relating to the admissibility of electronic signatures as evidence in legal proceedings, while The Electronic Signatures Regulations 2002[31] implemented the provisions relating to the supervision of a certification-service provider,[32] their liability in certain circumstances and data protection requirements concerning them. These regulations define 'electronic signatures' as 'data in electronic form which are attached to or logically associated with other electronic data and which serve as a method of authentication.'

The Library Regulations require the requester to sign the statutory declaration form. Therefore it is not acceptable for a librarian to sign the declaration form on behalf of the user; it must be the personal signature of the requester. Schedule 2 to these Regulations says that 'this must be the personal signature of the person making the request. A stamped or typewritten signature, or the signature of an agent, is NOT acceptable.' What would be the status of an electronic signature? The Patent Office understands that the Library Regulations already cover e-signatures.[33] The Regulations require that the signature must be in 'writing', and 'writing' is defined in the CDPA s178 as including any form of notation or code, whether by hand or otherwise.

Librarians can receive copyright declaration forms which have been signed electronically. The problem is that they must fulfil the requirements for a personal signature. The signature has to have a unique link to the requester which cannot easily be used by others. In short, this means that the signature must be linked to an authentication system, and it is unclear which systems would be deemed to fulfil the necessary legal requirements.

2.8 Ethical and professional issues and conflicts

Library and information service professionals find themselves in a difficult situation playing the role of 'piggy in the middle', acting as guardians of intellectual property whilst at the same time being committed to supporting their users' needs to gain access to copyright works and the ideas that they contain.

The CILIP Code of Professional Ethics[34] states that information professionals should aim to achieve an appropriate balance between the law, demands from information users, the need to respect confidentiality, the terms of their employment and the responsibilities outlined in the Code. It also says that information professionals should defend the legitimate needs and interests of information users, while respecting the moral and legal rights of the creators and distributors of intellectual property. The key point here is that the commitment to providing their users with information has to be tempered by the need to do so within the limits of the law, and that this includes respecting copyright law.

Similarly, the EIRENE code of practice for information brokers[35] also deals with a number of copyright-related issues stating that 'a broker shall abide by copyright law' (A.3) and that they shall 'clarify their copyright position vis-à-vis the information suppliers and inform the client of their copyright obligations as regards the information provided' (B.1).

The CLA has a whistleblowers line. There was an instance where a disaffected librarian, on leaving their job, rang the whistleblowers line to inform the CLA of the systematic copyright infringement of their former employer which had been undertaken over a long period of time. This led to the company paying out £50,000 in damages and costs, and also taking out a CLA licence.[36]

There may be times when an adamant user expects an information professional to undertake copying for them which falls outside of the permitted acts or exceptions set out in the CDPA. This is certainly an awkward situation for individuals to find themselves in. However, when this matter was raised on LIS-COPYSEEK, Charles Oppenheim said:

> I find the best way to deal with adamant staff members is as follows – demand that they sign a declaration stating that they understand that what they wish to do is potentially illegal and they agree that should the employer, or the librarian be sued, they will accept full liability, will pay all necessary legal costs to assist the employer or the librarian in its defence of the action, and indemnify the library/employer for any damages or costs awarded against them. In other words, he or she agrees in writing to take on the full legal and financial risks.

Figure 2.11 shows some helpful sites that offer advice on copyright.

2.9   Summary

In this chapter we have covered the general principles of copyright law; the legal and regulatory environment which governs the use of copyright mate-

CILIP's information and advisory service, available at info@cilip.org.uk
(for CILIP members only)

Libraries and Archives Copyright Alliance, available at www.cilip.org.uk/laca
(LACA lobbies the government and the EU on all aspects of copyright on behalf of UK
libraries, archives and information services and their users. People can contact committee members via the LACA website.)

IPR helpdesk, available at www.ipr-helpdesk.org

Intellectual Property, available at www.intellectual-property.gov.uk
(UK government-backed website)

JISC Legal Information Service, available at www.jisc.ac.uk/legal
(serving the higher and further education communities)

Fig. 2.11 *Where to go to seek copyright advice*

rial; the exceptions or permitted acts such as fair dealing and library privilege; licensing issues; the application of copyright law in the electronic environment; and a number of ethical and professional issues.

In the next chapter we will look at the general principles of data protection, the eight principles of good information handling, the rights of individuals and the responsibilities of those who process personal data.

2.10   Further information
British Library Copyright Office
Boston Spa, Wetherby, West Yorkshire LS23 7BQ
Tel: 01937 546 255; Fax: 01937 546 478
Website: www.bl.uk/copyright

Copyright Licensing Agency
90 Tottenham Court Road, London W1P 0LP
Tel: 020 7631 5555; Fax: 020 7631 5500; E-mail: cla@cla.co.uk
Website: www.cla.co.uk

Design Artists Copyright Society
Parchment House, 13 Northburgh Street, London EC1V 0AH
Tel: 020 7336 8811; Fax: 020 7336 8822
Website: www.dacs.co.uk

European Commission Directorate General XV

http://europa.eu.int/comm/internal_market/en/index.htm

HMSO

Enquiry Officer, Her Majesty's Stationery Office, The Licensing
Division, St Clements House, 2–16 Colegate, Norwich NR3 1BQ
Tel: 01603 621000; Fax: 01603 723000; E-mail: enquiries@hmso.gov.uk
Website: www.hmso.gov.uk

Newspaper Licensing Agency

7–9 Church Road, Wellington Gate, Tunbridge Wells TN1 1NL
Tel: 01892 525273; Fax: 01892 525274; E-mail: copy@nla.co.uk
Website: www.nla.co.uk

Ordnance Survey

Customer Contact Centre (Copyright), Romsey Road, Southampton
SO16 4GU
Tel: 023 8030 5030; E-mail: copyrightenquiries@ordsvy.gov.uk
Website: www.ordsvy.gov.uk

Patent Office

Intellectual Property and Innovation Directorate, Harmsworth House,
13–15 Bouverie Street,   London EC4Y 8DP
Tel: 020 7438 4777; Fax: 020 7306 4455
Website: www.patent.gov.uk

World Intellectual Property Organization

PO Box 18, CH-1211 Geneva 20, Switzerland
Tel: 0041 22 338 9111; Fax: 0041 22 733 5428;
E-mail: COPYRIGHT.mail@wipo.int
Website: www.wipo.int

Notes and references

1   *Sui generis* is a Latin term which literally means 'of its own kind [or type]', con-
stituting a class of its own. In relation to database right it refers to the rights that
were newly created in order to protect databases.

2   Adopted by the United Nations General Assembly on 10 December 1948. Available at www.unhchr.ch/udhr/lang/eng.htm.

3   Publishers and distributors in the United Kingdom and the Republic of Ireland have a legal obligation to send one copy of each of their publications to the Legal Deposit Office of the British Library within one month of publication. The other five legal deposit libraries (the National Library of Scotland, Edinburgh; Bodleian Library, Oxford; University Library, Cambridge; Trinity College Dublin and the National Library of Wales, Aberystwyth) are entitled to claim free of charge a copy of everything published in the United Kingdom, providing they make a claim in writing within a year of the date of publication.

4   The 'economic' rights are set out in S.16(1) of the CDPA.

5   Available at www.wto.org/english/tratop_e/trips_e/t_agm0_e.htm.

6   Cornish, W. R., *Cases and Materials on Intellectual Property*, 4th edn, Sweet & Maxwell, 2003.

7   SI 1989/1212 – The Copyright (Librarians and Archivists) (Copying of Copyright Material) Regulations 1989.

8   Norman, S., *Copyright in Industrial and Commercial Libraries*, 4th edn, Library Association Publishing, 1999, 30.

9   The Society of Authors, *Copyright and Moral Rights: Quick guide 1*, 2002.

10 Available at www.bl.uk/services/information/copyrightfaq.html.

11 Oppenheim, C., Directive on copyright, *Library & Information Update*, **1** (5), 2002, 26–7.

12 SI 1989/1212

13 Norman, S., *Copyright in Industrial and Commercial Libraries*, 4th edn, Library Association Publishing, 1999.

14 The Copyright (Librarians and Archivists) (Copying of Copyright Material) Regulations 1989: SI 1989/1212 [commonly known as the Library Regulations].

15 CDPA s136 – implied indemnity in schemes or licences for reprographic copying.

16 Directive 2001/84/EC of the European Parliament and of the Council of 27 September 2001 on the resale right for the benefit of the author of an original work of art. Official Journal L 272, 13/10/2001 P. 0032–0036.

17 Cm 4300, available at www.hmso.gov.uk/document/cpy-00.htm.

18 Cabinet Office press release CAB 020/03 of 14 April 2003. Government establishes advisory panel on crown copyright.

19 The Copyright and Rights in Databases Regulations 1997: SI 1997/3032.

20   British Horseracing Board (BHB) v. William Hill RPC 612, [2001] EWCA Civ
     1268, 31 July 2001, available at www.bailii.org/ew/cases/EWCA/Civ/
     2001/1268.html.
21   C-203/02. See Official Journal 'C', 180/14, 27 July 2002.
22   The reader should particularly look out for the form of words about on demand
     services which is used in the statutory instrument because this was one area where
     the Patent Office were responding to comments that came in during the con-
     sultation process. Available at www.patent.gov.uk/copy/notices/copy_direct2.htm.
23   Stepstone v. OFiR 2000 EBLR 87.
24   The Copyright and Rights in Databases Regulations 1997: SI 1997/3032.
25   Available at www.licensingmodels.com.
26   Available at www.eblida.org/ecup/licensing.
27   Available at www.library.yale.edu/consortia/statement.html.
28   Available at www.ukoln.ac.uk/services/elib/papers/pa/intro.html.
29   Available at www.ukoln.ac.uk/services/elib/papers/pa.
30   Directive 1999/93/EC of the European Parliament and of the council of 13
     December 1999 on a community framework for electronic signatures L13/12,
     published 19 January 2000.
31   The Electronic Signatures Regulations 2002: SI 2002/318.
32   A person who issues certificates or provides other services related to electronic
     signatures.
33   Statement by the Libraries and Archives Copyright Alliance [LACA] concern-
     ing electronic signatures on copyright declaration forms, June 2002, available
     at www.cilip.org.uk/committees/laca/e_sigs.html.
34   Code of professional ethics: draft for consultation, CILIP, 2003.
35   EUSIDIC (European Association of Information Services), E11A (European
     Information Industry Association) and EIRENE (European Information
     Researchers Network), *Code of Practice for Information Brokers*, 1993.
36   CLA, *Whistle blower leads to £50,000 court settlement for the Copyright Licensing
     Agency*, press release, 2 December 1996.

3 Data protection

3.1 Introduction

Information professionals process personal data as part of their daily work. Examples would include the maintenance of user registration records; circulation records; or management statistics on usage of the information service. They might be responsible for a contact database, or maintain an intranet or a website through which they collect and process personal data. In addition to the need to comply with the Data Protection Act, CILIP members also need to abide by the Code of Professional Ethics,[1] which applies professional principles to the management of personal data. The code states that information professionals should 'protect the confidentiality of all matters relating to information users, including their enquiries, any services to be provided, and any aspects of the users' personal circumstances or business.'

This chapter outlines the general principles of data protection (3.2), including the eight principles of good information handling (3.3). There is a section covering the processing of personal data (3.4), including the need to take additional care when processing sensitive personal data. The chapter then looks at notification (3.5) and the need for data processors to register with the Office of the Information Commissioner. Information professionals need to demonstrate good practice when processing personal data, but they are, of course, data subjects in their own right, who want to be able to protect their own information (3.6), and who should be aware of the rights that they themselves have as data subjects (3.7). The impact of data protection on employment is explored (3.8), including the contentious question of whether it is permissible to monitor an employee's internet, telephone or e-mail usage. Data protection compliance audits (3.10) can help to ensure that the data protection system in place is effective and that it works smoothly; and the very fact that an audit is undertaken can help to raise awareness of data protection issues and the need for compliance. The chapter then deals with issues relating to websites and intranets (3.11) such as the use of cookies[2] and other invisible tracking devices and the problem of spam or unsolicited commercial e-mail (3.11.2). It is also in this section that data protection statements are considered. Data protection and privacy statements are key documents that are well worth spending time drafting, because they will govern what an organization can do with personal data. The chapter concludes by considering the implications of data protection for librarians (3.12), including the question of how public librarians handle requests for access to electoral roll data (3.13) now that there are two versions of the electoral roll.

3.2   General principles

The Data Protection Act 1998 (DPA) came into force on 1 March 2000. It sets out how personal data should be handled. As far as the DPA is concerned, personal data means data which relates to an identified or identifiable living individual. The data could be about anyone in the world because the DPA applies either if control of the data is UK-based or if the data itself is held in the UK. It makes no difference how innocuous (e.g. the person borrows a book from the library and details of the loan are recorded on the library management system) or confidential (e.g. financial details) the data is – it all falls under the DPA.

The DPA sets out the rules for the processing of personal information and it applies to personal data held on computer and in some paper records where these form part of a 'relevant filing system'.[3] In essence, for manual records to be covered by the DPA, they need to fulfil three criteria:

- that they are not automatically processed
- that they are structured by reference to individuals or criteria relating to individuals
- that they contain specific information about individuals that is readily accessible.

Some manual records are covered by the DPA regardless of whether they are part of a relevant filing system. They include records relating to health matters, educational matters, housing and social security matters. The DPA also covers other media such as tape recordings and CCTV footage.

The DPA was introduced in order to ensure that UK law complied with the EU data protection directive.[4] Article 1 of the directive aims to protect the individual's rights of privacy. This principle is enshrined in Article 8 of the European Convention on Human Rights:[5] 'Everyone has the right to respect for his private and family life, his home and his correspondence.' – and it is important to recognize that the UK's data protection legislation is based on these human rights foundations (see Figure 3.1).

1980: OECD guidelines (Recommendations of the council concerning guidelines governing the protection of privacy and transborder flows of personal data, adopted by
the council 23 September 1980)
1981: Council of Europe convention (108/81) for the protection of individuals with
regard to automatic processing of personal data
1984: First UK Data Protection Act (now repealed)
1990: United Nations guidelines concerning computerized personal data files adopted by
the general assembly on 14 December 1990
1995: EU directive (95/46/EC) on the protection of individuals with regard to the processing of personal data and on the free movement of such data
1997: EU Telecommunications Data Protection Directive (97/66/EC)
1998: Data Protection Act
1998: Human Rights Act
1999: The Telecommunications (Data Protection and Privacy) Regulations 1999 (SI
1999/2093)
2000: Data Protection Act came into force
2000: Regulation of Investigatory Powers Act
2002: EU directive (2002/58/EC) on privacy and electronic communications

---

Fig. 3.1   *Legislative history of data protection laws*

3.3   The eight data-protection principles

The DPA says that those who record and use personal information must be open about how the information is used and must follow the eight principles of 'good information handling' (see Figure 3.2). These eight principles are set out in Schedule 1 to the Act. Since the eight principles are enshrined in law, data controllers are required to ensure that their handling of personal data is in line with these principles.

Data must be:

- fairly and lawfully processed
- processed for limited purposes (notified to the commissioner and to the data subject)
- adequate, relevant and not excessive
- accurate
- not kept for longer than is necessary
- processed in line with the data subject's rights
- kept secure
- not transferred to countries without adequate protection.

Fig. 3.2   *The eight principles of 'good information handling'*

3.3.1   First principle

The first data-protection principle says that personal data should be processed fairly and lawfully. The information must be processed in a way which complies with the general law and in a manner which is fair to individuals. The whole ethos of the legislation is that for processing to be fair there should be transparency. So, the data subject needs to be told the identity of the data controller, the purpose for which the information is going to be processed, and any other information necessary to ensure that the processing is fair.

3.3.2   Second principle

The second data-protection principle says that data must only be obtained for a specified purpose. You need to let individuals know the reason(s) why you are collecting the data. If you subsequently decide that data collected for one purpose would be useful for another purpose, you should first let the data subjects know what you are intending to do and give them an opportunity to opt out.

3.3.3   Third principle

The third data-protection principle says that personal data shall be adequate, relevant and not excessive in relation to the purpose for which it is processed. So you should only collect the minimum data necessary to fulfil the purpose for which you are processing it. This principle should be borne in mind when designing forms, and in the case of online forms you might want to make some of the fields optional.

3.3.4   Fourth principle

The fourth data-protection principle says that personal data shall be accurate and where necessary kept up to date. This requires data controllers to take reasonable steps to ensure the accuracy of the data. Upon a data subject's request you should correct, change or delete inaccurate details.

3.3.5   Fifth principle

The fifth principle requires that personal data should not be kept for longer than is necessary. Data controllers should have a clear policy on how long they keep data, and at the end of that period the data should be reviewed or destroyed as appropriate. But there are circumstances in which the destruction of personal data can be construed as unfair or damaging. Experian's guide to the DPA[6] uses an example to illustrate this: 'If sales records needed for the calculation of agreed retrospective discounts are destroyed, the customer can claim that their destruction is detrimental to his business.'

3.3.6   Sixth principle

The sixth data-protection principle states that personal data shall be processed in accordance with the rights of data subjects under the DPA. In other words, you are obliged to comply if a data subject wishes to assert his or her rights, and should do nothing to undermine those rights.

3.3.7   Seventh principle

Appropriate technical and organizational measures should be used to protect against unauthorized or unlawful processing of personal data and against accidental loss or destruction of, or damage to, personal data.

There has been a steady stream of stories in the papers about companies who have failed to keep personal data secure, and where customers' information, including their credit card details, have been accidentally made available to anyone through their website. It should be pointed out that the seventh principle covers not just technical measures, but also organizational measures. For example, library staff need to be careful about the positioning of VDUs at enquiry desks, ensuring that third parties cannot see the screen's contents. They also need to be wary of speaking on the telephone about a person's record within earshot of third parties.

The interpretation of this principle in Schedule 1 of the DPA says that 'the data controller must take reasonable steps to ensure the reliability of any employees of his who have access to the personal data.' Therefore it is necessary to consider, for example, whether you should ask temporary staff who are given access to personal data to sign a confidentiality agreement; or how you might ensure that visitors to your organization are not inadvertently given access to personal data.

3.3.8   Eighth principle

The eighth data-protection principle requires that personal data shall not be transferred to a country or territory outside the European Economic Area (EEA) unless that country or territory ensures an adequate level of protection for the rights and freedoms of data subjects in relation to the processing of personal data.

The EEA consists of the member states of the European Union plus Norway, Iceland and Liechtenstein. 'Transfer' covers not just deliberate export of data. It also includes making data available on a website that can be accessed and downloaded by anyone, wherever they may be located. No distinction is made between transfer to others within your organization or transfer to third parties.

The eighth data-protection principle causes practical difficulties for companies wishing to do business across national borders. There are, however, a number of initiatives to minimize those difficulties:

1   The US Department of Commerce developed a 'safe harbor' agreement, which was approved by the European Union in July 2000 (www.export.gov/safeharbor), but this only covers US companies who have agreed to abide by the 'safe harbor' principles.
2   The European Union has recognized the adequacy of the protection of personal data for the following countries:
    * Hungary
    * Switzerland
    * Argentina
    * USA (companies signed up to the 'safe harbor' agreement)
    * Canada.
    For up-to-date information on European Commission decisions on the adequacy of the protection of personal data in third countries, see

http://europa.eu.int/comm/internal_market/privacy/adequacy_en.htm.

3 The European Commission has adopted[7] a decision setting out standard contractual clauses ensuring adequate safeguards for personal data transferred from the EU to countries outside the Union. The decision obliges member states to recognize that companies or organizations using such standard clauses in contracts concerning personal data transfers to countries outside the EU are offering 'adequate protection' to the data.

There are a number of instances in which transfer of personal data to non-EEA countries is acceptable, and these are outlined in schedule 4 of the DPA. They include the following:

1 Individuals have given their consent.
2 It is necessary for the performance of a contract.
3 It is necessary for reasons of substantial public interest.
4 It is necessary for legal reasons (in connection with legal proceedings, obtaining legal advice, etc.).
5 The data subject has requested it.
6 It is necessary to protect the vital interests of the data subject.
7 The transfer is part of the personal data on a public register.

3.4   Processing of personal data

The DPA regulates the processing of information about individuals, and it defines processing widely to cover everything that can be done with personal information such as the obtaining, recording, holding, disclosing, blocking, erasure or destruction of personal data.

The DPA requires that personal data be processed 'fairly and lawfully'. Personal data will not be considered to be processed fairly unless certain conditions are met. These conditions are set out in Schedule 2 of the Act. Processing may only be carried out where one of the following conditions has been met:

1 Individuals have given their consent to the processing.
2 The processing is necessary for the performance of a contract with the individual.
3 The processing is required under a legal obligation.

4 The processing is necessary to protect the vital interests of the individual.

5 The processing is necessary to carry out public functions.

6 The processing is necessary in order to pursue the legitimate interests of the data controller or third parties (unless it could prejudice the interests of the individual).

The Act treats 'sensitive personal data' differently, giving it added protections. Figure 3.3 below outlines what is meant by 'sensitive personal data'.

Sensitive personal data refers to personal data about an individual's

- racial or ethnic origin
- religious or political beliefs
- trade union membership
- physical or mental health
- sex life
- criminal record.

Fig. 3.3 *Sensitive personal data*

The added protections state that it is necessary not only to comply with the fair processing conditions, but also to comply with further conditions which are set out in Schedule 3 of the Act. So, one of the conditions in Schedule 2 must apply plus one of the following conditions from Schedule 3:

1 Data subjects have given their explicit consent.

2 They are required by law to process the data for employment purposes.

3 It is necessary to protect the vital interests of the data subject or another person.

4 Processing is carried out in the course of its legitimate activities by any body which exists for political, philosophical, religious or trade union purposes, and which is not established or conducted for profit.

5 The information has been made public by the data subject.

6 It is necessary for the administration of justice or legal proceedings.

7 It is necessary for defending legal rights.

8 The processing is necessary for medical purposes and is undertaken by a health professional or someone with an equivalent duty of confidentiality.

9 It is necessary for equal-opportunities monitoring.

3.5   Notification

The DPA says that those who record and use personal information must notify the Office of the Information Commissioner that they process personal data. A register of data controllers is available on the website www.dpr.gov.uk. Each entry consists of:

- the data controller's name and address
- a description of the personal data being processed
- the categories of data subject to which they relate
- data classes such as employment details
- a description of the purpose(s) for which data is or may be processed
- a description of recipient(s) to whom the data will be disclosed
- the names of countries or territories outside the EEA to which the data is or might be transferred either directly or indirectly by the data controller.

Those who process personal data must provide access to the data that they hold on a person in order that the data subject can check and correct their records and prevent certain types of processing.

A data controller may only have one register entry. Therefore, even in the case of large organizations, there should only be a single entry on the register. Data controllers register for one year at a time at a notification fee of £35 for the year. They must ensure that the register entry for their organization is up to date and changes must be notified to the Office of the Information Commissioner within 28 days. Changes to the register entry can be made at any time free of charge. There is a notification helpline (01625 545740) and an e-mail address (mail@notification.demon.co.uk) for any questions about the notification process.

It should be noted that there are a number of people posing as data protection 'agencies' who offer to register your company on your behalf. They send out notices on headed notepaper requesting sums of £95 and upwards. Indeed, some people are even posing as collectors of data protection and are attending business premises requesting payment for Data Protection Registration. These 'collectors' produce identification cards and receipt books. They have no connection with the Office of the Information Commissioner, and anyone approached in this way is advised not to make any payment and to notify the local police. In fact, notification is relatively simple and the cost is only £35, and it can be done by companies themselves following the guidelines that are available on the website of the Office of the Information Commissioner.

3.6 How to protect your information

Personal information is a valuable commodity. It is important to read the data protection clauses at the end of documents very carefully and to ensure that you make full use of the 'opt out' or 'opt in' choices. Sometimes an organization will put several tick boxes at the end of a document and they may use a mixture of opt-ins and opt-outs. It is well worth taking the time to read through the wording of such documents to ensure that you have made the choices you intended. Think before you supply anyone with your personal data, and always ask yourself why an organization is asking for information about you. Do they need this information or are they asking for more information than is necessary? You may not have to provide it. They may, for example, be asking about your income, hobbies, interests or family life for possible future marketing campaigns. If someone wants to use your information for a purpose other than the reason for which the data is being collected, you should be told about it and given a choice. Of course, there will be times when you will need to give your personal information for legal reasons. If this is the case, this should be clearly explained. Figure 3.4 outlines the steps you should take to protect your privacy online

There are a number of different 'preference services' which are available if, for example, you want to stop unwanted marketing material being sent to you, or if you want to stop receiving uninvited telesales calls or telemarketing faxes (see Figure 3.5).

1	Limit the disclosure of your personal information.
2	Set up a separate e-mail account for e-commerce activities.
3	Reject cookies planted in your computer by intrusive businesses.
4	Use tools to protect privacy and enable you to surf anonymously [a URL is given which lists tools available at www.epic.org/privacy/tools.html].
5	Learn about your legal rights and be prepared to use them.

Fig. 3.4   *Five steps to protecting your privacy online*
Privacy@net, Consumers International, 2001.

Mailing Preference Service (MPS), Freepost 22, London W1E 7EZ	020 7766 4410
Telephone Preference Service	0845 070 0707
Fax Preference Service	0845 070 0702
e-mail Preference Service	www.e-mps.org/en

Fig. 3.5   *Preference services*

3.7   Rights of the data subject

The DPA gives certain rights to individuals. They are allowed to find out what information is held about them on computer and in some paper records. This is known as the 'right of subject access'. To assert this right they will need to write to the data controller at the organization which they believe holds the information. They should ask for a copy of all the information held about them to which the DPA applies (see Figure 3.6). If they are not sure who to write to within an organization, it is best to address it to the Company Secretary, Chief Executive or the contact name given on the register of data controllers[8] which is kept by the Office of the Information Commissioner.

Your address
The date

Dear Sir or Madam

Please send me the information which I am entitled to under section 7(1) of the Data Protection Act 1998.
 If you need further information from me, or a fee, please let me know as soon as possible.
 If you do not normally handle these requests for your organization, please pass this letter to your Data Protection Officer or another appropriate official.

Yours faithfully

Fig. 3.6   *Sample letter requesting a copy of the information held about you*

Some decisions are made by an automatic process. If the requester wishes to be informed of the logic involved in certain types of automated decisions which the controller may take (for example, your performance at work or credit-worthiness), after 'section 7(1)' in their letter, they should add 'including information under section 7(1)(d)'.

In response, the data subject should receive a copy of the information held about them. The DPA says that the information should be in permanent form (usually on paper). The information may therefore be sent as a computer printout, in a letter or on a form. The data subject should also receive a description of why their information is processed, anyone it may be passed to or seen by, and the logic involved in any automated decisions. The DPA requires that the information should be in an intelligible or understandable form, and so any codes should be explained.

Data controllers are obliged to reply. If the data subject does not receive a reply to their request within 40 days, they should send the organization a reminder by recorded delivery. If they still don't receive a reply fairly quickly, or if the information they receive is wrong or incomplete, then they should contact the Office of the Information Commissioner. The Commissioner can aid the data subject to get a reply, and if one of the principles has been broken, they can take enforcement action against the data controller.

It is best for data subjects to send their request by recorded delivery in the first instance, and it is important for them to keep a copy of the letter and any further correspondence. In many cases they will be asked to provide more details to confirm their identity. It will obviously help if the data subject provides the data controller with these details as quickly as possible. They are generally entitled to receive a reply within 40 days of providing these details as long as they have paid the required fee. There are different periods for copies of credit files (seven working days) and for school pupil records (15 school days). Many organizations choose not to charge a fee at all, but where a fee for access to information held about a data subject is levied, this cannot normally be more than £10. However, in the case of medical or educational records the amount can be up to £50; and in the case of credit records the fee is normally £2.

Usually the data subject can see all the information held about them. However, there are some exceptions (see Figure 3.7) – for example, if providing them with the information would be likely to affect the way crime is detected or prevented; catching or prosecuting offenders; or assessing or collecting taxes or duty. It should also be noted that material which infringes the privacy of third parties might be withheld. In some cases their right to see certain

Personal data collected for:

- national security
- crime and taxation
- health, school education and social work
- certain types of regulatory activity
- journalism, literature, art
- research, history and statistics
- legal proceedings
- domestic purposes.

Fig. 3.7   *Exceptions to the right of inspection*

health and social work details may also be limited. If a data subject thinks that information is being held back from them, they should contact the Office of the Information Commissioner.

The rights that a data subject has are:

1 Right of access to personal data – individuals have a right to know the identity of the data controller, the purposes for which their data will be used; the right to know where the data has come from and where it has gone to; and they also have a right to be given any other information that is necessary to make the processing fair such as details of likely disclosures (i.e. who is likely to have seen the data) or transfers.

2 Right to prevent processing that is causing, or likely to cause, unwarranted and substantial damage or distress to the individual, or to anyone else – according to Experian,[9] examples of causing substantial damage or distress would include sending letters to dead people or to their family relating to the deceased; or revealing payment details to a third party without consent.

3 Right to prevent processing for the purposes of direct marketing.

4 Right to be given an explanation as to how any automated decisions taken about you have been made.

5 Compensation – data subjects are entitled to claim compensation through the courts if damage has been caused as a result of a data controller not meeting any requirements of the DPA, and in particular if they have broken any of the data-protection principles. If damage is proved, the court may also order compensation for any associated distress. Data subjects can only claim compensation for distress alone in very limited circumstances, e.g. because of intrusion by the media.

6 Right to correction, blocking, erasure or destruction of inaccurate data.

7 Right to request an assessment by the Information Commissioner of the legality of processing that is occurring. However, the Information Commissioner is not obliged to respond to such a request.

3.7.1   Credit reference agencies

Credit reference agencies hold information to enable credit grantors to exchange information with each other about their customers. They also have access to the electoral roll and to publicly available financial information which will have a bearing on an individual's credit worthiness, including County Court judgments and Scottish decrees. If an individual wants to see the information that the credit reference agencies hold about their financial standing – their 'credit file' – the main credit reference agencies are:

Equifax Plc, Credit File Advice Service, PO Box 3001, Glasgow G81 2DT
Experian Ltd, Consumer Help Service, PO Box 8000, Nottingham NG1 5GX.

The data subject should send a fee of £2.00 and provide their full name and address, including postcode, any other addresses they have lived at during the last six years, and details of any other names they have used or been known by in that time. Unless the agencies require any further information to locate the file, they have seven working days from the receipt of the letter in which to supply the individual with a copy of their file.

If the data subject asks for information from a credit reference agency, unless they specifically say that they want any other information such as that referred to in the example letter (see Figure 3.6), the credit reference agency will only send them details about their financial situation.

3.8   Data protection and employment

In October 2000 the Office of the Information Commissioner issued a draft code of practice on the use of personal data in employer/employee relationships. This was followed in 2002 by the publication of a four-part Employment Practices Data Protection Code:

- Part 1 – Recruitment and Selection
- Part 2 – Records Management
- Part 3 – Monitoring at Work
- Part 4 – Medical Information.

The aim of the Employment Code is to strike a balance between a worker's legitimate right to respect for his or her private life and an employer's legitimate need to run its business. Compliance with the code will increase trust in the workplace; protect organizations from legal action; encourage workers to respect personal data; aid organizations in meeting other legal requirements such as the Human Rights Act 1998 and the Regulation of Investigatory Powers Act 2000; assist global business in complying with similar legislation in other countries; and help to prevent illegal use of information by workers. By contrast, a failure to comply with the code can lead to prosecution of both the company and/or the individual. Many companies would regard a serious breach of data protection rules as being a disciplinary offence.

As mentioned earlier, data protection covers personal data held on computer and in some paper records where these form part of a relevant filing system. In respect of the employment code, this would include information such as salary details, e-mails, notebooks and application forms of applicants, former applicants, employees, agency workers, casual workers, contract workers, volunteers and work experience placements.

Before an employer can store and process sensitive personal data (see Figure 3.3) at least one of the conditions set out in Schedule 3 must be met (see page 60). For example:

- it is necessary for the purposes of exercising any right or obligation – for example, to ensure health and safety, to avoid discrimination or to check immigration status
- the data subject has freely given explicit consent to the processing.

Employees are entitled to see their data. The request must be in writing and the company must respond within 40 days and can charge up to £10. There are exemptions from disclosure in areas such as criminal investigations or management planning (promotions, transfers or redundancies).

3.8.1   Recruitment and selection

The section of the Employment Code relating to recruitment and selection covers any data on applicants, employees, agency workers and casual workers (current and former) which is stored on a computer or on paper in a relevant filing system. It relates to the processing of data – that is, obtaining, keeping, using, accessing, disclosing or destroying it. This also applies to sensitive personal data, which includes information about racial or ethnic origin, political opinions, religious beliefs, physical or mental health or sex life. Figure 3.8 gives a checklist for employers to follow in order to make sure that they are in compliance with the Employment Code.

3.8.2   Employment records and references

Part 2 of the Employment Practices Data Protection Code covers records management issues relating to personal data stored on computer or on paper in a relevant filing system. It relates to the processing of data – that is, obtaining, keeping, using, accessing, disclosing and destroying it. This also applies to sensitive personal data (as defined in section 3.4), which includes information about racial or ethnic origin, political opinions, religious beliefs, physical or mental health and sex life.

References are subject to the DPA. The *writer* of a confidential reference is not obliged to provide the data subject with access to its contents, but the *recipient* of a reference is obliged to show the data subject the references if a subject access request is received. The employee is therefore able to obtain a copy of the reference from their new employer or would-be employer. It makes no difference whether the reference is marked 'confidential' or not. If the reference was fraudulent or negligent, the writer of the reference could be sued for compensation.

According to the Institute of Management, an employer does not have the right to demand an employee's home telephone number, unless it is specified in the contract that the employee has a duty to be available outside normal working hours. Telephone calls made by a manager to an employee at home could be held to be an invasion of privacy under the Human Rights Act 1998. Even when an employee has indicated a willingness to be called at home, managers should respect privacy and not make unnecessary or inappropriate calls.[10]

Recruitment and selection

- If possible, use the company name in recruitment advertisements.
- Only ask for information that is relevant to the selection process.
- When short-listing, use objective methods such as selection matrices and interview guides in order to avoid subjective decisions.
- Check that your selection criteria do not discriminate in terms of race, age, gender, etc.
- Keep CVs locked away. Only give access to those involved in the recruitment process.
- Explain what information will be checked if applicable, and how – for example, reference and qualification checks. Ask permission from the applicant if taking up references that they did not provide. If these checks suggest discrepancies, allow the applicant the opportunity to explain the inconsistencies.
- Take interview notes. Store them securely. Ensure the notes are relevant and justifiable for the process, e.g. make no assumptions based on age, appearance, etc. Candidates have the right to see these notes.
- Advise unsuccessful applicants if you intend to keep their details on file for future vacancies. Give them the opportunity to ask to have their details removed.
- Only transfer information from recruitment records to employment files where this information is relevant to ongoing employment.
- Remember that workers have the right to see their personal details.
- Keep personal data on staff secure.
- Include a privacy statement when seeking to capture personal data.

Employment records
- Ensure that new employees are aware of any information kept about them, how it will be used and who it will be disclosed to.
- Only collect necessary information and destroy it when no longer required.
- Ask the individual to check the accuracy of information.
- Put systems in place to avoid accidental loss or unauthorized access.
- Place confidentiality clauses in contracts.
- For discrimination reasons, keep sickness and accident records separately from absence records. Only disclose information for legal reasons or if the individual has given consent.
- Make sure the information is secure when being sent, e.g. password-protected.
- Anonymize any information where practical – for example, the author of an employment reference.
- Establish the identity of the person making the request for information. Only disclose information if you think it reasonable and appropriate.

Fig. 3.8   *Employment compliance checklist*

3.8.3   Employee monitoring

One of the most controversial parts of the employment code relates to monitoring at work of such things as e-mail, internet usage, telephone calls or CCTV footage. The DPA does not prevent monitoring. However, employers should ensure that the introduction of monitoring is a proportionate response to the problem that it seeks to address, and staff should be made aware that such monitoring might occur. In making that decision, employers should be absolutely clear about the benefits that monitoring will bring; whether there will be an adverse impact upon workers; whether comparable benefits can be obtained with a lesser impact; and the techniques available for carrying out monitoring.

The monitoring of employees' electronic communications such as telephone calls, fax messages, e-mails and internet access is governed by the Regulation of Investigatory Powers Act 2000, the Human Rights Act 1998 (HRA) and the Telecommunications (Lawful Business Practice) (Interception of Communications) Regulations 2000.[11]

While RIPA covers the *content* of communications, Part 11 of The Anti-Terrorism, Crime and Security Act 2001 covers access to *communications data*, which includes:

- traffic data – information such as a telephone number you call, when you made the call, where you were when you made the call and the location of the person you call
- service data – information about what telecommunications services you use, and when
- subscriber data – information about you that is held by your service provider, such as your name and address.

In March 2003 the Home Office issued two consultation papers on communications data.[12]

The simple listening-in, in real time, on telephone calls without recording them, does not involve the processing of personal data and therefore falls outside the scope of the DPA. However, if an employer carries out monitoring involving an interception which results in the recording of personal data, then they will need to ensure that they comply with the DPA, and that they have also taken account of other relevant statute law such as the RIPA and the HRA.

Monitoring of employees should only be undertaken if there are specific business benefits, and when an impact assessment has concluded that the impact of monitoring on workers is justified by the likely benefits. In making that assessment employers should consult trade unions or other workers' representatives. Where employers undertake monitoring in order to ensure compliance with regulatory requirements or to ensure that the company's policies are not breached, it is important to make sure that the rules and standards are clearly set out and that workers are fully aware of them. Workers should be told what monitoring is taking place and the reasons for it, and they should be periodically reminded that monitoring is undertaken unless covert monitoring can be justified. There should be proper safeguards in place to ensure that information obtained through monitoring is kept securely. One aspect of this would be to strictly limit those who have access to the information, and to include in their contracts a confidentiality clause. Another point would be to take care if sensitive personal data is collected, so that the requirements of Schedule 3 are complied with. It may be that where an organization undertakes monitoring that this results in the employer gleaning information which might be interesting, but which is not strictly relevant to the purpose for which the monitoring was originally put in place. If this happens the employer must avoid using that information unless it is quite clearly in the employee's interest to do so or it reveals activity which no reasonable employer could be expected to ignore.

Whilst employees of a company might know that monitoring of phone conversations is routinely undertaken, that will not automatically be true of those making calls to or receiving calls from employees of the company. They should therefore be made aware that the telephone call may be monitored. Figure 3.9 contains guidance for employers on monitoring at work, taken from the Employment Practices Data Protection Code.

E-mail is subject to the DPA. The ability for employees to send messages around the world at the touch of a button has its own problems such as attracting negative publicity, as was demonstrated by the case of Claire Swire,[13] who became a household name after an e-mail reached thousands of people around the world in a matter of minutes. Other potential problems are that e-mail might increase an employer's liability to actions for defamation, racial or sexual harassment, and that it can increase the chance of employees unintentionally creating contractual commitments for which their employers

1	Senior management should normally authorize any covert monitoring. They should satisfy themselves that there are grounds for suspecting criminal activity or equivalent malpractice and that notifying individuals about the monitoring would prejudice its prevention or detection.
2	Ensure that any covert monitoring is strictly targeted at obtaining evidence within a set timeframe and that the covert monitoring does not continue after the investigation is complete.
3	If embarking on covert monitoring with audio or video equipment, ensure that this is not used in places such as toilets or private offices.
4	If a private investigator is employed to collect information on workers covertly make sure there is a contract in place that requires the private investigator to only collect information in a way that satisfies the employer's obligations under the Act.
5	Ensure that information obtained through covert monitoring is used only for the prevention or detection of the criminal activity or equivalent malpractice. Disregard and, where feasible, delete other information collected in the course of monitoring unless it reveals information that no reasonable employer could be expected to ignore.

The Employment Practice Data Protection Code. Part 3: monitoring at work, Office of the Information Commissioner, 2003

Fig. 3.9   *Guidance on covert monitoring*

may be responsible. The CIPD has a booklet on data protection aimed at HR practitioners.[14] Figure 3.10 offers the employer an e-mail and internet access monitoring checklist.

3.9   The business case

Ensuring that your organization processes data in accordance with policies and procedures that meet the requirements of the DPA makes sound business sense. It is important that, in their dealings with users of their information services, information professionals build up a relationship of trust with them. Having a well thought-out data protection policy and a privacy statement will go a long way to inspiring confidence in users (see Figure 3.11, page 77).

Privacy is a strategic business issue that needs to be applied enterprise-wide. Many organizations recognize that they need to take privacy and data protection issues seriously, and that a failure to do so ultimately has the potential to harm their relationships with customers, business partners or employees. The consequences of not keeping data secure can manifest themselves in a number of different ways such as security breaches, hacking, credit card details getting into the wrong hands, or computer viruses causing disruption. Where

1	Make sure all employees password-protect their systems.
2	Employers should have written policies on e-mail and internet usage monitoring which outline clearly what is and what is not acceptable use of company systems, and what action will be taken should employees breach these policies.
3	Those who send e-mails to employees, as well as the employees themselves, need to be made aware of any monitoring and the purpose behind it, unless this is obvious.
4	Use simple, clear disclaimers on e-mails and web pages where necessary.
5	The policies on authorized access and acceptable use should be available at the login screen.
6	If it is necessary to check the e-mail accounts of workers in their absence, make sure that they are aware that this will happen.
7	Inform workers of the extent to which information about their internet access and e-mails is retained in the system and for what length of time.
8	Do not retain data for any longer than you need to.
9	Make sure that sensitive data is adequately secured.
10	Take into account the possibility of unintentional access to websites by workers when you are reviewing the results of any monitoring.
11	Train staff to exercise caution when using e-mail, just as much with other written documents.
12	Handle complaints in a fair, consistent and common-sense manner as they arise.
13	Ensure that any precautions taken are proportionate to the level of risk.
14	Where there is any doubt, seek legal advice.

Fig. 3.10   *E-mail and internet access monitoring checklist*

companies fail to protect the personal data of customers, clients, employees or partners, the consequence might be that a fine is imposed. But once news of an incident of poor management of personal data gets out, it can have a dramatic impact upon the organization's reputation, and it might even have a negative impact on the company's share price and result in a loss of clients.

In cases where the Office of the Information Commissioner issues an enforcement notice and this is then breached, the company would risk potential criminal prosecution.

A couple of examples of where things went wrong include a large US bank[15] who paid millions to settle a complaint that it sold customer data, including account numbers and balances, social security numbers and home phone numbers, to telemarketers; and an online ad agency which was hit with charges that it would violate consumer privacy if it merged anonymous user names with data from a company it acquired. After the Federal Trade Commission launched a probe, the agency's share price fell by over 20% in a week.[16]

3.10   Data protection compliance audits

A data protection compliance audit is a systematic and independent examination to determine whether activities involving the processing of personal data are carried out in accordance with an organization's data protection policies and procedures, and whether this processing meets the requirements of the DPA.

The key factors involved in data protection audits are that they should involve a systematic approach; that they should, where possible, be carried out by independent auditors; that they should be conducted in accordance with a documented audit procedure; and that their outcome should be a documented audit report.

There are a number of reasons why data protection audits should be carried out:

* to assess the level of compliance with the DPA
* to assess the level of compliance with the organization's own data protection system
* to identify potential gaps and weaknesses in the data protection system
* to provide information for a data protection system review.

The audit is a mechanism for ensuring that personal data is obtained and processed fairly, lawfully and on a proper basis. When carrying out a data protection audit in any area of an organization there are three clear objectives:

* to verify that there is a formal documented and up-to-date data protection system in place in the area
* to verify that all the staff in the area involved in data protection are aware of the existence of the data protection system, and that they understand and use that system
* to verify that the data protection system in the area actually works and is effective.

Undertaking a data protection audit facilitates compliance with the DPA. The very fact that an audit is taking place serves to raise awareness of data protection issues amongst both management and staff, and can act as a training tool. Additionally, where weaknesses are identified and then addressed, this can lead to improved customer satisfaction because it pro-actively tackles areas that might otherwise have led to complaints.

The auditor needs to check that the data protection procedures in place comply with the data protection legislation in the context of other pieces of legislation such as the Human Rights Act; that they comply with the data subject's rights; that there are clear policies, codes of practice, guidelines and procedures in place; that where personal data is processed there are proper quality assurance safeguards to ensure that the information is accurate, complete, up to date, adequate, relevant and not excessive; and that there are formal retention policies in place to ensure that appropriate weeding and deletion of information occurs automatically.

The Office of the Information Commissioner has produced a useful guide to data protection compliance auditing, which can be found at www.informationcommissioner.gov.uk/dpaudit. It contains a step-by-step guide to data protection auditing with a series of forms, checklists and basic auditing guidance to help ensure that even small organizations with limited auditing experience are able to undertake compliance audits.

3.11   Issues concerning websites and intranets

Anyone who hosts a website which processes personal data needs to ensure that users of that site are aware of:

- the identity of the person or organization responsible for operating the website
- the purposes for which the data collected is processed
- any other information that is needed in order to ensure the fairness of the processing of the data, such as whether the site uses cookies.

This requirement to process data fairly and lawfully can be achieved by developing a privacy policy statement (see Figure 3.11) which covers information about the data that you collect, the reasons for collecting it, and details of who it is passed on to. It is important to ensure that the statement provides the user with information which ensures that the processing of the data is fair. If, for example, your site uses invisible tracking devices such as cookies or web bugs, this could hardly be said to be fair unless you have made that clear to potential users of your site.

It is well worth investing time in developing a privacy statement, because it will govern what you are able to do with the data that you collect. Consumers are likely to have real concerns about giving out personal data through a website. They may be reluctant to engage in electronic transactions unless they can be reassured about the privacy of their personal data. Privacy policies are therefore a vital step towards encouraging openness and trust in electronic commerce among visitors to websites. Where an individual uses a website and looks up the data protection or privacy statement, they are then able to make an informed choice about whether or not to entrust their personal data to that organization, and whether or not they are willing to do business with that company. To assist in the process of putting together a data protection statement there is an OECD privacy statement generator, which can be found on their website at http://cs3-hq.oecd.org/scripts/pwv3/pwhome.htm.

The data protection statement should appear in a prominent position on the website. Recognizing that people can get to pages within a website by a number of different routes, you should always ensure that wherever personal data is being collected, the data subject always has the option to click on a link to see the privacy statement or at least an outline of the basic messages and choices, even where a more detailed explanation is provided elsewhere by means of a privacy statement. As well as having a privacy statement on your organization's website, you might also want to put a data protection statement onto your intranet or your library catalogue, depending on whether or not you use these to collect, process or hold personal data.

Websites and intranets might be used to collect or process personal data in a number of ways. For example, they might have a directory of employees, clients or business partners; or they might have a series of biographical information pages about members of staff, including photographs. Websites or intranets can also be used in order to collect data by means of online registration forms, requests for information or online research surveys. They might make use of invisible tracking devices such as cookies or web bugs. A key question that needs to be considered is whether or not any of the categories of data being collected fall within the definition of sensitive personal data (see section 3.4), in which case there are stricter safeguards to be considered.

> 1 Your company's name and address, so that customers can contact you if they need to.
> 2 The information that is gathered about a customer.
> 3 What you will do with this information.
> 4 If cookies are used to track a customer's movements, then this must be specifically drawn to their attention.
> 5 Details of how the customer will be contacted.
> 6 If your company is planning on sharing or disclosing personal information to any of its group companies or third parties, the customer must be informed of this.
> 7 The customer must have the opportunity to object to being marketed to.
> 8 Details of the rights of customers to access their personal data and rectify any inaccuracies.
> 9 How long you intend to hold the data on your system.
> 10 The choices available to customers about the processing of their personal information.
> 11 How data security is managed.
> 12 You must give the notice to your customers before they are asked to complete their details online.

Fig. 3.11   *What should be in a data protection/privacy statement?*

3.11.1 Directive on privacy in the electronic communications sector

The directive on privacy and electronic communications (2002/58/EC)[17] covers marketing via e-mail, SMS (short message service) messaging and other electronic communication methods; and it also regulates the use of invisible tracking devices such as cookies or web bugs. It replaces the Telecoms Directive[18] and introduces protection for subscribers to electronic communications services. In March 2003, the Department of Trade and Industry issued a consultation document,[19] and at the time of writing the Privacy and Electronic Communications (EC Directive) Regulations 2003 were due to be laid before Parliament and to come into force on 31 October 2003. Key features are outlined in Figure 3.12.

3.11.2 Spam

Spamming is the practice of bulk-sending unsolicited commercial e-mails in order to market and promote products and services. The e-commerce directive,[20] which was implemented in the UK in August 2002,[21] requires unsolicited commercial e-mail to be clearly identified as such in the title. This makes it easier for addressees to delete or filter out messages that they do not want to read. The directive on privacy and electronic communications

1	The EU set an important world-wide precedent by adopting a harmonized opt-in approach to unsolicited commercial e-mail. The opt-in also covers SMS messages and other electronic messages received on any mobile or fixed terminal.
2	Citizens have the right to determine whether their phone numbers for mobile or fixed lines, their e-mail addresses and physical addresses figure in public directories.
3	The use of privacy-sensitive location data indicating the exact whereabouts of mobile users is subject to explicit consent by the user. Moreover, users should have the possibility of temporarily blocking the processing of these location data such as 'cell of origin' data at any time.
4	Invisible tracking devices, such as cookies that may collect information on users of the internet, may only be employed if the user is provided with adequate information about the purposes of such devices and has the possibility of rejecting these tracking devices.

Fig. 3.12   *Key features of the directive on privacy and electronic communications 2002/58/EC*

(2002/58/EC) brings in further rules on the sending of spam, which require the prior consent of an individual before unsolicited commercial e-mail is sent unless there is an existing customer relationship. It also makes it unlawful to send junk mail anonymously or using a false identity. Whether the legislation will have the desired effect is quite another matter, since laws which are limited in geographic scope (in this case to data controllers established in the EEA) are of limited use when e-mail and the world wide web are truly global, and most spam comes from the USA.

The European Union undertook a study, which found that 'junk' e-mail costs internet users €10 billion a year worldwide.[22] There are a number of steps that can be taken to minimize junk mail:

1 Use the e-mail filters employed by your internet service provider (for example, it is possible within Hotmail to say that you only wish to receive e-mails from a list of people that you specify).
2 Contact one of the associations devoted to preventing junk e-mail such as:
   - CAUCE, available at www.cauce.org
   - EuroCAUCE, available at www.euro.cauce.org/en
   - SpamCon Foundation, available at www.spamcon.org
3 Use e-mail checking software such as Mailwasher, available at www. mailwasher.net.

If you have a problem with spam, it is good advice not to reply or request to unsubscribe unless you recognize the sender. Doing so only confirms that you are a real recipient. If you receive unsolicited e-mail and you can tell from the subject or sender that it is spam, you should delete it without opening it. In many cases, the senders track the opening of e-mails and use this to confirm that the recipient is real. They then send more.

The privacy and electronic communications directive requires the prior, positive consent (that is opt-in) for direct marketing via e-mail, SMS messages and other electronic messages received on any mobile or fixed terminal for new customers. In the case of existing customers,[23] a modified opt-out system applies in relation to sending them direct marketing by e-mail, mobile telephone or mobile text messaging.

Information about a user's movements within a site obtained by means of a cookie becomes personal data when it is combined with personal details submitted in a form. The cookie contains a unique number generated by the site, which is typically a series of numbers and letters intelligible only to the site, but it may also contain the user's account name and password or internet address. Cookies can be used to enable the website to 'recognize' a repeat visitor by linking the cookie to information the website has collected about the user's previous visits. This can be helpful to the user as it means that they don't need to enter their username and password on every visit. It can also help to develop the level of personalization of a website by storing preference details of the user. The directive permits cookies on an opt-out basis provided that recipients of the cookie are aware that a cookie will be deposited on their machine; that the purposes are clear for which the information collected via the cookie will be processed; and that they have been given an opportunity to opt out of receiving cookies.

Websites using cookies must ensure that the site's privacy policy or terms and conditions contain sufficient information to comply with the new requirements. They therefore need to provide the user with information as to which data is collected through the site, by whom, what will be done with the data, how long it will be kept, how it will be processed and how the user can disable cookies if they so wish.

The security provisions of directive 2002/58/EC include a new obligation on providers of publicly available electronic communications services to inform users if there is a security risk to the network where that security risk lies outside the scope of the provider's security measures. Service providers must also inform users of any possible remedies, including an indication of any likely costs. This information should appear in the general terms and conditions of use for services such as e-mail accounts or real-time chat-room facilities.

The directive requires that, before people are included in any public directory, they must be informed of this and they must be given the opportunity to opt out of that inclusion.

Article 6 of directive 2002/58/EC requires that traffic data must be erased or made anonymous by electronic communications service providers when it is no longer needed for the purpose of the transmission of a communication.

3.12   The implications for librarians

Library and information services are likely to process personal data as part of their day-to-day operations. Examples might include:

- user registration records containing user names and addresses
- circulation records
- library catalogues and databases containing the names of personal authors
- contact databases containing names, job titles, e-mail addresses and direct phone numbers
- staff records
- payroll and pension records
- management statistics on usage of the information service.

The CILIP Code of Professional Ethics in no way affects legal obligations under the Act, but it does supplement them with professional principles which apply to user information. Information professionals are required to protect the confidentiality of all matters relating to information users, including their enquiries, any services to be provided, and any aspects of the users' personal circumstances or business.

Where librarians are asked for confidential information by the police or any other agency, they should first request that a court order be obtained. The previous code[24] said that no breach of the code takes place when a librarian provides information, no matter how confidential, in response to a court order.

3.13   Electoral roll information in libraries

The Representation of the People Act 2000 has established a framework whereby there are two versions of the electoral register. The full register, containing everyone's details, is available only for electoral and a limited range of other purposes. The edited register, which continues to be available for sale for any purpose, does not include the details of those who have chosen to 'opt out'.

Before the Representation of the People Act 2000 entered into force, an elector brought a case to court against his local electoral registration officer (ERO) in Wakefield.[25] Mr Robertson was concerned that if he registered to vote he would have no right to object to the sale of his details for marketing purposes. In finding in Mr Robertson's favour the court ruled that the use of the electoral register for commercial purposes without an individual right of objection was in breach of the DPA.

Following the Robertson case, public librarians wanted clarification about how this would affect the making available of the registers in public libraries for inspection and consultation. The judge did say that EROs must consider and anticipate the purposes for which personal data are intended to be processed. If commercial data collection companies are allowed to access and copy the data in the public library for free, then EROs are likely to be forced to clamp down on this as well. It is anticipated that new regulations will restrict copying of the full registers held by libraries to something like 'making brief manuscript notes', that there will have to be a degree of supervision and that each council will have to decide whether its public libraries can offer such safeguards. Archive copies of previous full registers will also fall under these restrictions. Staffordshire Libraries and Information Services have produced a poster entitled 'Electoral Registers Clarification', which can be accessed via the LACA website at www.cilip.org.uk/committees/laca/er.html.

The Information Commissioner has expressed concerns[26] over other public registers such as the Register of Members ('Shareholders Register'), the Register of Directors and Secretaries, the Register of County Court Judgments and the Register of Medical Practitioners. Those who own shares, take on company directorships, get into debt or practise certain professions similarly have no choice but to have their details made available for marketing and other commercial purposes. Another potential danger is that the registers can also provide the basis for those wishing to establish false identities.

Having directors' home addresses on the public record is a key part of making sure business activity remains transparent and accountable. But when threats were made against the directors of the Cambridgeshire-based Huntingdon Life Sciences biotechnology firm by animal rights protesters, who had tracked down the directors using the information lodged at Companies House, the government decided that action needed to be taken to prevent such cases of intimidation. Legislation was introduced to bring those changes into effect. Section 45 of the Criminal Justice and Police Act 2001 inserted sections 723B to 723F into the Companies Act 1985. Those sections provide for a system for granting confidentiality orders to directors and secretaries of companies formed under the 1985 Act and to directors, secretaries and permanent representatives of oversea companies with a place of business, or to a branch in Great Britain within the meaning of the 1985 Act. This was then followed up by the Companies (Particulars of Usual Residential Address) (Confidentiality Orders) Regulations 2002: SI 2002/912 which enables the Secretary of State to issue confidentiality orders to individuals when they are satisfied that the availability for inspection of the usual residential address of that individual in the records of the registrar of companies creates, or is likely to create, a serious risk that the individual, or a person who lives with them, will be subjected to violence or intimidation. The effect of the order is that all notifications to the registrar of companies subsequent to the granting of the order in respect of the usual residential address of the beneficiary of an order are kept as confidential records by the registrar which do not form part of the records available for public inspection.

Figure 3.13 list some useful sources of help and advice on data protection.

3.14   Summary

In this chapter we have considered the general principles of data protection (3.2), including the eight data-protection principles (3.3). The chapter also

Information Commissioner	www.informationcommissioner.gov.uk
Privacy Laws & Business	www.privacylaws.com
JISC Legal Information Service	www.jisc.ac.uk/legal
Department for Constitutional Affairs – Freedom of Information and Data Protection Division	www.lcd.gov.uk/foi/foidpunit.htm

Fig. 3.13   *Where to go to seek data protection information or advice*

dealt with the legal requirements to be borne in mind before personal data can be processed (3.4), including the requirement for data controllers to notify the Office of the Information Commissioner that they process personal data (3.5). Recognizing that library and information professionals are data subjects in their own right, the chapter acknowledged that personal data is a valuable commodity which should be protected (3.6), and that data subjects have a number of rights under the DPA (3.7). Issues relating to employment matters were considered (3.8), including recruitment and selection, employment records and the controversial issue of whether it is permissible to monitor an employee's internet, telephone or e-mail usage. The chapter then discussed the role of data protection compliance audits (3.10) in ensuring that the legislative requirements are met, and how the mere fact that an audit is undertaken can help to raise awareness of data protection issues within the organization. The chapter discussed issues relating to websites and intranets such as the use of cookies, the problem of unsolicited commercial e-mail, and the implications of the directive on privacy in the electronic communications sector (3.11). This section also looked at the role of the data protection or privacy statement in informing users of a service about how their data would be handled, and how it could – if well drafted – reassure them that they are comfortable doing business with that organization. The chapter concluded by considering the implication of data protection for librarians (3.12), including the question of how public librarians handle requests for access to electoral roll data (3.13), now that there are two versions of the electoral roll.

If you process personal data, then you need to ensure that you are registered with the Office of the Information Commissioner and that your register entry adequately covers the scope of your operations. It is important that it is clear who within the organization has ultimate responsibility for data protection matters; but people also need to be clear about who would handle access requests, who would handle contractual or data transfer issues, or who would deal with complaints by customers about issues relating to their personal data.

In the next chapter the role of the Information Commissioner is considered; and the chapter seeks to clarify the data protection and freedom of information responsibilities of the Information Commissioner in the light of the creation of the post of Scottish Information Commissioner under the Freedom of Information (Scotland) Act 2002.

3.15   Further information

British Standards Institution

389 Chiswick High Road, London W4 4AL
Tel: 020 8996 9001
Website: www.bsi-global.com
[BSI publishes a data protection update service]

Department for Constitutional Affairs

Freedom of Information and Data Protection Division, Room 151 Selborne
House, London SW1E 6QW
Tel: 020 7210 8755; Fax: 020 7210 1415
Website: www.lcd.gov.uk/

Europa

Internal market – data protection homepage
E-mail: markt-info@cec.eu.int
Website: http://europa.eu.int/comm/internal_market/privacy/index_en.htm

JISC Legal Information Service

The JISC Legal Information Service, Learning Services, Level 3, Alexan-
der Turnbull Building, 155 George Street, Glasgow G1 1RD
Tel: 0141 548 4939; Fax: 0141 548 4216
Website: www.jisc.ac.uk/legal

OECD privacy statement generator

Website: http://cs3-hq.oecd.org/scripts/pwv3/pwhome.htm

Office of the Information Commissioner

Wycliffe House, Water Lane, Wilmslow, Cheshire SK9 5AF
Tel: 01625 545 745; Fax: 01625 524 510; E-mail: data@dataprotection.gov.uk
Website: www.informationcommissioner.gov.uk
(and for the Data Protection Register www.dpr.gov.uk).

Notes and references

1   CILIP code of professional ethics: draft for consultation, 2003.
2   A cookie is a small file that is placed on a user's hard drive by a website.

3   DPA 1998 s1.

4   Directive 95/46/EC on the protection of individuals with regard to the processing of personal data and on the free movement of such data.

5   Convention for the protection of human rights and fundamental freedoms – see the Council of Europe conventions website at http://conventions.coe.int.

6   Experian, *Data Protection Act 1998: a simplified guide to assist businesses holding personal information on customers, suppliers, directors, shareholders and others*, (no date).

7   Commission decision of 27 December 2001 on standard contractual clauses for the transfer of personal data to processors established in third countries under directive 95/46/EC, in Official Journal L6/52, 10 January 2002.

8   The register of data controllers can be found at www.dpr.gov.uk.

9   Experian, *Data Protection Act 1998: a simplified guide to assist businesses holding personal information on customers, suppliers, directors, shareholders and others*, (no date).

10 For further information see Institute of Management, *Guidelines for Managers on the Human Rights Act 1998*, 2001.

11 Telecommunications (Lawful Business Practice) (Interception of Communications) Regulations 2000: SI 2000/2699.

12 Home Office, *Access to Communications Data: respecting privacy and protecting the public from crime*, March 2003; Home Office, *Consultation paper on a code of practice for voluntary retention of communications data*, March 2003.

13 See, for example, 'Email woman in hiding', *BBC News Online*, 16 December 2000, available at http://news.bbc.co.uk/1/hi/uk/1072391.stm.

14 *Data Protection, Legal Essentials series*, CIPD, (no date).

15 Implementing privacy protection should be seen as an asset, not a cost, *The Business Journal*, 20 September 2002.

16 Privacy risks threaten bottom lines: why CFOs should worry about their companies' internet privacy policies, *CFO.com*, 22 February 2001.

17 Directive 2002/58/EC of the European Parliament and of the council of 12 July 2002 concerning the processing of personal data and the protection of privacy in the electronic communications sector (directive on privacy and electronic communications), 31 July 2002 L201/37, was adopted by the European Council on 25 June 2002 and came into force on being published in the Official Journal of the European Communities on 31 July 2002. Member states were required to implement its provisions into their national laws by 31 October 2003.

18 Directive concerning the processing of personal data and the protection of privacy in the telecommunications sector – 97/66/EC.

19 Department of Trade and Industry, Implementation of the directorate on privacy and electronic communications, 2003.

20   Directive 2000/31/EC of the European Parliament and of the council of 8 June 2000 on certain legal aspects of information society services, in particular electronic commerce, in the internal market OJ L178, 17 July 2000.

21   The Electronic Commerce (EC Directive) Regulations 2002: SI 2002/2013.www.legislation.hmso.gov.uk/si/si2002/20022013.htm

22   See http://europa.eu.int/comm/internal_market/privacy/studies/spam_en.htm. The report 'Unsolicited commercial communications and data protections', Commission of the European Communities, January 2001, is available at http://europa.eu.int/comm/internal_market/en/dataprot/studies/spamstudyen.pdf.

23   Until the Privacy and Electronic Communications (EC Directive) Regulations 2003 are passed, it is not clear how an existing customer relationship will be defined.

24   Library Association code of professional conduct.

25   R. v. City of Wakefield Metropolitan Council & another ex parte Robertson (16 November 2001).

26   In their annual report 2002, 22.

4 The Information Commissioner

4.1 Introduction

This chapter considers the role and functions of the Information Commissioner in relation to data protection and freedom of information (4.2). It examines the implications of devolved government and the appointment of Assistant Commissioners (4.3), and considers the functions of the Scottish Information Commissioner (4.4). Finally the chapter looks at how both the Information Commissioner and the Scottish Information Commissioner can charge for certain services (4.5).

4.2 The role of the Information Commissioner

The Office of the Information Commissioner is not a typical non-departmental public body. Such bodies usually have a relationship with ministers which is based on the delegation of ministerial powers. In the case of the Commissioner, it is a UK independent supervisory authority reporting directly to the UK parliament and has an international role as well as a national one.

The Information Commissioner enforces and oversees the Data Protection Act 1998 (DPA), the Freedom of Information Act 2000 (FOIA) and the Telecommunications (Data Protection and Privacy) Regulations 1999 (the Regulations) using only the powers which these pieces of legislation set out. Decisions of the Information Commissioner are subject to the supervision of the courts and the Information Tribunal.

The Commissioner was previously known as the Data Protection Commissioner and became the Information Commissioner on 30 January 2001,[1] when responsibility for freedom of information was added to the Commissioner's remit. This dual role enables the Commissioner to provide an integrated and coherent approach.

The mission statement of the Office of the Information Commissioner[2] says:

88 ESSENTIAL LAW FOR INFORMATION PROFESSIONALS

> We shall develop respect for the private lives of individuals and encourage the openness and accountability of public authorities: by promoting good information handling practice and enforcing data protection and freedom of information legislation; and by seeking to influence national and international thinking on privacy and information access issues.

The Information Commissioner participates in, and contributes to, European and international developments in the fields of data protection and freedom of information. For example, the Information Commissioner offered support to the Commonwealth Secretariat in producing model data protection law for use in Commonwealth countries. In September 2002, in conjunction with colleagues in Ireland, Jersey, Guernsey and the Isle of Man, the Information Commissioner hosted the annual international conference of data protection commissioners.

4.2.1   Data protection

The Information Commissioner's role in relation to data protection is set out in sections 51–4 of the DPA. Key elements of their role are:

- to promote good practice
- to make assessments
- to serve information notices
- to serve enforcement notices
- to use its powers of entry and inspection
- to commence proceedings for offences under the DPA
- to prepare and disseminate codes of practice for guidance on good practice.

The Information Commissioner has obligations to assess alleged breaches of the DPA. His office may serve information notices requiring data controllers to supply them with the information they need to assess compliance. Where there has been a breach, they can also serve an enforcement notice requiring data controllers to take specified steps (or to stop taking steps) in order to comply with the law. Appeals against these notices may be made to the Information Tribunal, which was formerly known as the Data Protection Tribunal.

The government decided that the Office of the Information Commissioner should also enforce the Telecommunications (Data Protection and Privacy) Regulations 1999 and the Amendment Regulations 2000 [The Telecommunications (Data Protection and Privacy) Regulations 1999 SI 1999/2093 and the Telecommunications (Data Protection and Privacy) (Amendment) Regulations 2000 SI 2000/157 will be replaced by the Privacy and Electronic Communications (EC Directive) Regulations 2003 which is anticipated to come into force by 31 October 2003] using the powers provided to that office under the DPA. This can involve issuing a detailed enforcement notice. Such notices can be, and usually are, appealed against, and whilst they are subject to appeal their application is suspended. Therefore, when a notice has been appealed it has no application until either the appeal is withdrawn or the Information Tribunal has adjudicated on the matter. Once a notice is in force, further contravention will, subject to a defence of reasonable diligence, be an offence. The Office of the Information Commissioner can then prosecute but has to collect further evidence before doing so. The whole enforcement process is time-consuming and makes significant demands upon the resources of the Office of the Information Commissioner. This means that, where a business chooses to ignore the requirements of the law, it can be many months before the Information Commissioner's Office are in a position to seek a criminal prosecution by the courts. In England, Wales and Northern Ireland, the Commissioner or the Director of Public Prosecutions may institute proceedings. In the case of Scotland there is no mention of this in section 60 of the DPA, although chapter 9 of the guidance states that all prosecutions must be brought by the Procurator Fiscal.

In recent years the Information Commissioner has taken enforcement action against a number of fax marketing companies following breaches of the Regulations in which unsolicited marketing faxes were sent to subscribers listed on the fax preference service register. Where an enforcement notice is in force, those who fail to comply with it will have commited a criminal offence punishable by a fine.

If an individual believes that one of the data protection principles has been breached (or any other requirements of the DPA), and they are unable or unwilling to sort the problem out themselves, they can ask the Information Commissioner to assess whether the requirements of the DPA have been met. The Commissioner will always try to deal with matters informally. However, if the Commissioner's assessment is that the requirements of the DPA have not been met and the matter cannot be settled informally, then his office may decide to take enforcement action against the data controller in question.

If the Commissioner takes enforcement action against a data controller, the controller can appeal to the independent Information Tribunal. However, if the Tribunal agrees with the Commissioner's enforcement action and the data controller continues to break the principles, a criminal offence can result for which the data controller can be prosecuted.

4.2.2   Freedom of information

The Information Commissioner is also responsible for freedom of information in England, Wales and Northern Ireland, and the general functions of the Commissioner are set out in Section 47 of the Freedom of Information Act 2000 (FOIA). With respect to freedom of information, the Commissioner's duties are:

* to approve or revoke publication schemes
* to promote the following of good practice by public authorities
* to promote public authorities' compliance with the FOIA and the provisions of the codes of practice made under sections 45 and 46, which relate respectively to dealing with requests for information and desirable practice in connection with the keeping, management and destruction of records
* to disseminate information about the operation of the FOIA and give advice about it
* with consent, to assess whether a public authority is following good practice
* to arrange for the dissemination of information about any other matters within the scope of their functions under the FOIA (he may give advice to any person about any of those matters)
* to report annually to Parliament.

The Information Commissioner is responsible for setting priorities for his Office and deciding how they should be achieved.

4.3   The Information Commissioner and devolved government

Data protection is a reserved matter. This means that the UK Parliament is responsible for data protection throughout the UK, and the legislation applies in England, Scotland, Northern Ireland and Wales. Freedom of information is not similarly reserved, and it can therefore be devolved to national legislatures. Consequently, the Information Commissioner is responsible for both data protection and freedom of information in England, Wales and Northern Ireland, but is only responsible for data protection in Scotland.

The Office of the Information Commissioner decided that, in view of the new constitutional arrangements for devolved government, they would establish an office presence in Scotland, Wales and Northern Ireland. On 3 April 2003, the Information Commissioner announced[3] the appointment of Assistant Commissioners for Scotland, Wales and Northern Ireland, and advised that regional offices would be opened by the end of 2003. The appointment of Assistant Commissioners is a recognition that local issues and sensitivities need to be fully understood and integrated into the promotion of good information handling across the UK.

The Assistant Commissioners, who all report directly to the Information Commissioner, are responsible for taking forward the Commissioner's work in promoting and enforcing both the DPA and the FOIA. In Scotland, Scottish public authorities are subject to the Freedom of Information (Scotland) Act (FOI(S)A), enforced by the Scottish Information Commissioner.[4] The Assistant Commissioner (Scotland) liaises closely with the Scottish Commissioner's office to uphold access to information rights under UK and Scottish legislation.

In England and Wales, proceedings for a criminal offence under the FOIA can be commenced by the Information Commissioner, or by or with the consent of the Director of Public Prosecutions; in Scotland, criminal proceedings will normally be brought by the Procurator Fiscal; whilst in Northern Ireland, proceedings for an offence under the FOIA can be begun by the Information Commissioner, or by or with the consent of the Director of Public Prosecutions for Northern Ireland.

4.4 Scottish Information Commissioner

The Freedom of Information (Scotland) Act 2002 (FOI(S)A)[5] was passed by the Scottish Parliament on 24 April 2002 and received Royal Assent on 28 May 2002. It established the freedom of information regime for devolved Scotland. It is the FOI(S)A that created the post of Scottish Information Commissioner. Section 43 of the FOI(S)A sets out the Scottish Information Commissioner's general functions. It places a duty on the Commissioner to promote good practice and Scottish public authorities' compliance with the FOI(S)A, their publication schemes and codes of practice. The Scottish Information Commissioner is also obliged, where he considers it expedient, to disseminate information to the public about the operation of the freedom of information regime. The Commissioner can also make 'practice recommendations' specifying what a Scottish public authority should do to comply with the codes of practice, and is required to lay annual reports before the Scottish Parliament.

The key functions of the Scottish Information Commissioner are:

• to promote good practice by Scottish public authorities in relation to the Scottish freedom of information regime
• to raise public awareness of the Scottish freedom of information regime
• to consider appeals from people seeking the disclosure of information.

The Scottish Information Commissioner is appointed by the Queen on the nomination of the Scottish Parliament. Once the FOI(S)A is fully in force, the public has direct access to the Scottish Information Commissioner, rather than only through the intervention of their MSP[6] (as has been the case with access to the Scottish Parliamentary Commissioner for Administration, who deals with complaints under the present Code of Practice on Access to Scottish Executive Information[7]).

The statutory rights under the FOI(S)A and the Scottish Information Commissioner's regulatory powers extend to information contained in historical public records, such as those held by the National Archives of Scotland.

4.5   Charging for services

The Information Commissioner can charge for certain services, with regard to both their data protection and their freedom of information responsibilities. This is set out in the legislation as follows:

DPA, section 51(8)
The wording used is that 'The Commissioner may charge such sums as he may with the consent of the Secretary of State determine for any serv-

ices provided by the Commissioner . . .' and a similar form of words is used in the FOIA.

This is also true of the Scottish Information Commissioner, who also has the right to charge for services, as outlined in the FOI(S)A section 43(5), where it states that 'the Commissioner may determine and charge sums for services provided under this section.'

4.6   Summary

This chapter has looked at both the role and the functions of the Information Commissioner in relation to data protection and freedom of information (4.2). It has examined the implications of devolved government on the remit of the Information Commissioner (4.3); and the functions of the Scottish Information Commissioner have been outlined (4.4). The chapter finished off by outlining how both the Information Commissioner and the Scottish Information Commissioner are able to charge for certain services (4.5).

The next chapter considers freedom of information and includes an overview of the general principles of freedom of information; the use of publication schemes by public authorities as a means of outlining what they routinely publish or intend to publish; the rights of individuals to request information; and the rights of redress where people feel that the FOIA or the FOI(S)A have not been followed.

4.7   Further information

Department for Constitutional Affairs

Freedom of Information and Data Protection Division, Room 151, Selborne House, London SW1E 6QW
Tel: 020 7210 8755; Fax: 020 7210 1415
Website: www.lcd.gov.uk/

Information Commissioner

Wycliffe House, Water Lane, Wilmslow, Cheshire SK9 5AF
Tel: 01625 545745; Fax: 01625 524510; E-mail: data@dataprotection.gov.uk
Website: www.dataprotection.gov.uk

JISC Legal Information Service

Learning Services, Level 3, Alexander Turnbull Building, 155 George Street, Glasgow G1 1RD
Tel: 0141 548 4939; Fax: 0141 548 4216
Website: www.jisc.ac.uk/legal

Scottish Executive. Freedom of Information Unit

St Andrew's House, Regent Road, Edinburgh EH1 3DG
Tel: 0131 244 4615; Fax: 0131 244 2582; E-mail: foi@scotland.gsi.gov.uk
Website: www.scotland.gov.uk/government/foi

Notes and references

1   By virtue of sections 18(1) and 87(2)(a) of the Freedom of Information Act 2000.
2   As set out on page 5 of the *Information Commissioner Annual Report and Accounts for the Year Ending 31 March 2002*, HC 913, The Stationery Office, June 2002.
3   Information Commissioner press release of 3 April 2003: 'Information Commissioner appoints new assistant commissioners for Scotland, Wales and Northern Ireland.'
4   Who at the time of writing was Kevin Dunion.
5   (2002 asp 13), available at www.scotland-legislation.hmso.gov.uk/legislation/scotland/acts2002/20020013.htm.
6   Member of the Scottish Parliament.
7   The code of practice is available from the website of the Campaign for Freedom of Information at www.cfoi.org.uk/pdf/scotcop.pdf, and there is also a set of web pages from the Scottish Executive on Freedom of Information at www.scotland.gov.uk/government/foi/.

5 Freedom of information

5.1 Introduction

Library and information professionals are uniquely placed and skilled to defend and deliver freedom of information. This chapter outlines the general principles of freedom of information (5.2). It then looks at a number of freedom of information initiatives which are already in operation for UK citizens (5.3) covering access to government information (5.3.1), public records (5.3.2), openness in the NHS (5.3.3), environmental information (5.3.4), local government information (5.3.5), European Union documents (5.3.6) and rights of access under the DPA (5.3.7). The Freedom of Information Act 2000 (FOIA) is discussed (5.4), and the manner in which the freedom of information regime it introduces will operate. The chapter then looks at how publication schemes are used as guides to what a public authority routinely publishes or intends to publish (5.5). The chapter outlines some of the copyright implications of complying with the FOIA (5.6). It then outlines the rights of an individual to make a request for information from a public authority, and the process involved (5.7). The chapter looks at the exemptions in the Act, and how most of these require public authorities to consider a test of prejudice and a public interest test, although there are some absolute exemptions. The chapter examines the appeals process (5.8) – where individuals consider that the FOIA has not been followed, they can apply to the Information Commissioner for a decision on whether or not the legislation has been adhered to (5.9). The chapter looks at the separate freedom of information regime in Scotland (5.10), and concludes by highlighting the discrepancies which exist between the freedom of information and data protection legislation (5.11).

5.2 General principles of freedom of information

Freedom of information is a fundamental human right and is the touchstone of all the freedoms to which the United Nations is consecrated – as stated in the United Nations General Assembly Resolution 59(i), which was passed at its first session on 14 December 1946.

Representing its membership of around 23,000 information staff, the Chartered Institute of Library and Information Professionals (CILIP) attaches a high value to freedom of information, which is considered to be a core responsibility of its members. The Institute believes that the library and information professional is uniquely placed and skilled to defend and deliver freedom of information.

CILIP's policy on information access states:

> . . . the right of access to information is essential for a civilized society. If citizens are to exercise their democratic rights, and to make information choices, they must have access to political, social, scientific and economic information. If our culture is to thrive and to grow, people need access to the widest range of ideas, information and images.[1]

CILIP's code of professional ethics binds its members to uphold its policy on access to information:

> The conduct of information professionals should be characterized by commitment to the defence of, and the enhancement of, access to information.[2]

The Westminster Parliament and the Scottish Assembly should both be applauded for overseeing the introduction of a freedom of information framework. However, it is unclear whether the government really does have a genuine commitment to the principles of freedom of information. When the Labour Party won the 1997 general election, they said that they were committed to the introduction of a radical Freedom of Information Act. With the appointment of Dr David Clark as Chancellor of the Duchy of Lancaster with responsibility for overseeing freedom of information, and with the publication in late 1997 of the White Paper *Your right to know: freedom of information*,[3] it certainly looked very promising. A year later, however, David Clark was once again a backbencher, and freedom of information legislation was not given parliamentary time for several years into the Labour administration.

At the end of April 1998 Lord Irvine said:

> I have no doubt that journalists and campaigners will take advantage of our
> regime of greater openness to reveal data which may be uncomfortable for
> officials and ministers. That is their job. Investigative journalism has an
> important role in making open government a reality.[4]

The original freedom of information proposals created a new criminal
offence for the wilful or reckless destruction, alteration or withholding of
records relevant to an investigation. Section 77 of the FOIA deals with the
offence of altering records with intent to prevent disclosure; however, the
words 'wilful or reckless' in connection with the destruction, alteration or
withholding of records do not appear and the criminal offence that was
proposed has instead become a civil offence punishable by a fine.

Information professionals have a key role to play in facilitating freedom
of access to information; because the libraries, information and advice centres of public authorities can provide citizens with details of what freedom
of information means to them, they can guide enquirers towards the information which their authority makes routinely available through the publication schemes, and they can also alert people to their rights to access
information that are not covered by the publication schemes.

Back in 1998, CILIP unsuccessfully argued the case for the FOIA to
include a statutory right for public libraries to claim a deposit copy, without
charge, of any publication produced by public authorities in their geographic
area. They said that public libraries are, and will remain, the most widely used,
accessible and popular point of access for most people to official information.
However, this idea was not adopted by the government.

5.3   Existing procedures for freedom of information

Even before the FOIA received royal assent, UK citizens had a freedom of
information regime of sorts, under which information was made available
to the public. This regime, however, was somewhat piecemeal as it consisted
of a number of different access regimes. The Lord Chancellor's Department's
annual report on the implementation of the FOIA[5] reproduces the text of these
schemes.

5.3.1   Code of practice on access to government information

There is a sense in which for democracy to be able work, members of the public must have access to information in order that they can reach informed decisions. It was in that spirit that the White Paper[6] on open government was published in 1993. This was a precursor to the 1994 open government code, which said that 'open government is part of an effective democracy. Citizens must have adequate access to the information and analysis on which government business is based.' The code of practice on access to government information is now in its 2nd edition (1997) and includes five commitments:

- to supply facts and analysis on major policy decisions
- to open up internal guidelines about departments' dealings with the public
- to supply reasons with administrative decisions
- to provide information under the Citizen's Charter about public services, what they cost, targets, performance, complaints and redress
- to respond to requests for information.

There is also an accompanying set of guidance notes on the interpretation of the code of practice on access to government information. The government also publishes an annual monitoring report on the code of practice.[7] Where individuals have made an unsuccessful application for access to government information, they can challenge such secrecy by making a complaint to the ombudsman.[8] However, such a complaint about the way in which the code is being implemented has to be channelled through a member of parliament.

In the summer of 2002, Sir Michael Buckley, the then parliamentary and health service commissioner (parliamentary ombudsman), resigned soon after being involved in a row over the refusal by Tony Blair to release information under the government's 'open government' code. Sir Michael had criticized stonewalling by ministers and civil servants, such as the way in which the government obstructed his inquiry into the Hinduja passport affair. According to a story in the *Financial Times*,[9] Sir Michael said that 'some departments are resisting the release of information, not because they have a strong case under the code for doing so, but because to release the information could cause them embarrassment or political inconvenience.' The Parliamentary Ombudsman retains responsibility for policing the Code of Practice on Access to Government Information until the FOIA comes fully into effect in January 2005.

5.3.2   Public records

Official documents are subject to the 30-year rule under Public Records Acts,[10] and retention and release is administered by the National Archives. [On 2 April 2003, the Public Record Office (PRO) and the Historic Manuscripts Commission (HMC) joined together to form a new organization known as the National Archives.] The National Archives are a national resource for anyone interested in, or with responsibility for, documents relating to British history, and they house records from across UK central government and, in smaller numbers, from the central courts. They are the national archive for England and Wales; while the National Archives of Scotland and the Public Record Office of Northern Ireland play this role in the devolved administrations. The National Archives provide advice to records managers in central and local government, and to archivists in public and private archives, on a wide range of archival issues such as electronic records management, conservation and digital preservation.

Records held by the National Archives may be closed for periods longer than 30 years ('extended disclosure'), or retained by the government department concerned. There are various reasons for this – some records may contain distressing personal information about people and events; or release may damage national security or international relations; or records may have been supplied subject to certain confidential undertakings. The release of other types of information may be barred under legislation which overrides the provisions of the Public Records Acts.

5.3.3   Code of practice on openness in the NHS

The code of practice on openness in the NHS works on the principle that the NHS should respond positively to requests for information whilst also ensuring that patients' records are kept safe and confidential. So, for example, whilst you can request information about yourself, you are not entitled to see information about other people. The code covers regional health authorities, family health service authorities, district health authorities, NHS trusts, the Mental Health Act Commission and community health councils. It also covers family doctors, dentists, opticians and community pharmacists.

There are a number of other means apart from the code of practice on openness in the NHS through which people are entitled to see medical information:

1 Under the DPA you have a right of access to your health record as long as the data controller is satisfied that you understand what it means to exercise your right. In England, Wales and Northern Ireland this is the case regardless of your age, whereas in Scotland you are presumed to understand what it means from the age of 12.

2 The Access to Medical Reports Act 1988 gives you the right to see any medical report on you that a doctor has written for an insurance company or an employer. This includes any doctor who is, or has been, responsible for your medical care – your general practitioner, hospital doctor, consultant or any other doctor who has treated or advised you. It does not include an independent doctor acting exclusively for the insurance company or employer. The Act does not extend to Northern Ireland.

5.3.4 Environmental information

The Environmental Protection Act 1990[11] requires the Pollution Inspectorate and local authorities to keep registers with considerable detail of pollution standards applying to individual firms, monitoring data relating to those firms, applications by them to release more pollution and other useful information. The Environmental Information Regulations[12] created a general right of access to environmental information held by public authorities, subject to broad exemptions, although the regulations are enforceable only by judicial review. This right stems from European Community directive 90/313/EEC on the freedom of access to information on the environment, and is an example of the beneficial effects of EC directives. Access to environmental information has more recently been formalized in the Convention on Access to Information, Public Participation in Decision-making and Access to Justice in Environmental Matters (known briefly as the Aarhus Convention[13]), which was drawn up by the United Nations Economic Commission for Europe, and signed by 39 states and the European Union in 1998.

The FOIA extends these rights to allow access to all the types of information held by public authorities, whether it is personal or non-personal, so long as it is not exempt. Section 74 of the FOIA contains an order-making power to allow environmental information regulations to be made. It is also anticipated that there will be an EIR code similar to the code under s45 of the FOIA.

The rules of procedure of the Information Tribunal will be amended to enable the Tribunal to consider appeals under the Environmental Information Regulations and appeals under the full access rights.

Destroying information with the intention of preventing disclosure is an offence under both the FOIA and the DPA, and this will apply equally with respect to environmental information.

5.3.5 Local government

The Local Government Act 1972 applies to district, borough and county councils. It provides both the press and the public with access to meetings and connected papers of the full council and its committees and sub-committees five days before a meeting takes place, unless confidential or exempt (see Figure 5.1). The Local Authorities (Executive Arrangements) (Access to Information) (England) Amendment Regulations 2002: SI 2002/716 – issued under the Local Government Act 2000 – cover access to meetings, documents and reasons for decisions, and they in turn amend an earlier set of regulations.[14]

The Local Government Act 2000 introduced 'cabinet'-style government, whereby executive decisions can be taken at meetings. These may be held in private except where 'key decisions' are to be made (see Figure 5.2).

1	Meetings of local authority executives must be held in public when they are discussing or voting on key decisions, unless the item is confidential or exempt, or would disclose the advice of a political adviser.
2	Agendas and reports to any public meeting must be made available at least five days beforehand.
3	A written record of all key decisions and other executive decisions must be made available 'as soon as is practicable' after the meeting. This also applies to decisions taken by individual members.
4	These documents must include the reason for the decision, any alternatives considered and rejected, and a record of any conflict of interest.
5	Every council must publish a 'forward plan', containing details of the key decisions it is likely to make over a four-month period. The plan, which must be updated monthly, must include documents related to those decisions and information on who will take the decision and on those the council will consult.
6	Meetings of backbench 'scrutiny committees' will be open to the press and public, with advance agendas and papers available beforehand.

Fig. 5.1 *Access to local government information*

A key decision means one that is likely

- to result in the local authority incurring expenditure or making savings that are significant, having regard to the local authority's budget for the relevant service or function
- to be significant in terms of its effects on communities living or working in an area comprising two or more wards or electoral divisions.

Fig. 5.2   *Key decisions*

5.3.6   European Union documents

The Amsterdam Treaty introduced a new Article 255, which gives citizens a right of access to European Parliament, Council and Commission documents. It was under this article on 30 May 2001 that European Union regulation 1049/2001[15] was passed on access to European Parliament, Council and Commission documents.

---

1   Make the request in writing and send it by post, fax or e-mail.
2   Check to see if the document you want is listed in the document register on the Europa server at http://europa.eu.int.
3   If it is there, quote the reference number of the document you require.
4   If it is not, make your request as detailed as possible to help the Commission to be able to identify the document you want.
5   The request can be made in any one of the 11 Community languages.
6   Send the request to the Commission's Secretariat-General or directly to the department responsible.
7   Receipt of applications will be acknowledged.
8   Within 15 working days from registration of your application, you will either be sent the document you requested or will be given the reasons for its total or partial refusal.
9   Documents of no longer than 20 pages are provided free of charge.
10   Where a charge is made, this will never be more than the real cost of producing and sending the copies.

Europe Direct website: http://europa.eu.int/europedirect/en/index_en.html; e-mail address: mail@europe-direct.cec.eu.int.
(This was set up to answer questions of a general nature from the public.)

The Secretariat-General, European Commission, Unit SG/B/2, B-1049, e-mail: sg-acc-doc@cec.eu.int.

Fig. 5.3   *How to access European Union information*

People can request access to any unpublished documents (subject to exemptions) as in Figure 5.3. This covers documents which have not been finalized or which are not intended for publication. It also includes documents from third parties, received and kept by the Commission.

5.3.7   Rights of access under the Data Protection Act 1998 (DPA)

The DPA gave individuals the right to find out what structured information was held about them by organizations in both the public and the private sectors, and to obtain a copy of that information. But in the case of public authorities, section 69 of the FOIA extended this to give individuals a right of access to *all* the personal data held about them. Manual records only fall within the remit of the DPA where they are structured; but the FOIA says that for public authorities individuals have a right of access to all personal data, whether structured or unstructured. (Chapter 3 deals with data protection in more detail.)

5.4   The Freedom of Information Act 2000 (FOIA)

The purpose of the FOIA[16] is to promote greater openness by public authorities (see Figure 5.4 for categories covered). The FOIA gives a general right of access to all types of 'recorded'[17] information held by public authorities; it sets out a number of exemptions from that right and it also places a number of obligations on public authorities.

Initially around 70,000 public bodies were covered by the FOIA. The list

---

- central government
- local government
- non-departmental public bodies
- NHS bodies
- schools
- colleges
- universities
- the police
- House of Commons
- House of Lords
- Northern Ireland Assembly
- National Assembly of Wales

Fig. 5.4   *Public authorities covered by the Freedom of Information Act 2000*

is set out in Schedule 1 of the FOIA, which can be supplemented by Statutory Instruments adding further public bodies – see, for example, SI 2002/2623, which added more public bodies.[18] It is anticipated that there will be an annual exercise to identify any public bodies which fulfil the necessary criteria but which are not yet subject to the FOIA.

Private entities, such as spin-off companies, that are wholly or largely owned by a public authority will also be subject to the FOIA. However, the FOIA does not apply to information held by the Security Service, the Secret Intelligence Service, the Government Communications Headquarters (GCHQ), the Special Forces or any unit or part-unit assisting GCHQ.

As far as libraries are concerned, relevant organizations covered by the Act include:

- Advisory Council on Libraries
- British Library
- Library and Information Services Council (Wales)
- National Library of Wales
- Resource: The Council for Museums, Archives and Libraries
- Staff Commission for Education and Library Boards (Northern Ireland).

The FOIA will be brought fully into force by January 2005, and it will be enforced by the Information Commissioner. The Information Commissioner's role is to promote good practice; to approve and advise on the preparation of publishing schemes; to provide information as to the public's rights under the FOIA; and to enforce compliance with the FOIA. He is also required to report annually to Parliament (Chapter 4 gives a more comprehensive overview of the role of the Information Commissioner). Public authorities have two main obligations under the Act (as shown in Figure 5.5).

Responsibility for freedom of information and data protection comes

---

| 1 | They have to produce a 'publication scheme' as a guide to the information that they hold which is publicly available. |
| 2 | They also have a duty to deal with individual requests for information – this will come into effect in January 2005. |

Fig. 5.5   *Obligations of public authorities under the Freedom of Information Act 2000*

within the remit of the Department for Constitutional Affairs. In November 2001 the government announced[19] the setting up of an advisory group to provide advice regarding the progress of implementation of the FOIA. The advisory group's membership includes representatives from:

- the Local Government Association
- the National Association of Local Councils
- the Association of Chief Police Officers
- the British Medical Association
- the Health Service Confederation
- Universities UK
- the National Association of Governors and Managers
- the Newspaper Society.

The Information Commissioner enforces the DPA throughout the United Kingdom, but only has responsibility for Freedom of Information in England, Wales and Northern Ireland. There is a separate FOI(S)A which was passed by the Scottish Executive on 28 May 2002[20] and is overseen by a Scottish Information Commissioner (see 5.10).

There are currently two codes of practice issued under the FOIA which provide guidance to public authorities:

1 About responding to requests for information and associated matters[21]
   This code provides guidance on:
   - the provision of advice by public authorities to those making requests for information
   - the transfer of requests from one public authority to another
   - consultation with third parties to whom the information requested relates or who may be affected by its disclosure
   - the inclusion in contracts entered into by public authorities of terms relating to the disclosure of information
   - the development of procedures for handling complaints from applicants.
2 Records management[22]
   This code aims to give advice to public authorities subject to the Public Records Act 1958 and the Public Records (Northern Ireland) Act 1923 as

to desirable practice in record keeping, and also advises on the practices to be followed when transferring records to the National Archives (formerly known as the Public Records Office and the Historic Manuscripts Commission) or the Public Records Office of Northern Ireland in the context of the FOIA. The DPA, the Public Records Act 1958 and the Public Records (Northern Ireland) Act 1923 are amended. One of the most significant amendments to the DPA[23] is that the definition of 'data' will be extended, as far as public authorities are concerned, to cover *all* personal information held. This includes both 'structured' and 'unstructured' manual records, as noted above.

It is anticipated that, once the revised Environmental Information Regulations are issued, the Department for Constitutional Affairs will issue a further code of practice to govern these.

5.5   Publication schemes

The FOIA places a duty on public authorities to adopt and maintain publication schemes, which must be approved by the Information Commissioner. A publication scheme is essentially a guide to information that a public authority routinely publishes or intends to publish; and the word 'publication' should be defined widely to cover not just items to be found in bound or printed form, but also computer printouts, information downloaded from a website, etc. The emphasis is on information rather than documents. Such schemes must set out the types of information the authority publishes, the format and details of any charges.

The FOIA has provided a tremendous opportunity for information professionals to play a key part in the development of publication schemes. Library and information professionals have considerable information management expertise that can be utilized by carrying out information audits so that public authorities can produce a detailed inventory of what they produce. The FOIA has also increased pressure for public authorities to have effective records management systems in place. Only by managing their records in a professional manner can public authorities be confident that they have a comprehensive overview of the information that they hold; and that knowledge can then assist those authorities to respond to requests effectively and to speedily identify cases where an exemption might be relied upon. Public authorities need to have formal records management procedures in place, including the development of proper retention, destruction and archiving policies. Sound principles of information handling and retrieval are the foundation of freedom of information.

The code of practice on records management (www.lcd.gov.uk/foi/codesprac.htm) recognizes that any freedom of information legislation is only as good as the quality of the records to which it provides access, and the National Archives also point out that records management can exist without freedom of information but freedom of information cannot exist without records management.[24] Some civil servants are more concerned about being able to fulfil the requirement to confirm or deny whether or not an item exists, based on the way in which records are managed, than with disclosure of the item.

Section 19(1)(c) of the FOIA requires public bodies to keep their publication schemes under review. They can submit a revised publication scheme for approval at any time after first approval. They are not permitted to remove a class of information from the scheme without first obtaining the approval of the Information Commissioner; and following a modification to the guidance from the Information Commissioner,[25] 'where a public authority chooses to add new classes to those which are included in their approved publication scheme they will be required to inform the Commissioner.' It is important to ensure that, once the scheme has been approved and is active, the process is not seen as being complete. Publication schemes will be time-limited, and though a public body may not be required to re-submit the scheme for as much as four years, the scheme itself should not be seen as in any way static.

The right of access to all types of 'recorded' information held by public authorities comes into force in January 2005, and once authorities start receiving access requests, these should be monitored to see whether the information requested should be made available routinely, and the publication scheme amended accordingly. Indeed, it would be good practice for authorities to keep a log of requests made for information which is not already included in their publication schemes, and to consider adding the class of information into which it falls as a new class to be covered by the scheme. The log itself could fall into a class for publication under the scheme. Public authorities have an incentive to add new classes of material into their publication schemes in response to the requests for information that may not have been anticipated initially, since the authority could then refer enquirers to their publication scheme for those items. Expanding the range of material covered by the publication scheme would therefore be likely to lead to a reduction in the number of individual freedom of information requests for specific pieces of information.

The Information Commissioner can approve model publication schemes for groups of similar bodies. There are model publication schemes available for a wide range of public bodies. These include:

• parish and town and community councils
• parish meetings
• fire authorities
• internal drainage boards
• district drainage commissioners
• information for health sector bodies
• passenger transport authorities
• port health authorities
• strategic health authorities
• primary care trusts
• opticians and optometrists
• mental health trusts
• general practitioners
• dentists
• community pharmacists
• ambulance trusts
• acute trusts
• universities.

There may be further model schemes published in the future.

It is left to the public authority to decide how to publish its scheme. The Information Commissioner's guidance[26] makes clear that making the publication scheme available on the web is not sufficiently universal to render it the sole means by which a scheme is delivered. Public authorities must cater for the needs of those who do not have web access; and they must also pay due attention to the needs of people with disabilities. They need to take account of their obligations under the DDA. The guide should be available to all who request it and, in normal circumstances, public authorities should not charge users for copies of it.

A publication scheme specifies 'classes' of information which the public authority publishes or intends to publish. These 'classes' might be described as groupings of information having one or more common characteristic. Including a 'class' of information within a scheme commits the public authority to publishing the information that falls within it. It is therefore important that a public authority, and its staff, understand what material is covered and that the coverage is clear to the user. Where it is intended that certain information is not included, this must also be clear to users.

If, for example, a public authority chose a heading such as 'recruitment', then they would be required to make available all information connected with the recruitment process. This is unlikely to be appropriate. They could, however, break this down further into headings for 'vacancies', 'induction', and 'job descriptions'. The lower-level headings then become the classes of information, rather than the broader heading of 'recruitment' – see Figure 5.6.

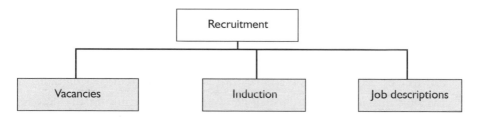

Fig. 5.6   *Classes of information*

The timetable announced by the Lord Chancellor on 13 November 2001 set out a phased adoption of publication schemes in which all public authorities in England and Wales would have to have schemes in place by June 2004; and it has been agreed that the implementation of the Act in Northern Ireland will follow a similar timetable to that for England and Wales.

A list of the 'first wave' of publication schemes is available on the Information Commissioner's website,[27] but this does not contain hyperlinks to each individual scheme.

5.6   Copyright implications of the Freedom of Information Act 2000

Documents which are disclosed under freedom of information, whether they are covered by a publication scheme or sent to an individual in response to a freedom of information request, will in most cases be subject to copyright protection.

The Code of Practice under s45 of the FOIA says:

> Public authorities should be aware that information which is disclosed under the Act may be subject to copyright protection. If an applicant wishes to use any such information in a way that would infringe copyright, for example by making multiple copies, or issuing copies to the public, he or she would require a licence from the copyright holder.

Section 50 of the Copyright Designs and Patents Act 1988 (CDPA), says:

> **Acts done under statutory authority**
> **50.—(1)** Where the doing of a particular act is specifically authorised by an Act of Parliament, whenever passed, then, unless the Act provides otherwise, the doing of that act does not infringe copyright.
> **(2)** Subsection (1) applies in relation to an enactment contained in Northern Ireland legislation as it applies in relation to an Act of Parliament.
> **(3)** Nothing in this section shall be construed as excluding any defence of statutory authority otherwise available under or by virtue of any enactment.

This indicates that, where the disclosure of a document is required under the FOIA, disclosure does not breach either Crown copyright or a third party's copyright in the document, and there is no suggestion that copyright would prevent the initial disclosure of the material under the FOIA.

Experts do not agree on this matter, though, as some take the view that if copyright in documentation belongs to a third party, then an organization is entitled to refuse to supply copies of that material under freedom of information because it will infringe that third party's copyright.

What is clear is that the recipient of that information is not free to further reproduce the material in ways that would breach the third party's copyright.

Under copyright law, the enquirer cannot make further copies of the documents without obtaining the permission of the copyright owner.

Some public authorities have been concerned at having to rely on copyright law to protect the information that they disclose. As a result, a number of organizations have spent time developing copyright policies which state in a clear and concise manner that citizens cannot simply do whatever they want with the information that has been disclosed to them under the freedom of information regime.

For example, where a public authority has produced some materials where quite a lot of work had gone into their creation, they might well be reluctant to include them in their publication scheme. To do so would make them routinely available to anyone who is interested, including their competitors. Where the information is subject to a freedom of information request, they would be protected by copyright law. But some people worry about whether this is an effective deterrent to wholesale copying.

HMSO have issued guidance on Freedom of Information publication schemes in relation to Crown Copyright.[28] This guidance draws a distinction between the supply of information held by public authorities under freedom of information legislation and the re-use of that information, and explains those circumstances where formal licensing is required. The guidance includes a sample form of words which can be used in order to explain who owns copyright in the information and contact details for obtaining a copyright licence.

5.7   Freedom of information rights and request procedures

When the individual right of access to information comes into force across all public authorities on 1 January 2005, anyone, anywhere can make a request for information from a public authority provided that the request satisfies all the relevant conditions (for procedure see Figure 5.7). The request must include sufficient information to enable the authority to identify the information requested. You do not have to live in the United Kingdom in order to ask for information, you do not have to be a British citizen and you do not have to say why you want the information. There are no limits on the kinds of information you can ask for, although there are limits on the information that the authority has to provide. Applicants have the right to be told what information is held by the public authority and they also have the right to receive the information

When making a request, you must:
- ask for the information in writing, which includes fax and e-mail
- give your name and address
- describe the information you want.

When responding to requests, public authorities must observe the following:
- they must respond to requests promptly and in any event within 20 working days
- they may charge a fee, which has to be calculated according to the Fees Regulations
- if a fee is required, the 20 working days will be extended by up to three months until the fee is paid
- they must tell the requester whether they hold the information that is being requested
- where the authority has grounds not to release the information requested, they must give reasons for their decision and must tell the applicant of their right to complain.

Fig. 5.7   *Freedom of information requests procedure*

(unless one of the exemptions disapplies or qualifies that right). The right of access covers information recorded both before and after the FOIA was passed. Applicants do not have to mention the FOIA or the DPA when requesting information.

When making a request under the FOIA, you can specify how you want the information to be given to you, and the public authority should give you the information in the form you prefer, if it is reasonably practical to do this. The FOIA lists three ways in which you might ask for the information to be provided:

- as a copy, in permanent form or some other form acceptable to you
- by an opportunity to inspect the information
- as a summary or digest.

The authority can consider the cost when deciding how practical your preference is.

Public authorities have 20 working days within which to respond to requests, and they can charge a fee, which has to be calculated according to the Fees Regulations.[29] Where a fee is required, the 20 working days is extended by up to 3 months until the fee is paid. The question has been asked whether charges will exclude people from exercising their rights. The government sees the maximum fee (where this is charged) not as a significant deterrent to potential applicants, but as an encouragement to think clearly about the request they wish to make.

5.8 Exemptions and appeals

Whilst the FOIA creates a general right of access to information held by public bodies, it also sets out 23 exemptions where that right is either disapplied or qualified (see Figures 5.2 and 5.3). The exemptions relate to information held for functions such as national security, law enforcement, commercial interests and personal data.

Most of the exemptions require a public authority to consider a test of prejudice *and* a public interest test:

1 The *test of prejudice* means that, for example, where a public authority considers the information to be exempt because it is held in connection with law enforcement, they can only withhold that information if its release would prejudice the prevention or detection of a crime.

2 In the case of the *public interest test*, this requires a public authority to consider whether the public interest in withholding the exempt information outweighs the public interest in releasing it; and the balance lies in favour of disclosure, in that information may only be withheld if the public interest in withholding it is greater than the public interest in releasing it.

In the run up to implementation, public authorities may wish to consider identification of those exemptions which are likely to be relevant to them in particular. They might also want to undertake legal research into any relevant case law from other jurisdictions on where the public interest may lie – a task which information professionals working for public authorities are well placed to undertake.

Public authorities do need to take care when applying the exemptions. Where a requested document contains some exempt information, only those specific pieces of exempt information can be withheld and the remainder of the document must be released.

Usually the public authority will give you a special notice explaining why it is not providing the information you have asked for. A public authority is not required to give you a full explanation if this would involve giving you

s22   Information intended for future publication
s24   National security (other than information supplied by or relating to named security
      organizations, where the duty to consider disclosure in the public interest does
      not arise – see section 23)
s26   Defence
s27   International relations
s28   Relations between administrations in the United Kingdom
s29   The economy
s30   Investigations and proceedings conducted by public authorities
s31   Law enforcement
s33   Audit functions
s35   Formulation of government policy
s36   Prejudice to effective conduct of public affairs (except information held by the
      House of Commons or the House of Lords)
s37   Communications with Her Majesty, etc. and honours
s38   Health and safety
s39   Environmental information [Regulations covering environmental information may be
      made under section 74]
s42   Legal professional privilege
s43   Commercial interests

Fig. 5.8   *Exemptions where the public interest test applies*

information that is itself exempt. So in some circumstances you will only be given a partial explanation. However the notice will:

- explain how you can complain to the particular authority about the way your request has been handled, or explain that the authority has no complaints procedure
- explain your right to ask the Information Commissioner to decide whether your request has been properly dealt with.

The exemptions from the right of access which appear in the FOIA are far more widely drawn than those envisaged in the White Paper (see Figures 5.8 and 5.9). Cases that 'would, or would be likely to prejudice' the specified interest mean that the exemptions could be used even where the likely prejudice is actually quite small. The final list of exemptions proved to be hugely controversial. It is well worth reading the article by Tom Cornford – 'The Freedom of Information Act: genuine or sham?'[30]

Absolute exemptions are those where, if the exemption applies, there is no duty to consider where the public interest lies:

s21   Information accessible to the applicant by other means
s23   Information supplied by or relating to bodies dealing with security matters
s32   Court records
s34   Parliamentary privilege
s36   Prejudice to effective conduct of public affairs
s40   Personal information (access is given in accordance with the rules in the DPA)
s41   Information provided in confidence
s44   Prohibition on disclosure where a disclosure is prohibited by an enactment or
        would constitute contempt of court

Fig. 5.9   *Absolute exemptions*

5.9   Enforcement

A person who has made a request for information may apply to the Information Commissioner for a decision as to whether the request has been dealt with according to the FOIA. In response the Information Commissioner may serve a decision notice on the public authority and applicant setting out any steps which are required in order to comply.

The Information Commissioner has the power to serve information notices and enforcement notices on public authorities. In certain circumstances the Information Commissioner may issue a decision or enforcement notice requiring disclosure of information in the public interest. However, this may be subject to an 'executive override'. In such a case the public authority has 20 days from receipt of the notice to obtain a signed certificate from a Cabinet Minister overriding the Information Commissioner's notice. There is no right of appeal against the ministerial certificate. All notices may be appealed to the independent Information Tribunal. The Information Commissioner may issue a practice recommendation in respect of non-conformity with either code of practice.

5.10   Freedom of information in Scotland

Access to information held by certain public authorities may be gained through the Scottish Executive's Code of Practice on Access to Scottish Executive Information[31] (1999) and the UK Government's Code of Practice on Access to Government Information.[32] Both codes are non-statutory and will cease to operate once freedom of information legislation comes into force in the respective jurisdictions.

The Scottish Executive's objectives in passing the FOI(S)A 2002 were:

- to establish a legal right of access to information held by a broad range of Scottish public authorities
- to balance this right with provisions protecting sensitive information
- to establish a fully independent Scottish Information Commissioner to promote and enforce the freedom of information regime
- to encourage the proactive disclosure of information by Scottish public authorities through a requirement to maintain a publication scheme
- to make provision for the application of the freedom of information regime to historical records.

The FOI(S)A requires full implementation by 31 December 2005; however, the Scottish Executive – in consultation with the Scottish Information Commissioner – have decided to bring the Act fully into force by January 2005, in line with the rest of the UK. A detailed list of the public authorities covered by the Act is contained in Schedule 1. It includes:

- the Scottish Executive and its agencies
- local authorities
- NHS Scotland
- schools, colleges, and universities
- the police
- the Scottish Parliament.

The Act provides for other authorities to be added later, and for organizations to be designated as public authorities if they exercise functions of a public nature or provide a service under contract which is a function of a public authority. This provision would enable private companies to be brought within the scope of the Act should they be involved in significant work of a public nature such as major PFI contracts. In such cases, only the company's involvement in work of a public nature would come within the freedom of information remit.

As part of the devolution settlement, UK government departments operating in Scotland and cross-border public authorities such as the Ministry of

Defence are not covered by Scottish freedom of information legislation, but instead by the UK FOIA.

Scottish public authorities will be required to respond to requests within 20 working days, as is the case for the UK. But in certain circumstances the Keeper of the Records of Scotland will have 30 working days to respond to requests.

A set of freedom of information fee regulations will be issued, as for the UK legislation. During the parliamentary passage of the Freedom of Information (Scotland) Bill 2002, the executive proposed the following:

1 Any request costing under £100 to fulfil will be free of charge to the applicant.
2 For requests costing between £100 and an upper cost threshold (likely to be set between £500 and £600), the applicant will be charged 10% of prescribed costs.
3 Authorities will not be required to respond to requests costing in excess of the upper cost threshold, but they may do so if they wish.

As far as the exemptions are concerned (see Figure 5.10), a key difference is that the test is whether the information would *prejudice substantially* the purpose to which the exemption relates. In other words, the exemptions are harder to justify in Scotland than in England and Wales.

The Scottish Executive's website contains useful advice on the application of freedom of information in Scotland, such as:

• Freedom of Information (Scotland) Act 2002 overview[33]
• code of practice on the discharge of functions by public authorities under the FOI(S)A[34]
• code of practice on records management[35]
• frequently asked questions about freedom of information.[36]

5.11 Freedom of information and data protection

Under the FOIA and the FOI(S)A, citizens are entitled to make a request for information from a public body without specifying whether or not they are doing so under freedom of information legislation. This could potentially become a cause of confusion once both the FOIA and the FOI(S)A are

---

FOI(S)A Part 2 – Exempt information (ss25-41)

Exemptions to which the public interest test *does not* apply
  25 Information otherwise accessible
  26 Prohibitions on disclosure
  36 Confidentiality
  37 Court records, etc.
  38 Personal information

Exemptions to which the public interest test *does* apply
  27 Information intended for future publication
  28 Relations within the United Kingdom
  29 Formulation of Scottish Administration policy, etc.
  30 Prejudice to the effective conduct of public affairs
  31 National security and defence
  32 International relations
  33 Commercial interests and the economy
  34 Investigations by Scottish public authorities and proceedings arising out of such investigations
  35 Law enforcement
  39 Health, safety and the environment
  40 Audit functions
  41 Communications with Her Majesty, etc. and honours

Fig. 5.10   *Exemptions under the Freedom of Information (Scotland) Act 2002*

fully in force, because the legislative regime conflicts significantly with the data protection legislation in several ways.

In October 2002, the Lord Chancellor's Department issued a consultation paper on 'Data Protection Act 1998: subject access'. This flagged up three key areas where there were discrepancies between the freedom of information and the data protection legislation:

5.11.1   Fees and charges

5.11.1.1   Data protection fees

Organizations can charge people who make subject access requests under the data protection legislation. Many organizations do not make a charge, but where they do, this can be up to a maximum of £10. In the case of credit records the fee would be £2, and in the case of medical and educational records the maximum fee is £50.

5.11.1.2   Freedom of information fees

In the case of freedom of information requests, the costs will be based on a set of Fees Regulations. These have not yet been issued and there is a set of Draft Fees Regulations.[37] The Regulations say that public bodies are entitled to charge 10% of prescribed costs for the first £550 of such costs – in other words that the maximum is £55. Where the prescribed costs are over £550, public bodies are not required to provide the information; but, with the agreement of the enquirer, they can charge the full prescribed costs for any costs above £550. In addition, the full costs for disbursements such as photocopying and postage and packing can be charged back to the enquirer.

With the Freedom of Information regime it is important to make a clear distinction between costs associated with answering freedom of information requests and costs for items within the publication scheme. The publication scheme should set out what is free and what is chargeable, but the prices charged should not be listed within the publication scheme itself. Otherwise, every time you wanted to change the price of an item, you would need to make an amendment to the publication scheme. The best solution, therefore, is to have a separate schedule of charges to which the publication scheme can make reference. A public authority might make some information in their publication scheme available free of charge on their website; but they might levy a charge to cover the costs of printing information from their website for those without web access.

5.11.2   The time limit for responding to requests

Under data protection legislation, data controllers have 40 days to respond to requests. The legislation simply says 40 days; it does not specify whether or not these are working days. There are different periods for copies of credit files (seven working days) and school pupil records (15 school days).

Under the Freedom of Information legislation, public bodies have 20 working days following receipt of the request within which to provide the information to the enquirer.

5.11.3   The exemptions

The third key area where the two legislative regimes differ is in the list of exemptions. Even if the government wanted to harmonize the two systems, they wouldn't have a completely free hand because in the case of data pro-

Section 28:	Provides an exemption to protect national security.
Section 29:*	Covers personal data processed for: (a) the prevention or detection of crime; (b) the apprehension or prosecution of offenders, or (c) the assessment or collection of any tax or duty or of any imposition of a similar nature.
Section 30:*	Provides powers for the Secretary of State to make orders providing exemptions in relation to health, education and social work records. Orders relating to all three categories of record have been made.
Section 31:*	Covers personal data processed for the purposes of discharging a wide range of regulatory functions.
Section 32:	Covers personal data processed for journalistic, literary or artistic purposes.
Section 33:	Covers personal data processed only for research, statistical or historical purposes, subject to certain conditions.
Section 34:	Covers personal data which are statutorily made available to the public.
Section 38:	Provides a power for the Secretary of State to make orders providing exemptions where disclosure of information is statutorily prohibited or restricted, subject to certain conditions.
Schedule 7	
Paragraph 1:	Covers confidential references given by data controllers in relation to education, employment or the provision of services.
Paragraph 2:*	Provides an exemption to protect the combat effectiveness of the armed forces.
Paragraph 3:	Covers personal data processed for the purposes of making appointments of judges and QCs, and the conferring of honours or dignities.
Paragraph 4:	Provides a power for the Secretary of State to make orders providing exemptions in relation to Crown appointments. An order designating a limited number of appointments has been made.
Paragraph 5:*	Covers personal data processed for the purposes of management forecasting or management planning.
Paragraph 6:*	Provides an exemption for personal data processed for corporate finance services.
Paragraph 7:*	Covers personal data consisting of records of the data controller's intentions in relation to negotiations with the data subject.
Paragraph 8:	Modifies the 40-day maximum period for dealing with subject access requests in relation to examination marks.
Paragraph 9:	Covers examination scripts.
Paragraph 10:	Covers personal data in respect of which legal professional privilege could be claimed. Legal advice is that this exemption covers legal advice given by departments' in-house lawyers.
Paragraph 11:	Provides an exemption for circumstances in which by granting access a person would incriminate himself in respect of an offence other than one under the 1998 Act.

* Note: exemptions including 'case by case' restriction.

Fig. 5.11   *Data Protection Act 1998: subject access exemptions*

Office of the Information Commissioner	www.dataprotection.gov.uk/dpr/foi.nsf
Department for Constitutional Affairs	www.lcd.gov.uk/foi/foidpunit.htm
Freedom of Information and Data Protection Division	
National Archives	www.nationalarchives.gov.uk/footer/freedom.htm
JISC Legal Information Service	www.jisc.ac.uk/legal
Campaign for Freedom of Information	www.cfoi.org.uk
Freedominfo.org	www.freedominfo.org
Privacy International	www.privacy.org

Fig. 5.12   *Where to go to seek freedom of information advice*

tection they are obliged to follow EC directive 95/46/EC. The exemptions under the FOIA are set out in Figures 5.8 (exemptions where the public interest applies) and 5.9 (absolute exemptions); and the exemptions under the FOI(S)A are set out in Figure 5.10. Figure 5.11 lists subject access exemptions under the Data Protection Act 1998. Figure 5.12 lists some helpful sources of advice about freedom of information.

5.12   Summary

In this chapter we looked at the general principles of freedom of information (5.2), and in particular at how this applies in the UK through the FOIA and the FOI(S)A. The chapter looked at the initiatives for freedom of information which already existed before the FOIA in areas such as government information (5.3.1), public records (5.3.2), openness in the NHS (5.3.3), environmental information (5.3.4), local government information (5.3.5) or European Union documents (5.3.6). We considered how publication schemes are being used as guides to what public authorities publish or intend to publish as a matter of routine. The chapter also outlined the right of access to information, and the appeals process that exists where individuals are not satisfied that their request for information has been handled properly. The chapter concluded by highlighting the discrepancies between the data protection and freedom of information legislation (5.11). In the next chapter, we will look at the general principles of libel and defamation law, and in particular the pitfalls that exist when applying defamation law to the internet and to news archives.

5.13   Further information

The Campaign for Freedom of Information
Suite 102, 16 Baldwins Gardens, London EC1N 7RJ
Tel: 020 7831 7477; Fax: 020 7831 7461; E-mail: admin@cfoi.demon.co.uk
Website: www.cfoi.org.uk

Charter 88
18A Victoria Park Square, London E2 9PB
Tel: 020 8880 6088
Website: www.charter88.org.uk

Department for Constitutional Affairs
Freedom of Information and Data Protection Division, Room 151,
Selborne House, London SW1E 6QW
Tel: 020 7210 8755; E-mail: fidp@lcdhq.gsi.gov.uk

freedominfo.org
Suite 701, Gelman Library, The George Washington University,
2130 H. Street NW, Washington DC 20037
E-mail: email@freedominfo.org
Website: www.freedominfo.org/

The Guardian
Special report on freedom of information, available at
www.guardian.co.uk/freedom

Office of the Information Commissioner
Wycliffe House , Water Lane, Wilmslow, Cheshire SK9 5AP
Tel: 01625 545745; Fax: 01625 524510; E-mail: data@dataprotection.gov.uk
Website: www.informationcommissioner.gov.uk

Parliamentary Ombudsman
Millbank Tower, Millbank, London SW1P 4QP
Tel. 0845 015 4033; E-mail: OPCA.Enquiries@ombudsman.gsi.gov.uk

Scottish Executive. Freedom of Information Unit

St Andrew's House, Regent Road, Edinburgh EH1 3DG

Tel: 0131 244 4615; Fax: 0131 244 2582; E-mail: foi@scotland.gsi.gov.uk

Website: www.scotland.gov.uk/government/foi

Scottish Information Commissioner

being established in St Andrews, Fife but at the time of writing can be contacted at:

Scottish Information Commissioner, c/o Citigate Smarts, 1 Albert Quay, Edinburgh EH6 7DN

Tel: 0131 555 0425; E-mail: itspublicknowledge@citigatesmarts.co.uk

Website: www.itspublicknowledge.info

Notes and references

1 *Your Right to Know: freedom of information*, CILIP, 1998. Available at www. la-hq.org.uk/directory/prof_issues/yrtk.html.
2 Code of Professional Ethics: draft for consultation, CILIP, 2003.
3 Cm 3818 ISBN 0101381824, 1997.
4 'We will deliver a Freedom of Information Act and it will deliver', Lord Chancellor's Department press notice 114/98, 28 April 1998.
5 *Freedom of Information: annual report on bringing fully into force those provisions of the Freedom of Information Act 2000 which are not yet fully in force*, HC 6, 2002/3, November 2002.
6 White Paper on open government, Cm 2290, HMSO.
7 Available at www.lcd.gov.uk/foi/codpracgi.htm.
8 Publications of the Parliamentary and Health Service Ombudsman are available at www.ombudsman.org.uk/publications.html.
9 Guha, K., Ombudsman Hits at Government Obstruction, *Financial Times*, 4 July 2002.
10 Public Records (Northern Ireland) Act 1923 and Public Records Act 1958.
11 Environmental Protection Act 1990 (c43). Available at www.legislation. hmso.gov.uk/acts/acts1990/Ukpga_19900043_en_1.htm.
12 The Environmental Information Regulations 1992: SI 1992/3240. A new set of Environmental Information Regulations is due out in 2003.
13 Available at www.unece.org/env/pp/welcome.html.
14 The Local Authorities (Executive Arrangements) (Access to Information) (England) Regulations 2000: SI 2000/3272.

15 Regulation (EC) No 1049/2001 of the European Parliament and of the Council of 30 May 2001 regarding public access to European Parliament, Council and Commission Documents, Official Journal L145/43, 31 May 2001.
16 Freedom of Information Act 2000, chapter 36, available at www.legislation. hmso.gov.uk/acts/acts2000/20000036.htm, and explanatory notes, available at www.legislation.hmso.gov.uk/acts/en/2000en36.htm.
17 In section 84 of the Freedom of Information Act 2000, the interpretation of the word 'information' is explained as meaning 'information recorded in any form'.
18 The Freedom of Information (Additional Public Authorities) Order 2002: SI 2002/2623. Available at www.legislation.hmso.gov.uk/si/si2002/20022623.htm.
19 'Freedom of Information – new advisory group', LCD Press Notice 411/01, 29 November 2001.
20 Freedom of Information (Scotland) Act 2002 asp 13. Available at www.scotland-legislation.hmso.gov.uk/legislation/scotland/acts2002/20020013.htm.
21 Code of practice on the discharge of the functions of public authorities under part I of the Freedom of Information Act 2000. Available at www.lcd.gov.uk/foi/codepafunc.htm.
22 Code of practice on the management of records, Lord Chancellor's Department, 2002. Available at www.lcd.gov.uk/foi/codemanrec.htm.
23 See section 69 of the Freedom of Information Act.
24 *Records Management News* (PRO), November 2002.
25 *Freedom of Information Act 2000. Preparing for implementation. Publication schemes. Guidance and methodology*, February 2003.
26 *Freedom of Information Act 2000: preparing for implementation – publication schemes methodology: p4, v1.0*, Office of the Information Commissioner, February 2002.
27 Available at www.informationcommissioner.gov.uk/psfw.html.
28 HMSO guidance note 19 is available on HMSO's website at www.hmso.gov.uk/g-note19.htm.
29 The Freedom of Information (Fees and Appropriate Limit) Regulations have not yet been issued, but there is a set of Draft Fees Regulations at www.lcd.gov.uk/foi/secleg.htm
30 Cornford, T., The Freedom of Information Act 2000: genuine or sham?, *Web Journal of Current Legal Issues* (2001) 3 Web JCLI, available at http://webjcli.ncl.ac.uk/2001/issue3/cornford3.html.
31 Available at www.cfoi.org.uk/pdf/scotcop.pdf.
32 Cabinet Office, *Code of practice on access to government information*, 2nd edn, 1997.
33 Available at www.scotland.gov.uk/government/foi/foioverview.pdf.
34 Available at www.scotland.gov.uk/government/foi/reviseds60.pdf.

35   Available at www.scotland.gov.uk/government/foi/s61revised.pdf.
36   Available at www.scotland.gov.uk/government/foi/faqs.pdf.
37   Available at www.lcd.gov.uk/foi/secleg.htm.

6 Defamation

6.1 Introduction

Defamation law attempts to strike a balance between society's interest in freedom of speech and the individual's interest in maintaining their reputation. It is relevant to information professionals, whether they be responsible for intranets, extranets, publicly available websites or online databases; users of their organization's internet e-mail system; members of internet e-mail discussion groups; or authors of books or articles in their own right. The chapter looks at the general principles of defamation law (6.2), and what constitutes slander (6.3) or libel (6.4). It then outlines the defences that can be used in libel cases (6.5); and the remedies that the law provides (6.6). The application of defamation law to the internet is then considered (6.7), including the issues surrounding the liability of internet service providers (6.7.1), the application of the limitation period to online archives (6.7.2), the question of jurisdictions and applicable law in cases of internet defamation (6.7.3), and the risk of prosecution for contempt of court that newspaper and magazine publishers face when they operate online archives (6.7.4). Finally, the potential dangers involved in the use of internet e-mail in terms of defamation and cyberliability are outlined (6.7.5).

6.2 General principles

English law distinguishes between libel (written) and slander (spoken). An item is defamatory if one of the following tests is satisfied:

1 The matter complained of tends to lower the plaintiff in the estimation of society.
2 It tends to bring them into hatred, ridicule, contempt, dislike or disesteem in society.
3 It tends to make them shunned, avoided or cut off from society.

In Scottish law, libel and slander are virtually indistinguishable with regard to both the nature of the wrongs and their consequences. The terminology of Scottish defamation law differs from that of English law. Scots law does not recognize the offence of criminal libel. Where individual English litigants enjoy absolute privilege for what they say in court, their Scottish counterparts have only qualified privilege. 'Exemplary', or 'punitive', damages are not awarded by the Scottish courts. According to D. M Walker,[1] 'Absolute privilege protects all statements made in judicial proceedings, whatever the rank of the court or the position of the person sued, so long as it is not a gratuitous observation.' However, the footnote confirms that in Scotland, a party only has qualified privilege in his pleadings. This also extends to tribunals if the procedures are similar in essence to a court.

6.3   Slander

Slander is oral defamation – the use of the spoken word to injure another person's reputation. To be the basis of a legal action, a publication of the words complained of must demonstrably have taken place – that is, they must have been uttered within the hearing of a third party. It should be noted that the Scottish position is different, as Scots law does not require that a defamatory statement be communicated to third parties before it is actionable. Among statements considered slanderous per se are:

- those that impute the commission of a felony, such as calling someone a murderer
- those that impute an individual to be suffering from a communicable disease such as gonorrhoea
- those that are injurious to an individual in their trade or profession – for example, saying that an accountant fiddles the figures.

The party charged with the slander may hold, as a defence, that the words spoken were in fact true, inasmuch as true statements result in no injury to reputation. Defining slanderous language is sometimes difficult. The disputed words themselves may not be slanderous but may hold a hidden meaning, or innuendo, that hearers may understand, and that may therefore result in damage to the reputation of the slandered party. A defendant in a slander action cannot claim as a defence that another party had made the slanderous statement and that the defendant was merely repeating the statement; nor can the defendant claim that they gave the name of the informant and expressed no opinion as to the truth. In some cases, words that would otherwise be considered actionable, or subject to laws of slander, may be uttered as a privileged communication. Privileged communications are words uttered for a purpose or in a context which is protected by law. Words uttered with qualified privilege for example, when giving an oral reference, are protected as long as the speaker is not motivated by malice. Words uttered with absolute privilege – for example, in Parliament – can never be slander.

6.4   Libel

Defamation published in permanent form (such as writing, printing, drawings, photographs, radio and television broadcasts) is known as libel. You libel someone if you *publish* a *defamatory statement* about them which you cannot defend. *Published* in the legal sense means communicated to a person other than the plaintiff. So, for example, if a manuscript is sent to a publisher it would be deemed to have been published in the legal sense. A *defamatory statement* is one that damages a person's reputation. For example, it is defamatory to say that someone has committed a criminal offence.

The courts will evaluate matters from the perspective of the ordinary person, so a statement would not be regarded as defamatory unless it would make ordinary readers think worse of the person concerned. An ordinary person[2] in this context would be someone with the following characteristics:

- not naïve
- not unduly suspicious
- able to read between the lines
- capable of reading in an implication more readily than a lawyer
- capable of indulging in a certain amount of loose thinking
- not avid for scandal.

You can libel individuals, companies, partnerships and businesses. You cannot libel the dead and you cannot libel local authorities or other government bodies, although you can libel the individuals employed by those organizations. It is possible to libel someone even if you do not name them. Only people who are identified by the offending material can sue, but it is important to bear in mind that you might be identifying someone inadvertently. If, for example, there is only one 27-year-old male librarian living in a particular village, then describing him as such could identify him whether you name him or not. Small groups may also be identifiable and all its members may be able to sue. For example, if you were to write that 'one of the members of the ethics committee has been convicted of murder', and the ethics committee only consisted of five people, this casts suspicion on all five people as it could be referring to any of them. As such the statement would be actionable.

In an action for damages for libel, the plaintiff is required to establish that the matter they complain of:

• has been published by the defendant (publication)
• refers to the plaintiff (identification)
• is defamatory (defamatory words or gestures).

If the plaintiff does this, they establish a prima facie case – that is, they provide sufficient evidence for proof of the case. However, the defendant could still escape liability if they can show they had a good defence.

6.5 Defences to libel

The defences to a libel action are:

• justification/veritas in scotland – being able to prove that what you wrote was substantially true
• fair comment – showing it was an honest expression of opinion
• privilege – special protection to which the law determines that certain kinds of report are entitled
• offer to make amends (ss2–4 of the Defamation Act 1996).

6.5.1 Justification/veritas

The law of defamation exists to protect individuals who suffer damage to their reputation. It follows, therefore, that the law does not protect the reputation that a person does not possess. If you can prove that what you have written is true both in substance and in fact, then you have a defence against an action for damages. The key point is that you have to be able to prove that what you have written is true. Ultimately, it is not what you know or believe that matters, but rather whether your evidence will stand up in court, to the satisfaction of the jury. So if you will be relying on witness evidence:

1 Make sure your witnesses are likely to be available at trial. Relying solely on written statements from overseas witnesses will have far less impact in front of a jury.
2 Do not rely on witnesses who have spoken to you only off the record.
3 Only rely on witnesses who
   • are credible
   • are independent
   • have first-hand knowledge of what they are telling you.

It is important to keep safely any supporting documentation such as a notebook, tapes or documents which might be used in evidence, because you might have to produce this material in court.

Like justification, the defence of veritas in Scotland is a complete defence. It is governed by Section 5 of the Defamation Act 1952.

6.5.2   Fair comment

The defence of fair comment provides for the right of freedom of speech for individuals. For a defence of fair comment to succeed, you must show that:

• the comment was made honestly and in good faith, based on true facts or on privileged material, as opposed to being inspired by malice
• it was on a matter of public interest, and
• if the claimant alleges malice, that you were not motivated by malice.

The distinction between the defences of justification and fair comment is that justification/veritas protects the publication of facts whereas fair comment protects the expression of opinion. In some cases it can be particularly difficult to distinguish between whether a statement is fact or opinion. If you can prove a statement, it is fact. If you are drawing an inference from the facts, or if there are at least two possible views on the matter, then it is an opinion.

6.5.3   Privilege

Privilege affords a defence for certain types of report whether or not they are true. Many of these are specified by statute, and include fair and accurate reports of court proceedings, parliamentary proceedings, reports in Hansard, public inquiries and international organizations; also a range of public meetings and the findings of governing bodies and associations.

Absolute privilege means that the statement can in no circumstances be the subject of libel proceedings. It covers contemporary, fair and accurate reports of court proceedings, communications within the government, and communications between solicitor and client about legal cases. Proceedings in parliament are similarly protected, because the courts refuse jurisdiction over parliamentary affairs.

Qualified privilege is available where the defendant acts without malice – that is, acts for the reasons for which the privilege exists, and not principally to harm the plaintiff. It applies generally to all communications that the defendant has a legal or moral duty to make, or makes, in protecting his or her own legitimate interests. Such a defence is wide-ranging and includes reports on most public proceedings and references on employees.

6.5.3.1 Qualified privilege for general media reports

Reynolds v. Times Newspapers Limited[3] was a case which arose as a result of a newspaper article that implied that Albert Reynolds, the former prime minister of Eire, had lied. In its judgement (28 October 1999) the House of Lords developed the common law defence of qualified privilege to general media reports on matters of public interest. The defence applies when the circumstances are such that a 'duty to publish' and a 'right to know' test is satisfied. Lord Nicholls set out ten factors which need to be taken into account (the tests have an emphasis on responsible journalism):

1 The seriousness of the allegation. The more serious the charge, the more the public is misinformed, and the individual harmed, if the allegation is not true.
2 The nature of the information, and the extent to which the subject-matter is a matter of public concern.
3 The source of the information. Some informants have no direct knowledge of the events. Some have their own axes to grind, or are being paid for their stories.
4 The steps taken to verify the information.

5   The status of the information. The allegation may have already been the subject of an investigation which commands respect.

6   The urgency of the matter. News is often a perishable commodity.

7   Whether comment was sought from the plaintiff. He may have information that others do not possess or have not disclosed. An approach to the plaintiff will not always be necessary.

8   Whether the article contained the gist of the plaintiff's side of the story.

9   The tone of the article. A newspaper can raise queries or call for an investigation. It need not adopt allegations as statements of fact.

10   The circumstances of the publication, including the timing.

6.5.4   The offer to make amends

The procedure for the offer to make amends is set out in sections 2–4 of the Defamation Act 1996. The defendant must make an offer in writing to publish a suitable correction and apology and to pay damages and costs. When an offer of amends is made, a claimant must decide whether to accept or reject it. If they accept it, no further proceedings can be taken, except to decide disputes over apologies and the amount of any compensation payable. If they reject it, then the defendant may rely on the offer as a defence to an action of defamation where the maker did not know nor had reason to believe that the statement complained of referred to the pursuer and was false and defamatory.

It is no defence to libel to say that you were just reporting what someone else said. Therefore you cannot avoid liability by the use of words such as *alleged* or *claimed*. Nor is it a defence to show that someone has published the allegations before. Newspapers and magazines are liable for the contents of whatever they publish, including material not written by them such as readers' letters and advertisements.

It isn't sufficient for newspapers and magazines to ensure that the articles they publish are libel-proof. They also have to pay careful attention to headlines and picture captions, because these can be a lucrative source of damages. In the case of picture captions, the words and the pictures should match.

6.6   Remedies

The remedies available are a civil action for damages, the awarding of costs, an injunction (interdict in Scotland) to prevent repetition, or a criminal prosecution to punish the wrongdoer by means of a fine or imprisonment; although it is far more common for cases of libel to result in a civil action for damages or an injunction/interdict to prevent repetition.

6.6.1 Civil action for damages

Damages can be colossal, even though the Court of Appeal can now reduce libel awards. The main aim of a libel claim is in order to compensate the plaintiff for the injury to their reputation. A jury can give additional sums either as 'aggravated' damages, if it appears a defendant has behaved malevolently or spitefully, or as 'exemplary' or 'punitive' damages where a defendant hopes the economic advantages of publication will outweigh any sum awarded. Damages can also be nominal if the libel complained of is trivial (see Walker/Stewart on Delict[4] as awards are assessed on very different principles in Scotland from England).

Malice is irrelevant in awards for damages, although the award may be mitigated where it is shown that there was no malice involved in the defamatory statement. There is also a principle in Scots law that provocation may mitigate. Malice is not defined in the Defamation Act 1952.

However, under the ECHR, damages must be necessary and there are controls on excess – see Tolstoy v. UK, 1995 (English law).[5]

6.6.2 Costs

Costs go up all the time. If you were to lose a libel case, then you would have to pay the claimant's expenses as well as your own, which would be likely to add at least a six-figure sum to the bill for damages. Indeed, in many of the high-profile libel cases of the past decade, the costs have often exceeded the damages.

6.6.3 An injunction/interdict to prevent repetition

Any individual or organization can seek an injunction either to stop initial publication of an article or to prevent any further publication. Injunctions/interdicts may be granted, temporarily and for a short while, ex parte, meaning that only the claimant is represented before the judge. If both parties appear before the judge, the defendant would have to argue on grounds of public interest or, for potential libels, be ready to declare on affidavit that they could justify the story.

Injunctions/interdicts against any publication bind all other publications that are aware of the injunction. To breach an injunction is a severe contempt of court that could lead to an offender's imprisonment.

6.6.4   Criminal prosecution to punish the wrongdoer by fine or imprisonment

Where libel occurs, it can lead to a criminal prosecution against those responsible, who include the author/artist/photographer, the publishers and the editor of the publication in which the libel appeared. To be a criminal offence the libel needs to have been calculated to provoke a breach of the peace or that there is some other public interest. Criminal prosecutions are rare. The main types of writing which have the potential to lead to a criminal prosecution are:

• defamatory libel
• obscene publications
• sedition
• incitement to racial hatred
• blasphemous libel.

Section 8 of the Defamation Act 1996 introduced a summary procedure under which a judge may dismiss a plaintiff's claim if it has no realistic prospect of success, or give judgment for the claimant and grant summary relief, which means ordering the defendant to publish a suitable correction and apology and pay damages.

6.7   Defamation and the internet

The Law Commission has investigated the application of libel laws to the internet.[6] In February 2002 they sent out a questionnaire to a number of interested parties, including online publishers, internet service providers, barristers and solicitors. The responses highlighted four areas of concern:

• the liability of internet service providers for other people's material (6.7.1)
• the application of the limitation period to online archives (6.7.2)
• the exposure of internet publishers to liability in other jurisdictions (6.7.3)
• the risk of prosecution for contempt of court (6.7.4).

6.7.1   The liability of internet service providers for other people's material

ISPs offer services such as website hosting and newsgroups where they do not exert editorial control over the material. Where a defamatory statement appears on a website, the ISP is considered to be a 'secondary publisher' – they are involved in disseminating the defamatory statement even though they are not the author, editor or commercial publisher, and can be held liable if they exercise discretion over how long material is stored or if they have the power to remove the material.

Under section 1(1) of the Defamation Act 1996, an innocent disseminator such as a printer, distributor, broadcaster or ISP who is considered by the law to be a secondary publisher has a defence if:

• he was not the author, editor or publisher of the statement complained of
• he took reasonable care in relation to its publication
• he did not know, and had no reason to believe, that what he did caused or contributed to the publication of a defamatory statement.

The section builds upon the common law defence of 'innocent dissemination'. It does not apply to the author, editor or publisher of a defamatory statement but is intended for distributors. It is of particular relevance to ISPs. However, as soon as a secondary publisher such as an ISP has been told that something on a newsgroup or a web page is defamatory, they cannot use the section 1 defence.

ISPs are seen as tactical targets and regularly receive complaints that material on websites and newsgroups is defamatory. In such instances, the safest option for them is to remove the material immediately, even if it appears to be true; and to remove not just the page in question but the entire website, although this is at odds with freedom of speech.

In view of the amount of e-mail messages, newsgroup postings or web pages that are uploaded daily, it is doubtful whether it would be practical for ISPs to pre-screen all content; and even if it were possible, whether they could do so in a cost-effective manner. It is, however, more reasonable for internet service providers to undertake post-screening. If an ISP is told that material is defamatory, they should act promptly and responsibly by:

- removing the defamatory statements once they have been notified
- posting a retraction
- making a reasonable effort to track down the originator of the defamatory remarks in order to prevent future postings.

Failure to do so would suggest that the ISP had not acted responsibly and that they should be held accountable for the consequences. ISPs are well placed to block or remove obscene, illegal, infringing or defamatory content.

In their response to a Law Commission consultation process, the industry made three criticisms of the current position:

1 Receiving and reacting to defamation complaints was 'costly and burdensome'.
2 The industry felt uncomfortable about censoring material that may not in fact be libellous.
3 It was suggested that customers might be attracted to US ISPs, who had greater protection against being held liable for defamation, and who could therefore offer their customers more attractive terms.

ISPs should certainly take complaints seriously. In order to protect themselves, they should obtain warranties and indemnities from content providers, and post notices such as acceptable use policies on their services.

The Electronic Commerce (EC Directive) Regulations[7] implement the Electronic Commerce Directive 2000/31/EC.[8] The Regulations provide that intermediaries such as ISPs and telecommunications carriers are not liable for damages or criminal sanctions for unlawful material provided by third parties where the intermediary:

- is a mere conduit[9] (the intermediary does not initiate the transmission, does not select the receiver of the transmission, and does not modify the information it contains)
- simply caches the information,[10] as part of automatic, intermediate, temporary storage, without modifying it
- simply hosts the information[11] (such as a newsgroup or website) so long as the intermediary:

— does not have actual knowledge or awareness of the unlawful activity

— upon obtaining such knowledge or awareness acts expeditiously to remove or disable access.

Godfrey v. Demon Internet Ltd [2001] QB 201

This case concerns a posting to a newsgroup which was distributed to Usenet subscribers. An unnamed USA resident posted a contribution on another ISP purporting to come from Laurence Godfrey, which the judge described as 'squalid, obscene and defamatory'. When Dr Godfrey heard of the posting, he informed Demon Internet that the posting was a forgery and asked them to remove it from their Usenet server. They failed to do so and the posting was left on the site for a further 10 days until it was automatically removed. Demon Internet argued that they had a purely passive role similar to that of a telephone company. However, it was held that, as the defendants had chosen whether to store the material and for how long, they could not be said to have played only a passive role.

Following the decision in Godfrey v. Demon Internet [2001] QB 201, ISPs are often seen as tactical targets. They are regularly put on notice of defamatory material and they find themselves facing a difficult choice – whether to surrender in the face of a claim which may be without merit, or continue to publish on the basis of indemnities and assurances from primary publishers that the material, although defamatory, is not libellous.

Totalise plc v. Motley Fool Ltd (2001) 4 EMLR 750

Totalise took action against two websites in order to get them to disclose the identity of an individual who had posted defamatory messages on those sites. The judge decided that Totalise was entitled to know the identity of the individual in order to decide how best to protect their rights, whether or not they then undertook legal proceedings.

The defence of innocent dissemination also applies to booksellers, libraries and newsagents. The case of Weldon v. Times Book Co Ltd[12] indicates that while a library is not expected to review the contents of every book it possesses, some works may call for a more searching examination, taking account of the type of book in question, the reputation of the author, and the standing of the publisher. The Law Commission report on defamation and the internet[13] quotes from a response to their consultation on aspects of defamation procedure by the Booksellers Association of Great Britain and Ireland, which says that the provisions of section 1 of the Defamation Act 1996 . . .

have encouraged plaintiffs or prospective plaintiffs with dubious claims who are unwilling to commence proceedings against the author or publisher of the allegedly defamatory publications to take or threaten action against book-sellers to force them to remove such publications from their shelves. As those plaintiffs and their legal advisers clearly realise, booksellers are not in a position to put forward a substantive defence of justification because they have no direct knowledge of the subject matter of the alleged libel.

Bookshop Libel Fund

Two independent bookshops – Housmans Bookshop and Bookmarks Bookshop – faced potentially ruinous legal proceedings for stocking the anti-fascist magazine *Searchlight*, and the Bookshop Libel Fund was originally set up in 1996 to support small shops such as these who were caught up in libel cases.

The case is not about defamation and the internet, but it is relevant here because of the innocent disseminator defence in section 1(1) of the Defamation Act 1996.

The case was first brought in 1996 and six years later the bookshops had to relaunch their appeal for funds as the case was still continuing. British law allows anyone who claims they have been libelled to sue any shop, distributor or library handling the allegedly libellous publication, as well as or instead of suing the author, editor and publisher. Housmans and Bookmarks fought the case with a defence of 'innocent dissemination', in effect arguing that it is impossible for bookshops, particularly small independents, to check – and take responsibility for – the content of the thousands of publications in stock at any one time. They felt it was important to try to take a stand, otherwise there might be no end to this sort of 'legal intimidation'.

The litigant had been referred to as a plagiarist in one sentence in a 136-page pamphlet stocked in the shop. He had chosen to sue only the shop, not the author or publisher concerned.

Although he had at one stage demanded that the shop pay him £50,000 to drop the case, the jury awarded him just £14. Because he had already rejected a settlement offer higher than that, he was also ordered to pay most of the shop's legal costs; however, it was not anticipated that he had the resources to do so.

Where tactical targeting of this kind does occur, it is open to secondary publishers to protect themselves by seeking indemnities from the primary publisher. The primary publisher could also apply to be joined in the action as a defendant in order to provide the necessary evidence for a defence of justification.

6.7.2   The application of the limitation period to online archives

The Defamation Act 1996 reduced the limitation period for defamation actions from three years to one year, although courts have discretion to extend that period. However, the application of this limitation to online archives has proved to be extremely contentious. For, while the limitation period is one year, in the case of Loutchansky v. Times Newspapers Limited,[14] the Court of Appeal held that this limitation period commenced every time someone accessed a defamatory internet page. In other words every 'hit' on an online article could be regarded as a fresh publication of that article. The judgment means that a piece put on the internet five years ago could still be the subject of legal action today so long as the relevant pages are accessible. The effect of this is that the limitation period is potentially indefinite.

Similarly, in the Scottish case of Her Majesty's Advocate v. William Frederick Ian Beggs,[15] the judge ruled that information held on the internet archives of newspapers was published anew each time someone accessed it. This potentially lays newspaper publishers and editors open to charges of contempt of court unless they remove material relating to the previous convictions and other relevant background material of anyone facing criminal proceedings (see section 6.7.4). The judge did not take the same view of the paper archives held by public libraries, and this distinction takes into account the ease with which material on the internet can be accessed.

One also has to bear in mind the way in which certain search engines and websites are automatically caching and/or archiving the content of a vast number of websites, thus making web pages available even after the site owner has removed the content from their site.

A number of people have suggested that we should adopt the US single publication rule in which the limitation period starts running on the date of the first publication of the defamatory article, even if it continued to be sold or 'webcast' for months or years afterwards. This matter is of direct relevance to library and information professionals, who make regular use of online archives in order to carry out their research and enquiry roles, and for whom any reduction in the availability of online archives would hamper their work. The Law Commission report[16] says that 'online archives have a social utility and it would not be desirable to hinder their development.'

6.7.3   Exposure of internet publishers to liability in other jurisdictions

England's libel laws are regarded as being 'plaintiff-friendly'. British courts, for example, do not have the First Amendment protections to consider and apply that United States courts do.[17] The nightmare scenario for online and internet publishers is for potential litigants to be able to undertake 'foreign shopping' or 'forum shopping', whereby they can launch an action in a country of their choosing, where the defamation laws are the most stringent. Foreign individuals or companies may, for that reason, be particularly interested in pursuing a British-based publication.

If pursued by overseas claimants, British publications face tricky issues in mounting a defence because subpoenaing foreign witnesses is impossible, although there is a procedure for taking written evidence abroad through foreign courts. Even if the claimant is not particularly well known here, the compensation that could awarded for damage suffered elsewhere in the world can still be substantial.

Dow Jones v. Gutnick

In the Australian case Dow Jones & Company Inc v. Gutnick [2002] HCA 56, the High Court agreed that a person in Victoria was entitled to bring an action for defamation in Victoria in respect of the publication on the internet of an article about the tax affairs of Joseph Gutnick, even though the article was uploaded to the web by Dow Jones in America.

The court said potential litigants needed to consider practical issues, such as whether they had assets or reputations in the jurisdiction where the material was published. Otherwise, the court would rule that it was not the appropriate place to hear the case. In Australia, the tort of defamation depends on publication, and therefore the fundamental question to be decided was that of determining the place of publication of the alleged damaging article. However, the High Court clearly distinguished between jurisdiction and applicable law. It was said that a court may have jurisdiction but that it may equally be bound by the applicable rules of a foreign jurisdiction.

In Dow Jones v. Gutnick, The Australian High Court justified their position, in part, by reference to the International Covenant on Civil and Political Rights,[18] which provides, among other things, that everyone shall be protected from 'unlawful attacks on his honour and reputation'. However, the covenant also provides that:

- everyone shall have the right to hold opinions without interference
- everyone shall have the right to freedom of expression; this right shall include freedom to seek, receive and impart information and ideas of all kinds, regardless of frontiers, either orally, in writing or in print, in the form of art, or through any other media of his choice.

As an article in *The Australian*[19] points out, the Gutnick decision would seem to put all of this in peril. There have been cases in the USA which have taken the opposite view to the Gutnick decision, but of course US libel law is not as plaintiff-friendly as is the case in the UK.

Traditional publishers are able to restrict sales of their publications by geography, but internet publishers do not seem to have that option, because simply by choosing to publish on the internet they are in theory subjecting themselves to the laws of every nation from which the internet can be accessed. The court dismissed Dow Jones' contention that it would have to consider the defamation laws from 'Afghanistan to Zimbabwe' in every article published on the internet. 'In all except the most unusual of cases, identifying the person about whom material is to be published will readily identify the defamation law to which that person may resort,' the court said. Online publishers are concerned that by publishing content to the internet they have to contend with a significant burden of legal risk. What they want are greater levels of certainty and clarity over which laws should be applied to them and their intermediaries. These publishers might feel it necessary to turn to technology for a solution. They might, for example, seek out the development of software that could let sites identify where visitors come from and then block them if they are deemed to expose the publishers to a high risk of potential lawsuits.

In an unprecedented move, the reporter who wrote the piece that Joe Gutnick objected to has responded by filing a writ at the United Nations Human Rights Commission, claiming that he has been denied the right of free speech[20] and that Australia is in breach of Article 19 of the United Nations International Covenant on Civil and Political Rights.

Some people argue that the UK should follow the US example and exempt ISPs from liability for material published. However, the Law Commission found that this would not prevent legal action against UK-based internet service providers in foreign courts. An international treaty would be required in order to solve the problem of unlimited global risks.

6.7.4 The risk of prosecution for contempt of court

Material is held to be in contempt of court if it poses a substantial risk of serious prejudice to the administration of justice. Serious prejudice is likely to arise from publication of the following matters:

- a defendant's previous convictions
- details of a defendant's bad character
- suggestions that a witness's (particularly a defendant's) testimony is likely to be unreliable
- details of evidence that is likely to be contested at trial.

The law of contempt does not stop you writing about a case; it simply places certain limits on what you may say. For the purposes of contempt, criminal proceedings become active from the time of arrest or charge, or from the time a warrant for arrest is issued, and civil proceedings are active from the time arrangements are made for trial. The closer the case is to trial, the greater the risk of prejudice.

The rulings in Loutchansky v. Times Newspapers Limited[21] and Her Majesty's Advocate v. William Frederick Ian Beggs[22] (see section 6.7.2) that a web page is published each time a user accesses that page in effect means that the limitation period is indefinite. The UK does not have the single publication rule that applies in the USA. Consequently, online publishers are concerned over the risk of being held to be in contempt of court because their websites and online archives may well contain records of a defendant's previous convictions or acquittals which jurors could research during a trial. In order to eliminate those risks, newspapers would either have to monitor every criminal case throughout the country and to remove any offending material from their online archive for cases that were active – which would be impractical – or they could opt for the more cost-effective option of taking down the online archives of their publications in their entirety, which would clearly be to the detriment of historians and researchers.

6.7.5 E-mail libel

The use of e-mail is fraught with dangers. The informal nature of the internet increases the likelihood that people will make defamatory statements in e-mails, on discussion groups or in chat rooms. These defamatory statements can reach the far corners of the world in a matter of seconds, whether through e-mails being directed to a large number of recipients, or through the forwarding or copying of e-mail correspondence that typically happens.

It is extremely easy and indeed quite common for people to send an e-mail to unintended recipients. Some discussion groups, for example, have as a default setting that when you reply to a message from an individual, the response goes to all members of the group. Many is the time that I have seen people apologizing for sending out a rather candid e-mail to an entire discussion group when they had only intended to send the message to one person. Another common mistake is that of including the wrong file attachment in a message. The user may have published an item which they had never intended to publish, and thereby perpetrated an accidental defamation. Similarly, it is all too easy to forward a long e-mail without reading the whole message. If the end of the e-mail contains a defamatory statement, the act of forwarding the e-mail would mean that the user had unwittingly repeated the defamatory statement and could be held liable for their actions.

The use of e-mail disclaimers is becoming more common. Whilst the disclaimer may be of dubious legal validity in the absence of any contractual relationship between the sender and the recipient, the sender will be in a better position if the unintended recipient has notice of the potentially confidential nature of the e-mail and is advised what to do with it. Therefore disclaimers may help to limit certain legal liability, but they will not of themselves be a defence to an action for defamation.

There have been a number of legal cases dealing with defamation and cyber-liability. One case which was settled out of court involved defamatory remarks made on the internal e-mail system of Asda Supermarkets in 1995 accusing a policeman of fraud.[23]. Asda paid substantial damages to the complainant.

Norwich Union v. Western Provident Association

In 1997 Western Provident started an action against Norwich Union, a rival private healthcare insurance provider, when it was discovered that Norwich Union were circulating messages on their internal e-mail system which contained damaging and untrue rumours about their competitor to the effect that they were in financial difficulties and being investigated by the DTI. Western Provident sued for libel and slander. Norwich Union publicly apologized to Western Provident and paid £450,000 in compensation for damages and costs.

The Norwich Union case showed that the courts are willing to step in to order employers to preserve the evidence. The High Court in an interlocutory hearing ordered Norwich Union to preserve all the offending messages and to hand over hard copies of them to its rival. The fact that e-mail creates a discovereable document means that employees should be aware that apparently deleted e-mail may be held on the system for some time or be accessible from backups.

If an employee makes a defamatory statement using their company's internal e-mail system, or posts a defamatory comment on the company intranet, then it is possible for a legal action to be brought against the organization as employer by way of 'vicarious liability' for acts of their employees.

It is important for employers to issue guidelines such as an e-mail and internet policy with the employee's contract of employment, prohibiting defamatory statements so as to be able to prove that employees or other categories of e-mail, intranet and extranet users have acted contrary to guidelines. It is also good practice to have employees click on an 'accept' button of the e-mail and internet policy before they are able to gain access to the computer system. You need to ensure that users are aware of such guidelines by incorporating them into the intranet home page and elsewhere, as appropriate. However, such action is not a guarantee of immunity from legal actions.

6.8   Checklist

1 Does your organization have a guide to acceptable use of e-mail, the intranet, and the internet?
2 Does this mention anything about offensive, defamatory or derogatory material?
3 Is this covered in the staff handbook?
4 Is the policy mentioned as part of the induction process?
5 Emphasize disciplinary action for breaches of e-mail and internet policy.
6 Treat e-mails with the same care that you would show when composing a letter or a fax.
7 Educate and train employees as to the legal implications of sending messages which may be read by tens of thousands of users, and on the acceptable use of internet/e-mail.
8 Bear in mind that there is likely to be a backup of the correspondence.
9 Use a disclaimer on e-mail correspondence.
10 Consider insurance cover for liability in defamation.

6.9   Summary

In this chapter we looked at defamation law, including oral defamation (slander)(6.3) and written defamation (libel) and the law of defamation in Scotland (6.4). Defamation law is relevant to information professionals, whether they be responsible for intranets, extranets, publicly available websites or online databases; users of their organization's internet e-mail system; or members of internet e-mail discussion groups. The chapter then outlined the defences that can be used in libel cases (6.5) and the remedies that the law provides (6.6). The 'innocent disseminator' defence is relevant for information professionals in the hard copy world, where people can target libraries and bookshops as 'secondary publishers', just as much as in the internet era, where publishers face a wide range of legal hazards – including the application of the limitation period to online archives (6.7.2), the question of jurisdictions and applicable law in cases of internet defamation (6.7.3), and the risk of prosecution for contempt of court that newspaper and magazine publishers face when they operate online archives (6.7.4). The chapter concluded with an examination of the dangers of cyberliability in relation to e-mail.

In the next chapter we will consider the general principles of breach of confidence and privacy.

Notes and references

1   *Principles of Scottish private law*, volume 2, 4th edn, 1988, 637–8.
2   See Skuse v. Granada Television Ltd [1996] EMLR 278 and Gillick v. British Broadcasting Corporation [1996] EMLR 267.
3   Available at www.parliament.the-stationery-office.co.uk/pa/ld199899/ldjudgmt/jd991028/rey01.htm.
4   Walker, D. M., *The Law of Delict in Scotland*, 2nd rev. edn, 1981, Edinburgh, W. Green.
5   Tolstoy v. UK, unreported ECHR, 13 July 1995 (English law).
6   Law Commission, *Defamation and the internet : a preliminary investigation, Scoping study no. 2*, December 2002, available at www.lawcom.gov.uk/files/defamation2.pdf.
7   The Electronic Commerce (EC Directive) Regulations 2002: SI 2002/2013.
8   EC directive 2000/31/EC of 8 June 2000 on certain legal aspects of information society services, in particular electronic commerce, in the Internal Market, Official Journal L178/1, 17 June 2000.
9   SI 2002/2013 regulation 17.
10 SI 2002/2013 regulation 18.
11 SI 2002/2013 regulation 19.
12 Weldon v. Times Book Co Ltd [1911] 28 TLR 143.

13   Law Commission, *Defamation and the internet : a preliminary investigation, Scoping study no. 2*, December 2002, 11, available at www.lawcom.gov.uk/files/defamation2.pdf.
14   Loutchansky v. Times Newspapers Limited [2001] EWCA Civ 1805. Available at www.bailii.org/ew/cases/EWCA/Civ/2001/1805.html.
15   Her Majesty's Advocate v. William Frederick Ian Beggs, High Court of Judiciary (2001).
16   Law Commission, *Defamation and the internet : a preliminary investigation, Scoping study no. 2*, December 2002, available at www.lawcom.gov.uk/files/defamation2.pdf.
17   The first amendment of the US constitution says that Congress shall make no law respecting an establishment of religion, or prohibiting the free exercise thereof; or abridging the freedom of speech, or of the press; or the right of the people peaceably to assemble, and to petition the government for a redress of grievances.
18   International Covenant on Civil and Political Rights, New York, 19 December 1966, ATS 1980 no. 23.
19   High court throws a spanner in the global networks, *The Australian*, 11 December 2002.
20   Australian laws challenged at UN, smh.com.au, 18 April 2003, available at www.smh.com.au/articles/2003/04/18/1050172745955.html.
21   Loutchansky v. Times Newspapers Limited [2001] EWCA Civ 1805.
22   Her Majesty's Advocate v. William Frederick Ian Beggs, High Court of Judiciary (2001).
23   Caught in the net, *The Guardian*, 25 April 1995.

7 Breach of confidence and privacy

7.1 Introduction

This chapter considers what constitutes a breach of confidence (7.2). It explores how human rights legislation has been used in privacy actions (7.3), and the differences that exist between the law on obligation of confidence and actions for breach of privacy (7.4). The implications of the obligation of confidence on the freedom of information regime are discussed (7.5). The role of regulatory codes of practice are then considered (7.6). The chapter concludes by looking at remedies available for breach of confidence, and relevant case law in which breach of confidence was used to protect the privacy of individuals.

7.2 General principles

The common law tort of breach of confidence deals with unauthorized use or disclosure of certain types of information and provides protection for that information to be kept secret.

This branch of the law is based upon the principle that a person who has obtained information in confidence should not take unfair advantage of it. The main means used to achieve this is the interim injunction (interdict in Scotland), which is an order of the court directing a party to refrain from disclosing the confidential information. A document may be considered confidential where there is:

- an obligation of non-disclosure within a particular document
- a duty in certain papers involving professional relationships
- a duty of confidence, which arises where a reasonable individual may determine that a document contains confidential material.

Breach of confidence is most commonly used to prevent publication of private material. The law protects confidential information from unauthorized disclosure, and an injunction may be granted unless you can show that the publication is in the public interest, usually by exposing some wrongdoing. The injunction can in extreme circumstances be against the whole world, such as the injunction granted to protect the new identities of the killers of James Bulger.

In the James Bulger case, Dame Elizabeth Butler-Sloss gave the killers of James Bulger the right to privacy throughout their life. The media were already prevented from publishing their identities as a result of information obtained from those who owed the pair a duty of confidence, such as police officers and probation service officials; but Dame Elizabeth went further and said the pair had an absolute right to privacy. In May 2003 the child killer Mary Bell and her daughter won a high court injunction guaranteeing them lifelong anonymity.

There are three elements of a breach of confidence. In 1968 Mr Justice Megarry[1] said:

1   The information must have 'the necessary *quality of confidence*' – namely it must not be something which is public property and public knowledge.
2   The information must have been imparted in circumstances imposing an *obligation of confidence*.
3   There must be an unauthorized use of that information to the *detriment* of the party communicating it.

If someone wishes to seek redress for disclosure of confidential information, then each of these elements must be present. Furthermore:

1 Companies use breach of confidence to protect sensitive commercial information and trade secrets.
2 Governments use breach of confidence to protect information they regard as secret.
3 Individuals use it for the same purpose and also to protect their privacy.

The duty of confidence is, as a general rule, also imposed on a third party who is in possession of information which he knows is subject to an obligation of confidence.[2] If this was not the law, the right would be of little practical value. There would, for example, be no point in imposing a duty of confidence in respect of the secrets of the marital bed if newspapers were free to publish those secrets when they were betrayed to them by the unfaithful partner in the marriage. Similarly, when trade secrets are betrayed by a confidant to a third party, it is usually the third party who is to exploit the information, and it is the activity of the third party that must be stopped in order to protect the owner of the trade secret.

The use of breach of confidence by individuals wishing to protect their privacy was boosted by the implementation of the European Convention on Human Rights in UK law through the Human Rights Act 1998 (HRA), because this Act gives individuals a right to privacy.

Between February and April 2003, the Culture, Media and Sport select committee held an inquiry into privacy and media intrusion,[3] and whether there was a need for legislation on privacy. The inquiry did not aim to come to the aid of public figures who have problems with the press; rather, they were concerned with ordinary people whose lives can be affected, perhaps adversely, by their relations with the media. It is about 11 years since the previous enquiry on this topic by the then National Heritage Committee. The fact that the committee undertook a new enquiry on privacy and media intrusion was a recognition that things have moved on a considerable degree since that time.

7.3   Privacy and the Human Rights Act

There has never been an absolute 'right to privacy' in English or Scots law. Yet Britain has been bound to comply with the European Convention on Human Rights (ECHR) for decades, which states that 'everyone has the right to respect for his private and family life, his home and his correspondence.' A number of the rights which are enshrined in the ECHR are in conflict with one another, and there will always be a tension between them. In particular, the right to privacy (article 8) and the right to freedom of expression (article 10) often conflict (see Figure 7.1). In every situation, a balance needs to be struck between those two rights; and the courts would need to consider the issues on a case by case basis. What is clear is that the right to privacy is not an absolute right.

Article 8 – Right to respect for private and family life

1   Everyone has the right to respect for his private and family life, his home and his correspondence.

2   There shall be no interference by a public authority with the exercise of this right except such as is in accordance with the law and is necessary in a democratic society in the interests of national security, public safety or the economic well being of the country, for the prevention of disorder or crime, for the protection of health or morals, or for the protection of the rights and freedoms of others.

Article 10 – Freedom of expression

1   Everyone has the right to freedom of expression. This right shall include freedom to hold opinions and to receive and impart information and ideas without interference by public authority and regardless of frontiers. This article shall not prevent States from requiring the licensing of broadcasting, television or cinema enterprises.

2   The exercise of these freedoms, since it carries with it duties and responsibilities, may be subject to such formalities, conditions, restrictions or penalties as are prescribed by law and are necessary in a democratic society, in the interests of national security, territorial integrity or public safety, for the prevention of disorder or crime, for the protection of health or morals, for the protection of the reputation or rights of others, for preventing the disclosure of information received in confidence, or for maintaining the authority and impartiality of the judiciary.

Fig. 7.1   *European Convention on Human Rights*

Since the HRA came into force in 2000, the courts have had to interpret existing law in ways which secure this right. The existing law, however, remains piecemeal, and privacy complaints are usually found in actions for breach of confidence, harassment, trespass, malicious falsehood and data protection legislation or pursued under regulatory codes of practice (see 7.6).

Courts have been reluctant to establish a right to privacy as a separate cause of action in UK law. The court of appeal, by allowing the *Mirror*'s appeal against Naomi Campbell's award for damages[4] for the publication of details about her private life, resisted the chance to declare once and for all whether there is a freestanding actionable wrong in English law for breach of privacy.

To date the court of appeal has expressly eschewed a right to make claims based directly on the articles of the ECHR and has instead determined cases in accordance with existing causes of action. The cases have proceeded historically by applying the law of confidence.

The professions are subject to obligations of confidentiality. The CILIP Code of Professional Ethics[5] addresses the question of confidentiality from several different perspectives:

1 One of the general principles states that the conduct of information professionals should be characterized by respect for confidentiality and privacy in dealing with information users.
2 One of the specific responsibilities to information users says that information professionals should protect the confidentiality of all matters
   relating to information users, including their enquiries, any services to be
   provided, and any aspects of the users' personal circumstances or business.
3 In the list of responsibilities to society it says that information professionals
   should aim to achieve an appropriate balance between the law, demands
   from information users, the need to respect confidentiality, the terms of
   their employment, and the responsibilities outlined in the Code.

Section A.3 of the EIRENE (European Information Researchers Network)
Code of Professional Conduct[6] says that

A broker shall:

- hold the affairs of the client in the strictest confidence, except where
  the law requires disclosure
- declare any conflicts of interest if they are likely to undermine confidentiality
- undertake not to re-use or misuse information gained as part of the
  client contract for personal or professional gain.

7.4   Obligation of confidence v. breach of privacy

An obligation of confidence, by definition, arises firstly from the circumstances in which the information is given. By contrast, a right of privacy
in respect of information would arise from the nature of the information itself;
it would be based on the principle that certain kinds of information are cat-
egorized as private and for that reason alone ought not to be disclosed. In many
cases where privacy is infringed, this is not the result of a breach of confidence.

In the late 1980's the UK government used the law of confidence to try
to silence former members of the security services (in particular Peter
Wright, author of *Spycatcher*) and journalists trying to report their disclosures.
It has been established that the public have a legitimate interest to be

weighed against other interests in knowing how they have been governed. It has always been accepted that Cabinet deliberations are confidential. As a result of the publication of Richard Crossman's diaries, a case was taken by the Attorney General against the publisher for breach of confidence.[7] It was held that the public interest in disclosure outweighed the protection of information given in confidence once the material was sufficiently old. In this particular case that period was taken to be 10 years. The courts appear to retain for themselves the role of arbiter of the public interest and will consider each case on its merits.

Kaye v. Robertson [1991] FSR 62

A reporter and a photographer tricked their way into the private hospital room of the actor Gorden Kaye who was lying semi-conscious. They did so in order to 'interview' and photograph him. The court held that there was no actionable right to privacy in English law and that no breach of confidence had taken place because there wasn't a recognized relationship between Mr Kaye and the journalists (such as that between a doctor and his patient) which could be used in order to impose an obligation to keep confidential what Mr Kaye had said.

This case might be seen as the low-point in the laws of privacy and breach of confidence; but since that time a lot has happened with the implementation of the Human Rights Act 1998 and case law which has further refined and developed the laws relating to privacy and breach of confidence.

7.5   Obligation of confidence and the Freedom of Information Act

Section 41 of the FOIA provides for an absolute exemption for information provided in confidence (see Figure 7.2). However, the exemption provided for in section 41 only applies if information has been obtained by a public authority from another person, and the disclosure of the information to the public, otherwise than under the Act *would constitute a breach of confidence actionable by that, or any other person*.

The s45 code of practice issued by the Lord Chancellor's Department[8] states that authorities must consider the implications of freedom of information before agreeing to confidentiality provisions in contracts and accepting information in confidence from a third party more generally. In any event, public authorities should not agree to hold information 'in confidence' which is not in fact confidential in nature.

In some cases the disclosure of information pursuant to a request may affect

41. (1) Information is exempt information if

(a) it was obtained by the public authority from any other person (including another public authority), and
(b) the disclosure of the information to the public (otherwise than under this Act) by the public authority holding it would constitute a breach of confidence actionable by that or any other person.

(2) The duty to confirm or deny does not arise if, or to the extent that, the confirmation or denial that would have to be given to comply with section 1(1)(a) would (apart from this Act) constitute an actionable breach of confidence.

Fig. 7.2   *Freedom of Information Act 2000, section 41, exemption*

the legal rights of a third party – for example, where information is subject to the common law duty of confidence or where it constitutes 'personal data' within the meaning of the Data Protection Act 1998 (DPA). Public authorities must always remember that, unless an exemption provided for in the DPA applies in relation to any particular information, they will be obliged to disclose that information in response to a request.

When entering into contracts with non-public authority contractors, public authorities may be under pressure to accept confidentiality clauses in order that information relating to the terms of the contract, its value and performance will be exempt from disclosure. Public authorities should reject such clauses wherever possible. Where, exceptionally, it is necessary to include non-disclosure provisions in a contract, an option could be to agree with the contractor a schedule of the contract which clearly identifies information which should not be disclosed. But authorities will need to take care when drawing up any such schedule, and be aware that any restrictions on disclosure provided for could potentially be overridden by their obligations under the DPA.

A public authority should only accept information from third parties in confidence if it is necessary to obtain that information in connection with the exercise of any of the authority's functions and it would not otherwise be provided. Acceptance of any confidentiality provisions must be for good reasons, capable of being justified to the Information Commissioner.

7.6   Regulatory codes of practice

There are a number of codes of practice governing the media, and in any cases relating to privacy or breach of confidence, the courts would have regard to any relevant privacy code. These codes include:

• newspapers and magazines (Press Complaints Commission Code of Practice[9])
• BBC TV (producers' guidelines[10])
• other TV (Broadcasting Standards Commission[11])
• radio (Radio Authority's Radio Code[12])
• Independent Television Commission (ITC Programme Code[13])

For example, in considering whether to grant an injunction (interdict in Scotland), courts would have regard to the standards the press has itself set in voluntary codes of practice. Under the Press Complaints Commission Code, a publication will be expected to justify intrusions into any individual's private life without consent.

In March 2003, the 11th edition of the *British Code of Advertising, Sales Promotion and Direct Marketing*[14] was launched by the Committee on Advertising Practice (CAP). The code applies to non-broadcast marketing communications in the UK and is endorsed and administered independently by the Advertising Standards Authority (ASA).

The code takes account of the UK's distance selling regulations[15] and the EU's directive on privacy and electronic communications.[16] As far as the obligation of confidence is concerned, the code states that 'the ASA and CAP will on request treat in confidence any genuinely private or secret material supplied unless the courts or officials acting within their statutory powers compel its disclosure.'

7.7   Remedies

The main means of ensuring that information obtained in confidence is not unfairly taken advantage of is the use of an injuction (interdict in Scotland). A prohibitory injunction can be used in order to direct the party to refrain from disclosing the information. There are a number of remedies available to the courts:

• fines
• court order to reveal source

- court order that a confidential matter be 'delivered up' or destroyed
- account for the profits where a person misusing confidential information may be asked to account to the person who confided the information
- damages claim by the person whose confidences have been breached in the publication of confidential material
- contempt of court action where injunction/interdict is breached.

7.8   Case law on breach of confidence

The past few years have witnessed a number of high-profile cases in which well known personalities have used the law relating to breach of confidence in order to try and protect their privacy.

Even a public figure is entitled to a private life, although he or she may expect and accept that his or her circumstances will be more carefully scrutinized by the media. If the claimant has courted attention, this may lead the claimant to have fewer grounds upon which to object to the intrusion.

Naomi Campbell v. Mirror Group Newspapers [2002] EWCA Civ 1373

The Naomi Campbell case was about confidentiality, privacy, the Human Rights Act and data protection.

Naomi Campbell sued the publishers of *The Mirror* for breach of confidence and breach of the DPA in respect of articles and photographs which showed that she was attending meetings of Narcotics Anonymous.

In this case the court applied the practical test for what information or conduct is to be considered private and confidential – the common law test of offensiveness – whether disclosure or observation of the information would be highly offensive to a reasonable person of ordinary sensibilities.

The footballer's case A v. B & another [2002] EWCA Civ 337

The claimant was a premier league footballer, who was granted an interim injunction restraining the first defendant B from publishing stories about his extramarital affairs with two women C and D.

The court considered the balance between article 8 of the ECHR on the right to respect for private life and article 10 on the right to freedom of expression. The court of appeal said that the judge had been wrong to reject any element of public interest in the publication of the proposed stories.

The Lord Chief Justice, Lord Woolf, said that the more stable the relationship, the greater would be the significance attached to it by the court. But the court should not protect brief affairs of the sort the footballer enjoyed with the two women, when the women wanted to talk about them. Banning the two women from telling their stories for publication was an interference with their freedom of expression.

Theakston v. MGN Ltd [2002] EWHC 137

Jamie Theakston sought an injunction to prevent publication of photographs and an article relating to his visit to a brothel. He relied on the grounds of breach of confidentiality and breach of his right to privacy as reflected in the Press Complaints Commission Code, and as contained in article 8 of the ECHR. Mr Theakston claimed that he had been in a private place with friends, that the events were private and confidential. and that he had never discussed the details of his private life or sex life in public.

The judge stated that he did not consider the brothel to be a private place. Mr Theakston had courted publicity regarding his private life, which had led to his enhanced fame and popularity.

Mr Theakston was successful in obtaining an injunction preventing publication of the photographs, but was unsuccessful in preventing publication of the article.

Douglas and others v. Hello! Ltd [2003] EWCH 786 (Ch)

Catherine Zeta Jones and Michael Douglas had signed an exclusive deal with *Hello!*'s rival, *OK!* to publish wedding photographs. *Hello!* magazine published photographs of the wedding in breach of confidence, and the celebrity couple won damages from *Hello!*

The couple's complaint about invasion of privacy was rejected because there was no privacy law and an action for breach of confidence provided the necessary protection. Commenting on the lack of a privacy law, Justice Lindsay said, 'That parliament has failed so far to grasp the nettle does not prove that it it will not have to be grasped in future.'

Lord Justice Lindsay concluded, 'I hold the *Hello!* defendants to be liable to all three claimants under the law as to confidence . . . It will have been noted that an important step in my coming to that conclusion has been that, on balancing rights to confidence against freedom of expression for the purpose of granting or withholding relief, I have been required by statute to pay, and have paid, regard to the code of the Press Complaints Commission . . . The *Hello!* defendants broke their own industry's code.'

7.9 Summary

This chapter has outlined the law relating to breach of confidence (7.2). It discussed how human rights legislation has been used in privacy actions (7.3) and the differences that exist between the law on obligation of confidence and breach of privacy (7.4). The FOIA has an absolute exemption for breach of confidence, but the code of practice issued by the former Lord Chancellor's Department makes it clear that the use of confidentiality should not be used to prevent disclosure without good reason which can be justified to the Information Commissioner. The chapter concluded by looking at the remedies available for breach of confidence, and details of a few high-profile cases in which breach of confidence has been used by individuals to protect their privacy.

The next chapter deals with professional negligence, and whilst there hasn't yet been a legal case of a UK librarian being sued on the grounds that their work has caused loss or damage, information professionals do need to be aware of the risks involved and need to try and minimize those risks.

Notes and references

1   Coco v. Clark [1969] RPC 41 at 47.
2   See Prince Albert v. Strange (1840) 1 Mac & G 25 and Duchess of Argyll v. Duke of Argyll [1967] Ch 302.
3   HC 458i-iv and HC 458-I Session 2002/03, available at www.parliament.the-stationery-office.co.uk/pa/cm/cmcumeds.htm.
4   Naomi Campbell v. Mirror Group Newspapers [2003] 2 WLR 80.
5   *Code of Professional Ethics: draft for consultation*, CILIP, 2003.
6   EUSIDIC (European Association of Information Services), EIIA (European Information Industry Association) and EIRENE (European Information Researchers Network), *Code of Practice for Information Brokers*, 1993.
7   Attorney General v. Jonathan Cape Ltd [1976] QB 752.
8   Lord Chancellor's code of practice on the discharge of public authorities' functions under part I of the Freedom of Information Act 2000, issued under section 45 of the Act. Lord Chancellor's Department, November 2002.
9   Available at www.pcc.org.uk/cop/cop.asp.
10 Available at www.bbc.co.uk/info/editorial/prodgl/index.shtml.
11 *Codes of Guidance*, Broadcasting Standards Commission, June 1998 (includes code on fairness and privacy; and a code on standards).
12 Available at www.radioauthority.org.uk/regulation/codes/codes-main.html.
13 *Programme Code*, Independent Television Commission, January 2002.
14 *British Code of Advertising, Sales Promotion and Direct Marketing*, 11th edn, The Committee of Advertising Practice, 2003 (came into force on 4 March 2003).
15 The Consumer Protection (Distance Selling) Regulations 2000: SI 2000/2334.
16 2002/58/EC covering the processing of personal data and the protection of privacy in the electronic communications sector (directive on privacy and electronic communications).

8 Professional liability

8.1 Introduction

This chapter considers professional liability from the perspective of library and information professionals. Although there hasn't been an instance of a UK librarian being successfully sued for negligence, that is no reason to become complacent. In December 2002, Mark Field reported[1] that professional liability issues were becoming a growing area in CILIP's casework.

The chapter looks at the general principles of professional liability (8.2), and how librarians could be held liable for their work under the law of contract (8.3) or the law of tort (delict in Scotland) (8.4). Specific types of liability are considered, including liability in relation to electronic information (8.5) and liability for copyright infringement (8.6).

Strategies for minimizing the legal liability risks that librarians face as professionals are examined (8.7), as well as the role of professional indemnity insurance as part of that strategy (8.8).

8.2 General principles

Liability means having legal responsibility for one's acts, errors or omissions. It is the duty of care that one individual or organization owes to another, and gives rise to the risk of being sued for damages if the individual or organization fails in that duty. It is certainly the case that by his contract with his client, a librarian owes the client a duty to exercise reasonable care; and this duty of care basically means that he should do the things that a prudent person would do in the circumstances and refrain from those things which they would not do.

Whilst there is no UK legislation which deals specifically with liability for information provision, librarians do need to be aware of the potential risk of facing a professional liability claim because they could be held liable for their work under contract law or the law of tort/delict.

Any organization whose professional employees provide advice, expertise, information or a consultancy service may be legally liable for a claim of malpractice where a breach of professional duty occurs. If you work for an employer, your employer is vicariously liable for the torts/delicts of his/her employees if they are committed in the course of the employees' employment. However, this only applies if the act were one of the type that the employee might have been expected to carry out in the normal course of their duties. The employer is likely to have insurance cover against any actions brought against the company – although it is well worth checking that this is the case rather than taking it for granted that it is. Self-employed information consultants and brokers should consider taking out professional indemnity insurance (see section 8.8).

Even if you work for an employer, there are potential dangers involved in assuming that your firm's professional indemnity insurance will protect you in the event that liability is established, as the case of Merrett v. Babb demonstrates.

Merrett v. Babb (Court of Appeal, 15 February 2001)

In the case of Merrett v. Babb, the Court of Appeal held that a surveyor employed by a firm of valuers who negligently prepared a mortgage valuation report for a lender owed a duty of care to the purchasers who relied on the surveyor's report when buying the property, and that the surveyor was personally liable for the purchasers' loss. Permission to appeal was refused.

In the mortgage valuation report prepared by Mr Babb on the property that Miss Merrett was about to purchase, it was noted that the property contained certain cracks, but the report failed to point out that settlement had taken place. Miss Merrett said that the property was worth £14,500 less than the valuation and she sued Babb in his personal capacity.

The surveyor was employed as branch manager of a firm of surveyors and valuers from February 1992 to January 1993. On 1 June 1992 he signed the relevant mortgage valuation report. A bankruptcy order was made against the sole principal of the firm on 30 August 1994. The principal's trustee in bankruptcy cancelled the firm's professional indemnity insurance without run-off cover in September 1994. The purchasers therefore brought an action in negligence against the surveyor personally rather than against the firm. The surveyor was not insured.

The implications of this case are that professional employees may be open to claims for negligent advice in situations where their firm has become insolvent or is otherwise under-insured. The case shows that there may be instances where individuals might need to take out personal insurance even after their employment has ended.

Taking the general principles of liability into account, it is necessary to consider how they relate to the information professional. You are expected to use reasonable skill and care when providing library and information services, and the key issue to establish is what is meant by 'reasonable'. 'Reasonable' would mean that which an information professional would be expected to do in the circumstances, and the judges of what is reasonable are other information professionals. So 'reasonable' really constitutes good professional practice, which could be established by testimony from expert witnesses.

Only when we can say what a quality product or service consists of and how it is identified can we speak of being liable for low-quality work. Is the service performed to the standard of an average professional? Ultimately your own reputation with colleagues and clients is the best guide.

Information professionals seek to provide their services as well as possible – that is, they should do their job with due care and attention. Did they fail to search an appropriate source and thereby miss something vital? Did they try to verify the accuracy of the information? Information professionals should also act ethically. They have a Code of Professional Conduct[2] to be followed (this is currently in the process of being replaced with a Code of Ethics[3]).

The CILIP draft Code of Ethics sets out a number of personal responsibilities of information professionals, which include that they should:

- ensure they are competent in those branches of professional practice in which qualifications and/or experience entitle them to engage
- avoid claiming expertise in areas of library and information work or in other disciplines where their skills and knowledge are inadequate.

According to the CILIP leaflet *Working for Yourself* (2002), 'As yet there is no record of a library or information professional being sued on the grounds that their work caused loss or damage to their client.' However, this should not lure people into a false sense of security. It begs the question of whether you want to be the first information professional in the UK to be sued because your advice caused a client loss or damage.

It may seem hard to think of a situation where provision of information could lead to a client suffering loss or damage, but information professionals need to think about the nature of the information they are dealing with and the levels of risk attached to different types of information. For example, if an enquirer were to ask you to find a set of instructions on how to make your own parachute, you would need to make it absolutely clear that you had not tested the validity of the instructions and give the enquirer a disclaimer along the lines that you could not take any responsibility for any damage caused to the enquirer if they were to follow the instructions that you had given them. That probably sounds like it is a rather frivolous example, but where you are dealing with legal, financial, patent or medical information, you would need to be particularly careful. If you obtained a credit rating on a company for a user, it is quite feasible that, if the credit rating was out of date or was inaccurate, the user could end up experiencing financial loss if they were to do business with the company based largely on a healthy credit rating.

8.3 Contract

Contract law is relevant to the liability of information professionals. If, for example, an enquirer contacts the information centre and asks a member of staff to find some information for him, the researcher provides the requested information and the user accepts it, this whole transaction will be subject to contract law. This is the case even if there is nothing written down and no money has changed hands. Indeed, it is a common misunderstanding to think that for a contract to exist money has to be involved. It has to be said that where money does change hands clients have a higher expectation of the quality of service that is being provided; that is, they have higher customer expectations of the duty of care that is applied in delivering the service. In any question of liability, the courts too may well expect a higher level of duty of care for a priced service than is required for a free service. But even if a service is provided free of charge you cannot ignore issues of liability.

A contract is a legally binding agreement between two or more parties which is enforceable in a court of law. One party offers to do something for the other party and the other party accepts this offer. The essential elements of a contract are:

1 Offer – the proposal to make a deal. This offer must be communicated clearly to the other party and remain open until it is either accepted, rejected, withdrawn or has expired.
2 Acceptance – this is the acknowledgement by the other party that they have accepted the offer, except where a qualified acceptance is made, as this

amounts to a rejection of the offer and is instead regarded as a counter-offer, which also requires acceptance.

3 Consideration – this is what supports the promises made. It is the legal benefit that one person receives and the legal detriment on the other person. This could, for example, take the form of money, property, or services.

Consideration is not necessary for a contract in Scots law. Contracts arise where the parties reach agreement as to the fundamental features of the transaction; this is often referred to as 'consensus in idem' (meeting of the minds). To determine whether agreement has been reached, contracts in Scotland are analysed in terms of offer and acceptance.

The contract doesn't have to be a signed document. It could be entered into orally, although this does make it more difficult to establish whether or not there is a contract. A written contract contains the terms and conditions of the agreement and can be used in any dispute, although the very fact that someone has a carefully worded written contract can help prevent a dispute occurring because a written contract sets out clearly the rights and obligations of the parties.

The increasing trend for librarians to work for themselves as freelance consultants, who charge for their expertise, is accompanied by the ever-increasing risk that they could be held liable for their expertise and advice. In the case of consultants and information brokers, many will have a set of terms and conditions which they will send to the client before they start working on an assignment. It is in their interests to do so, because the terms and conditions will set out what the client can expect from the information broker, and there will be a number of disclaimers and exclusion clauses limiting the broker's liability.

Any contracts entered into with users should include a formal disclaimer of liability. However, this needs to be carefully worded, because if an exclusion clause is too general it could be deemed to be invalid. The exclusion clause should, therefore, be specific. It could put a limit on the extent of any potential liabilities, such as putting a maximum figure of £5,000 on any damages to be paid; stating that the liability is capped at the monetary value of the contract between the broker and the client; or in the case of an online service, allowing the subscriber to terminate the contract if he or she finds errors.

A number of information brokers use the Code of Practice for Information Brokers which was produced by EIRENE[4] – the European Information Researchers Network – in order to demonstrate competency in performing the services that they provide.

8.4   Tort (delict in Scotland)

Tort/delict refers to behaviour causing loss or harm to other people where no contract exists. It would cover the concept of negligence or carelessness, such as where a librarian carelessly provides inaccurate information to a user who suffers loss as a result. The legal basis for the law of tort/delict is the assumption that citizens owe each other a duty of care. If you cause your fellow citizens loss by your negligence, you lay yourself open to claims for compensation.

Tort/delict does not require any contractual relationship between the parties involved, and it therefore follows that third parties who suffer loss because of your actions can sue for compensation. For such an action to succeed, the injured party would need to establish the following:

• that the other party owed him a duty of care
• that this duty had been breached
• that there had been damage
• that the damage had been a direct result of the breach
• that the damage could have been reasonably foreseen.

The English law of tort and the Scots law of delict are similar but have considerable differences. For example, the law of defamation, nuisance, trespass and property, and the award of exemplary or penal damages, does not exist in Scotland. However, the law of negligence is now the same in both jurisdictions.

There are a number of key legal cases which set important precedents in the law of tort.

Donoghue v. Stevenson [1932] AC 562

The case of Donoghue v. Stevenson is important because it established the 'neighbourhood principle', which defines classes of persons to whom a duty of care is owed. In his judgment, Lord Atkin said that 'one owes a duty of care to one's neighbour', and he explained that 'neighbour' refers to 'such persons as are so closely affected by my acts or omissions that I ought reasonably to have them in my contemplation when directing my mind to the acts or omissions called into question.' This duty of care extends to financial loss where an expert is consulted, as illustrated by Hedley Byrne v. Heller.

Hedley Byrne & Co v. Heller and Partners [1964] AC 465

A bank advised that a certain business would be a good investment; it was not and the investor lost a lot of money. The case dealt with the question of whether someone who provides advice to another person without a contract being in place could be held liable for negligence. The House of Lords found that if the advice was being sought in circumstances in which a reasonable man would know that he was being trusted or that his skill or judgement was being relied upon, then if the person didn't clearly qualify their answer so as to show that they did not accept responsibility, then they accepted a legal duty to take such care as the circumstances required. The case established that a duty of care could arise to give careful advice and that a failure to do so could give rise to liability for economic loss caused by negligent advice. Liability arose because the individual consulted had claimed expertise in business investments, his advice would be relied upon and was intended to be definitive. Financial harm can be compensated only in such cases where specific expertise is consulted.

Anns v. London Borough of Merton [1978] A C 728

The case of Anns v. London Borough of Merton developed the 'neighbourhood principle' further. In this case Lord Wilberforce said that first the court should establish proximity, using the 'neighbourhood test'; and then, if proximity were established, the court must take account of any 'consideration which ought to negate, reduce or limit the scope of the duty or the class of persons to whom it is owed or the damages to which breach of it may give rise.' For example, in the case of a public library providing a free enquiry service, a court might decide in any claim for liability that it would not be in the public interest to set a precedent which allows users to sue public libraries providing their services free of charge.

See also Home Office v. Dorset Yacht Co. Ltd 1970 AC 1004.

Caparo Industries plc v. Dickman [1990] 2 AC 605

An important case in defining the duty of care in the field of information provision is Caparo Industries plc v. Dickman. The case dealt with the liability of auditors to potential investors. It established that the concept of 'duty of care' existed when a number of factors were present:

1   The information is for a specific purpose.
2   The purpose is made known at the time that the advice is given or that the advice is sought.
3   The advisor knows that his or her advice will be communicated to the advisee or recipient.

8.5   Liability and electronic information

In the late 1980s and early 1990s there was a lot of interest in the question of information quality and liability in relation to electronic information, as evidenced by the number of articles written on the topic at that time. Unlike the situation with hard-copy material, it isn't always possible with electronic information to browse the data or examine the indexes in detail, and then there are the added restrictions on time and cost. Users of online databases may find errors when they search for information, ranging from simple spelling errors, inconsistent use of controlled vocabulary through to factual errors. In the case of incorrect spellings, these can mean the difference between retrieving a record and not being able to retrieve that record.

To address such concerns, the Centre for Information Quality Management (CIQM) was established in 1993 under the auspices of the Library Association and the UK Online User Group (UKOLUG) with the aim of providing a clearing house through which database users could report quality problems. In a 1995 CIQM survey on the effects of poor data on workflow, a surprisingly high figure (31.11%) was returned for retrieval of unusable records (either missing data, badly formatted tables or erroneous data). The questionnaire was addressed to professional intermediaries and it was noted that end-user searchers might be affected more seriously.

If information professionals obtain data from an online service, the information provider is likely to have a liability exclusion clause in their contract making it more difficult to take action against them. Library and information professionals need to take steps which protect them from potential claims for liability. The CILIP draft Code of Ethics[5] sets out a number of responsibilities of information professionals, and as far as responsibilities to their users are concerned the first two that are listed in the code are particularly relevant:

1 Ensure that information users are aware of the scope and remit of the service being provided.
2 Indicate to information users the reliability of the information being provided.

Information professionals need to warn their users that output from the online service doesn't necessarily carry a guarantee of accuracy. You are not in a position to promise that all of the information retrieved from an online database is correct, complete and accurate because the database provider is responsible for that, and it is outside your control.

Librarians should watch out for signs of how reliable an online database is from:

- how frequently the database is updated
- whether it contains typographical errors
- any gaps in coverage
- any inconsistencies or errors in the indexing.

Where information workers have reservations about the accuracy, reliability or trustworthiness of an information source, they should convey these to the user and make the user aware that there is no guarantee of accuracy. Where the service is chargeable, your terms and conditions of service should make clear that you cannot accept responsibility for errors or omissions in the databases or other sources that you use in your search. Whenever possible the information professional should seek to double-check and verify the accuracy of the data. Information staff should maintain good records of the sources used to answer an enquiry. This is particularly important in cases where a fee is charged. The record that is kept can be used as a checklist to ensure that the key sources have all been consulted, and can also be referred back to in the event that a user of the service challenges you about not doing a thorough job.

8.6   Liability for copyright infringement

There are a number of instances where an information professional could potentially be held liable for copyright infringement. For example, with the implementation of the Copyright Directive,[6] copying for a commercial purpose is no longer permitted under the fair dealing provisions or the library regulations. In the case of the library regulations, librarians are given an indemnity to do copying on behalf of their users that users would themselves be entitled to make under s29 of the Copyright, Designs and Patents Act 1988 (CDPA). The copyright declaration is the librarian's indemnity and if this is false the onus is on the signatory and not the librarian. However, if a user is unsure as to whether or not a particular instance of copying is permitted, they may understandably turn to the librarian for advice before signing the declaration form. The librarian should be careful not to decide for people whether or not a commercial purpose applies, because they could be held responsible for a false declaration.

Library staff also need to be particularly careful to ensure that in answering a user enquiry they are not infringing someone's copyright. As the draft CILIP Code of Ethics says, 'Information professionals should defend the legitimate needs and interests of information users, while respecting the moral and legal rights of the creators and distributors of intellectual property.'

8.7 Risk management

It is important for librarians to be aware of how liability arises, in order to be aware of the risks involved and to be able to take steps to minimize the possibility of legal action. Jonathan Tryon says, 'In a litigious society every library administrator must take care to institute procedures which will minimise the likelihood of law suits based on harm caused by the library's negligence.'[7] However, whilst effective risk management can help reduce exposure to allegations of neglect, error or omission it can never completely eradicate that risk. A simple error, omission or mis-statement could potentially trigger a claim. The best defence against such claims is to:

- pay attention to your own professional development
- keep yourself up to date
- be aware of the range and content of the sources
- be aware of the accuracy, timeliness and reliability of the sources.

Indeed, the CILIP draft Code of Ethics[8] says that information professionals should 'ensure they are competent in those branches of professional practice in which qualifications and/or experience entitle them to engage', and also that they should 'undertake continuing professional development to ensure that they keep abreast of developments in their areas of expertise.'

In any promotional material about your information service, you might wish to note that you follow the code of ethics of the professional organization to which you belong – such as the Chartered Institute of Library and Information Professionals or the Society of Competitive Intelligence Professionals (SCIP).

The professional guidelines for the American Society for Information Science and Technology (ASIST)[9] state that as part of their responsibility to the profession, members are required to truthfully represent themselves and the information which they utilize or which they represent. ASIST sets out a number of key ways in which this is achieved. These include:

- not knowingly making false statements or providing erroneous or misleading information
- undertaking their research conscientiously, in gathering, tabulating or interpreting data; in following proper approval procedures for subjects; and in producing or disseminating their research results
- pursuing ongoing professional development and encouraging and assisting colleagues and others to do the same.

The Business Reference and Services Section of the Reference and User Services Association (RUSA) has produced a set of guidelines for medical, legal, and business responses,[10] in which they state that:

> Libraries should develop written disclaimers stating a policy on providing specialized information service denoting variations in types and levels of service. The level of assistance and interpretation provided to users should reflect differing degrees of subject expertise between specialists and non-specialists. When asked legal, medical, or business questions, information services staff should make clear their roles as stated in their library's specialized information services policies.[11]

In a case of professional liability, the courts would take into account a number of key factors:

1 The nature of the information service being provided. Was the information service, for example, a general service providing information about a wide range of subjects where it would be unreasonable to expect an information professional to be an expert in all of the areas covered by the information service? Or was it a specialist information service covering a narrowly defined subject area, where the information service had built up an international reputation and in which the information staff had specialist knowledge and which had made claims of having expertise in that field?
2 The level of knowledge of the user of the information service. If the topic that enquirers are asking about is one in which they themselves have considerable expertise, then they can be expected to use their own judge-

ment on the validity of the information received. Or was it a member of the general public who could not be expected to use professional judgement on the quality of information?

The EIRENE code of practice for information brokers[12] has a section relating to liability, in which it says that a broker shall

- clearly state the accuracy limits of the information provided, within their professional competence and available sources
- state clearly their liability and will not use total disclaimers
- abide by the existing local laws regarding liability, arbitration procedures or professional negligence, when providing information services
- accept limited liability up to the value of the contract between broker and client, and
- indicate their arbitration procedures in their terms of business.

8.8 Indemnity and insurance

Indemnity is protection or insurance against future loss or damage. Professional indemnity insurance is an insurance against a claim from a client or any other independent third party who suffers financial loss as a result of alleged neglect, error or omission.

Any organization whose employees provide advice, information or a consultancy service may be legally liable at law for a claim of malpractice where a breach of professional duty occurs. If you give professional advice, your clients will regard you as an expert. These days clients are often well aware of their legal rights and are ready to assert those rights, so you could find yourself facing a claim from a client who feels that they have received substandard advice.

CILIP recommends professional indemnity insurance for self-employed information consultants and brokers, particularly if they are giving advice that could result in financial loss to their clients, because if they work as a sole practitioner, they would be personally liable for negligence, if proven, whatever the legal form of their company. The insurance provides them with financial protection. CILIP says that 'clear and reasonable disclaimers are also helpful, for example stating that you have no liability for errors in published

sources. Pay attention to deadlines and keep records – ideally for six years.'[13]
Unlike the situation for some professions, professional indemnity insurance
is not compulsory for the library and information profession. Some information professionals might not be keen on the idea of taking out professional
indemnity insurance because of a perception that the premiums are quite high
and that they don't always provide the desired protection. However, in the
case of freelance workers it makes sound business sense and should not be
regarded as an expensive or unnecessary business overhead. Furthermore, for
freelance workers the premiums are tax-deductible.

At the moment it is quite difficult to obtain professional indemnity insurance (PII) after the terrorist attacks of recent years. Costs have increased in
some sectors by over 200%. But it is nonetheless worthwhile to discuss the
matter with an insurance broker who can advise on pros and cons.

8.9   Summary

This chapter has considered the question of professional liability and the general principles of this branch of the law (8.2), including how this relates to
the law of contract (8.3) and the law of tort (8.4). Information professionals need to be careful to avoid making any claims to have expertise in areas
of library and information work or in other disciplines where their skills and
knowledge are inadequate. It is important that they are honest with their users
about what the user can expect from the service being provided. Although
there hasn't been an instance of a UK librarian being successfully sued for
negligence, that is not a reason to be complacent. Specific types of liability
were considered such as liability for inaccurate information or liability for
copyright infringement (8.6). The chapter concluded by outlining some
strategies for minimizing the legal liability risks that librarians face as professionals (8.7), as well as the importance of professional indemnity insurance (8.8).

With a greater and greater reliance on electronic information, information
professionals are regularly having to negotiate licences or contracts in order
to use electronic journals, online databases or other fee-based information
services. The next chapter will look at some of the key issues involved with
licences and contracts, as well as highlighting a number of pitfalls and things
to watch out for.

Notes and references

1 Available at www.cilip.org.uk/practice/km_bulletin/num2.html (Mark Field is CILIP's Information and Knowledge Management Adviser).

2 *Library Association Code of Conduct and Guidance Notes*, 2nd edn, 1995.

3 *Code of Professional Ethics: draft for consultation*, CILIP, 2003.

4 EUSIDIC (European Association of Information Services), EIIA (European Information Industry Association) and EIRENE (European Information Researchers Network), *Code of Practice for Information Brokers*, 1993.

5 *Code of Professional Ethics: draft for consultation*, CILIP, 2003.

6 Directive 2001/29/EC of the European Parliament and of the council of 22 May 2001 on the harmonization of certain aspects of copyright and related rights in the information society.

7 Tryon, J. S., Premises Liability for Librarians, *Library and Archival Security*, **10** (2), 1990.

8 *Code of Professional Ethics: draft for consultation*, CILIP, 2003.

9 ASIST professional guidelines, available at www.asis.org/About ASIS/professional-guidelines.html (accessed 24 July 2002).

10 Guidelines for medical, legal and business responses. Originally prepared by the Standards and Guidelines Committee, Reference and Adult Services Division, American Library Association in 1992. Revised and updated by the Business Reference and Services Section, Reference and User Services Association in 2000 and 2001. Approved by the RUSA Board of Directors, June 2001. Available at www.ala.org/Content/NavigationMenu/Our_Association/Divisions/RUSA/Professional_Tools4/Reference_Guidelines/Guidelines_for_Medical_Legal_and_Business_Responses.htm.

11 *Guidelines for Medical, Legal and Business Responses at General Reference Desks*, prepared by the ALA's Reference and Adult Services Division in 1992.

12 EUSIDIC (European Association of Information Services), EIIA (European Information Industry Association) and EIRENE (European Information Researchers Network), *Code of Practice for Information Brokers*, 1993.

13 *Working for Yourself*, CILIP, 2002.

9 Contracts and licensing agreements

9.1 Introduction

Information professionals need to be able to negotiate licence agreements with information providers, because licences are often the means by which access to information products is controlled. This chapter sets the scene for licensing and contracts in a library setting (9.2), and then examines the issues that information professionals need to take account of when negotiating licence agreements (9.3). The key elements of a licence are outlined (Figure 9.1). The chapter then looks at a number of consortia and other initiatives which have led to model licence agreements being produced (9.4). Finally, there is a brief mention of how technology is increasingly being used to ensure compliance with licence agreements (9.5).

9.2 General principles

Information professionals are in the business of providing access to information, but they can only do so whilst respecting the moral and legal rights of the creators and distributors of intellectual property.

Some would argue that copyright exceptions and limitations have been rendered practically meaningless in the digital arena. How, for example, are the limitations and exceptions to be applied in the digital environment in view of the widespread deployment of technological protection measures?

The exceptions available under the CDPA are extremely limited in their application to electronic information sources. Consider, for example, matters such as multiple copying, converting from one format to another, or storage in a central repository. With the implementation of EC directive 2001/29/EC the exceptions are even less generous.

To get around these limitations, information professionals are increasingly turning to licences as the means of providing access to works. Licences are contracts that are binding on both parties. They are governed by the law of contract, and enable information professionals to reach agreement with rights holders to permit their users to have access to electronic information services such as online databases, e-journals, websites, or CD-ROMs in ways that meet their users' needs.

It is important to point out that a licence does not confer ownership rights. It merely specifies the conditions upon which databases and other copyright works can be used and exploited, and by whom. Typically, the licences that information professionals negotiate are non-exclusive, granting the same rights to many different users.

An effective licence can be granted orally or by implication from particular circumstances, but it is always better to have a written agreement in order that the terms and conditions of your relationship with the licensor are clear.

Contracts cannot be used in order to agree the few terms which have been set as non-negotiable in a statute. For example, regulation 19 of the Copyright and Rights in Databases Regulations 1997[1] says:

Avoidance of certain terms affecting lawful users
19. – (1) A lawful user of a database which has been made available to the public in any manner shall be entitled to extract or re-utilise insubstantial parts of the contents of the database for any purpose.
(2) Where under an agreement a person has a right to use a database, or part of a database, which has been made available to the public in any manner, any term or condition in the agreement shall be void in so far as it purports to prevent that person from extracting or re-utilising insubstantial parts of the contents of the database, or of that part of the database, for any purpose.

9.3　Negotiating licences

It may sound trite to say it, but it is important to read the licence terms thoroughly. When you get a licence to sign, this should be viewed as the starting point of a negotiation process. Every licence should be subject to the discussion of its terms, rather than being signed immediately. There are some instances, though, where there is no scope for negotiation – such as 'click through' licences or 'shrink wrap' licences.

Information professionals do need to be extremely careful when signing contracts. You might think that, if a contract contains unfair terms, the courts will overturn it. It is certainly the case that under the Unfair Contract Terms Act 1977 agreements should satisfy the test of reasonableness, but there are very limited circumstances in which the courts would overturn an unfair contract term.

In a Court of Appeal ruling in 2001,[2] Lord Justice Chadwick said that the courts should be reluctant to interfere in contractual relationships where each party has freely entered into a contract and where each party enjoys reasonably equal bargaining power:

> Where experienced businessmen representing substantial companies of equal bargaining power negotiate an agreement, they may be taken to have had regard to the matters known to them. They should, in my view, be taken to be the best judge of the commercial fairness of the agreement which they have made; including the fairness of each of the terms in that agreement. They should be taken to be the best judge on the question whether the terms of the agreement are reasonable. The court should not assume that either is likely to commit his company to an agreement which he thinks is unfair, or which he thinks includes unreasonable terms. Unless satisfied that one party has, in effect, taken unfair advantage of the other – or that a term is so unreasonable that it cannot properly have been understood or considered – the court should not interfere.

It is essential that you read and understand the whole contract. You cannot get out of contract terms on the basis that you didn't read that particular term. For example, the contract might be 13 pages long, but unless you spend time reading it in detail you won't spot that on page 8 it makes clear that the contract automatically renews unless you give three months' notice. In these instances you might want to consider handing in the signed contract and the cancellation notice at the same time, in order to have maximum flexibility at the time when the contract is due for renewal.

You also need to be careful about signing a contract if there is anything that you don't fully understand (see Figure 9.1 for common legal terms used in contracts). It is no defence to say that the contract is invalid because you didn't understand a particular clause. If there is something that you don't understand, ask the supplier for clarification or refer it to your in-house legal team (if you have one).

Parties: the full contractual names of the parties to the licence.

Key definitions: essential terms are defined (e.g. authorised users, licensed materials, library premises, secure network, term, permitted purpose, licence fee, intellectual property, etc.).

Services: description of the material to be licensed. This is likely to also explain how the form and content may change during the contract period, particularly if the provider is an information aggregator who is reliant on data from a range of publishers. However, you should check carefully how you will be told about any changes, and whether you are happy with those arrangements.

Usage rights and prohibited uses: sets out precisely what authorized users are entitled to do with the licensed materials such as access, use, display, download, print; and any restrictions on their use such as removing copyright notices, or altering, adapting or modifying the licensed materials.

Warranties and indemnities: it is essential that the licence contains a warranty which confirms that the licensor has the legal right to license use of the copyright material, and that this does not infringe any third-party intellectual property rights. The warranty should also be backed up by an indemnity to this effect.

Terms and termination: sets out the subscription period and the conditions under which the licence can be terminated by either party.

Force majeure: this 'acts of God' clause excuses the supplier for circumstances beyond their reasonable control (such as riots, war, floods, etc.).

Legal jurisdiction and dispute resolution: this clause makes clear which law governs interpretation of the licence, and any arrangements for the resolution of disputes.

Fees and payment: the subscription price, payment arrangements and details of any other charges such as taxes.

Assignment: whether or not the licence is transferable, either by the licensor or by yourself to another third party.

Schedules: there may be one or more schedules appended to the main licence agreement setting out a number of additional terms and conditions.

Fig. 9.1   *Contract clauses*

Information professionals are increasingly having to sign licences with information providers in order to sort out access to electronic information products. The negotiation process can sometimes be quite lengthy and involve discussion over very specific points. Where this is the case, there is likely to be a certain amount of correspondence in the form of letters, faxes and e-mails that relates to the licence, and these should be kept on file. You might, for example, have asked for clarification on access restrictions; service content; or acceptable download limits. You might have sought clarification on whether the definition of authorized users enables you to send information from the online service to your clients; or to staff in your overseas offices. You might even have managed to negotiate a special deal with your account manager which will give you the option of renewing the service at the same rate as for the current subscription period. It is essential to retain all this documentation – not just the licence, but all the accompanying e-mails, faxes and letters as well. Even where the clarification was given orally, you should keep a written record. You don't want to rely on staff working for the information provider being aware of what has been agreed, because that documentation will come in extremely useful if your account manager moves on to another job, or if a dispute arises.

Librarians need to develop their negotiation skills. There are several documents on licensing matters which information professionals will find particularly helpful when negotiating licences. In May 2001, the International Federation of Library Associations (IFLA) announced that they had approved a set of licensing principles[3] which should prevail in the contractual relationship and written contracts between libraries and information providers. These principles touch upon aspects such as the applicable law, access, usage and users, and pricing. There is a helpful guide to the licensing of electronic information[4] and the pitfalls to watch out for. It has been produced by EBLIDA, the European Bureau of Library, Information and Documentation Associations and is full of practical tips and advice. Finally, it is worth mentioning Lesley Ellen Harris's book *Licensing Digital Content*.[5]

There are a number of key issues which need to be considered when you negotiate a licence for an information product. These include:

1 **Applicable law** – this should preferably be the national law of where your organization is located. If you are based in the UK, for example, you would not want the applicable law to be that of the USA; otherwise, if there is a problem relating to the interpretation of your licence, you could end up having to travel to a US court in order to plead your case.
2 **Ensure that statutory rights are recognized** – to avoid any doubt, the licence should contain a term which explicitly acknowledges that nothing in the licence prevents the licensee from dealing with the licensed materials in ways which are expressly permitted by statute: 'This agreement is without prejudice to any acts which the licensee is permitted to carry out by the terms of the Copyright, Designs and Patents Act 1988 and nothing herein shall be construed as affecting or diminishing such permitted acts in any way whatsoever.' This is particularly important in preserving the right to copy materials under the fair dealing provisions of the CDPA.

3 **Perpetual access to the licensed material** – when libraries subscribe to a journal in hard copy, then even if they cancel their subscription, they still have the back issues available for future reference. This is not automatically the case with electronic products. Are there any arrangements outlined in the contract for perpetual access? Does it, for example, have a clause along the lines that 'on termination of this licence, the publisher shall provide continuing access for authorized users to that part of the licensed materials which was published and paid for within the subscription period or by supplying a CD-ROM to the licensee'?

4 **Warranties and indemnities** – the licence should contain a clear warranty that the publisher/licensor is the owner of the intellectual property rights in the licensed material and/or that they have the authority to grant the licence. This helps to protect the library against an author who subsequently claims that they are the real owner of the intellectual property rights; or against claims from a new owner that you have to buy a fresh licence from them. It is also common to have a clause that the licence will not be assigned to a third party without the agreement of the other. Indemnities back up a warranty with a promise to insure or compensate the other party against losses and expenses arising from a breach of the warranty. The licence should indemnify the library against any action by a third party over the intellectual property rights that are being licenced. This indemnity should cover *all* of the losses, damages, costs and expenses that are incurred, including legal expenses, on a full indemnity basis.

5 **End users** – the library should not incur legal liability for each and every infringement by an authorized user. It is perfectly reasonable to ask the library to notify the publisher/licensor of any infringement that comes to the library's notice and for them to co-operate with the publisher/licensor to prevent further abuse. Of course, if the library condoned or encouraged a breach to continue after being notified of the breach by the publisher/licensor, then they would be held liable.

6 **Non-cancellation clauses** – for example, there should be no penalty for cancelling the print version in order to sign up to the electronic version of an information source.

7 **Non-disclosure clauses** – if the licence contains a non-disclosure clause, it needs to be clear what information is subject to the obligation of confidence; and you need to decide whether this is reasonable. There are obvi-

ously some things – most notably the price – which it is in the supplier's interests to keep confidential, especially if you have negotiated a preferential rate.

8 **Termination clause** – licences should always contain a clause which sets out the mechanism or circumstances in which the licence terminates.

9 **'Reasonable effort' and 'best effort' clauses** – the phrases 'reasonable effort' or 'best effort' are ambiguous, and should, wherever possible, be avoided. If the licence contains one or more of these phrases, then you should negotiate an amendment which replaces the phrase with something that is clear and unambiguous.

9.4   Consortia and standard licences

Negotiating licences can be extremely time-consuming. If you have to negotiate separate licences with each information provider, this is not only going to take up a lot of time but it also creates practical issues relating to compliance. Can you really be expected to know each of the licences you have signed up to inside out, especially if you have to take account of the terms and conditions in the licences for a large number of products?

Consortia purchasing and/or the use of standard licences is a recognition of the amount of time and effort involved in negotiating licence terms. There are a number of initiatives to produce a standard form of licence. These include:

1 Licensingmodels.com[6] is an initative that was led by a number of subscription agents. Model standard licenses for use by publishers, librarians and subscription agents for electronic resources have been created. There are four different types of licence covering the whole range of library types: single academic institutions; academic consortia; public libraries; and corporate and other special libraries.

2 In the academic sector, the Joint Information Systems Committee (JISC) often negotiates access to digital materials on behalf of interested universities. There is also a model licence that was negotiated by JISC with the Publishers Association. The 'Standard Licensing Arrangements' working party was asked by the JISC and the Publishers Association to explore options for developing 'umbrella' licence models which individual publishers could employ. These generic tools were intended to cover differ-

ent products and different types of use and would set out the more routine conditions of use, but leave a limited number of commercial issues – such as price per access or territory – to be added by different suppliers.

3 The European Copyright Users Platform (ECUP)[7] have produced four model licences for public libraries,[8] national libraries,[9] university libraries,[10] and company libraries.[11] These contain clauses favourable to libraries.

4 The International Coalition of Library Consortia (ICOLC)[12] produced a statement of current perspective and preferred practices for the selection and purchase of electronic information back in 1998. This was primarily aimed at the higher education community, and in December 2001 there was an update to the original statement.

5 The JISC Model Licence for Journals[13] is based on the National Electronic Site Licence Initiative (NESLI) site licence.[14] It was approved in September 2002, the major changes being that JISC replaced the NESLI managing agent and that the licence no longer covers service delivery.

The corporate sector has not tended to work together to create consortia in order to negotiate agreements with information providers. There are a number of reasons for this. The sector is quite disparate, consisting of a wide range of organizational types: media, law, property, professional services, engineering, pharmaceutical, etc. There is also the competitive nature of the corporate sector to bear in mind. Many commercial organizations will not want their competitors to know of any specially negotiated contract terms, especially not the price agreed; and may even be cagey about what services they subscribe to. One example of where the corporate sector has worked together is the sample license for electronic journals produced by the Pharma Documentation Ring (www.p-d-r.com).

Some large companies have produced a standard contract for the supply of online information services, and have used their buying power to persuade information providers to let them have access to their products using the standard contract that they, the customers, have drafted.

9.5 Technology solutions

Compliance with the terms and conditions of licences for electronic products is certainly going to be a major concern for both publishers and librarians in the future, and suppliers will increasingly look to the technology that is available in order to control access to electronic information products.

SI 2003/xxxx,[15] which implements EU directive 2001/29/EC, recognizes electronic copyright management systems and promotes their adoption, protection and use. It also provides legal protection against circumvention of technological measures designed to restrict infringement of copyright.

Where a library purchases a journal article or book in electronic format, the supplier might require them to accept a set of terms and conditions restricting access to, and use of, the item being purchased. But they might not rely solely on a set of terms and conditions to protect their intellectual property. Rather, they may use the technology to build in a number of security settings. Examples of how this could be applied in practice might include building in settings such as:

1 Any use of the file is limited to the machine on which it is downloaded.
2 Printing is set to one copy only.
3 Saving and viewing of the article is permitted, but for a limited period of time.
4 Forwarding and copying functions are disabled.
5 Annotations and conversion to speech are permitted.
6 Encrypted data which ensures that the material can only be read by one person who has been given access to the software that unencrypts the data.

9.6   Summary

This chapter has looked at the use of contracts and licences by information providers as a means of controlling access to electronic information products (9.2). It outlined the key elements that are likely to form part of a licence agreement (Figure 9.1). A number of essential points to watch out for when negotiating licences, such as the applicable law under which any dispute would be resolved, or the warranties and indemnities that need to be present in a licence agreement, were outlined (9.3). There have been a number of instances where people have come together to prepare a model licence and examples of these were discussed (9.4). Information providers and users are both concerned about compliance issues, and the final part of the chapter looked at how technology is increasingly being used to ensure compliance with the licence terms (9.5).

The next chapter looks at internet and electronic commerce law, including buying goods and services over the internet; electronic signatures; issues relating to jurisdiction; advertising law; and electronic communications such as direct marketing which uses e-mail and SMS.

Notes and references

1 Copyright and Rights in Databases Regulations 1997: SI 1997/3032.
2 Watford Electronics v. Sanderson 2001 EWCA Civ 317 para 55.
3 Available at www.ifla.org/V/ebpb/copy.htm.
4 Giavara, E., *Licensing Digital Resources: how to avoid the legal pitfalls*, 2nd edn, EBLIDA, 2001.
5 Harris, L.E., *Licensing Digital Content: a practical guide for libraries*, American Library Association, 2002.
6 Available at www.licensingmodels.com.
7 Available at www.eblida.org/ecup/licensing/
8 Available at www.eblida.org/ecup/docs/heads/publib.htm.
9 Available at www.eblida.org/ecup/docs/heads/natlib.htm.
10 Available at www.eblida.org/ecup/docs/heads/unilib.htm.
11 Available at www.eblida.org/ecup/docs/heads/company.htm.
12 Available at www.library.yale.edu/consortia/statement.html.
13 Available at www.nesli.ac.uk/modellicence_info.html.
14 Available at www.nesli.ac.uk/modellicence8b.html.
15 See author's note at the beginning of Chapter 2.

10 Internet and electronic commerce law

10.1 Introduction and background

Internet and e-commerce law affects information professionals in a number of ways as the internet has fast become the primary method of communication. It governs the electronic purchase of goods and services, such as the online purchase of books or subscriptions to e-journals. Information professionals may make use of digital signatures when signing contracts. It is likely, for example, that when a recognized industry standard evolves, a large proportion of copyright declaration forms will be completed using digital signatures. Information professionals also need to be mindful of the regulations governing privacy and electronic communications, as they will need to ensure that, where their websites use cookies or web bugs, users are told about this; and that if they send out e-mail advertising, this only goes to those who have opted in – or are existing clients, in which case they should be given an option to unsubscribe.

Many English laws apply just as well to electronic commerce and the internet as they do already to the more traditional means of business and communication. With the exponential growth in the use of the internet, for both business and residential usage, there have been a number of pieces of legislation relating specifically to the use of the internet as a means of communication, as a tool for gathering information, and as a vehicle for undertaking electronic commerce. In the UK, the Distance Selling Regulations (10.2) and the Electronic Commerce (EC Directive) Regulations (10.3) provide a framework for regulating contracts which are concluded electronically. The past few years have also seen developments in the law relating to electronic signatures (10.4).

The internet is by its very nature global, whereas that is not the case with the law. There are, of course, international treaties and conventions – and European directives and regulations – in addition to specific UK law. But the use of the internet to do business and to promote services – whether they be free or chargeable – means that it is quite possible that the two parties to a contract are from different countries. This raises a number of questions such as where the contract would be said to have been concluded, what country's law is the applicable to that contract, and where any dispute would be considered should a problem arise. Questions of jurisdiction (10.5) are certainly not straightforward, although the situation is less complex in those instances where both parties have entered into a written contract.

The Electronic Commerce Directive (2000/31/EC) explicitly states that it does not affect private international law in relation to conflicts of law nor does it deal with the jurisdiction of the courts. However, article 3(2) of the directive says:

> Member states may not, for reasons falling within the coordinated field, restrict the freedom to provide information society services from another member state.

Consequently, any UK law which restricts the ability of other EU member states to provide such services in the UK would disapply.

There are also other issues to take into account such as the application of advertising law (10.6) to online advertisements such as pop-up banner advertising appearing on websites; and to advertisements in the form of e-mails. There are also data protection issues to be considered, and the Privacy and Electronic Communications (EC) Directive Regulations (10.7) deal with the application of data protection and privacy issues in the electronic environment. They regulate the use of invisible tracking devices such as web bugs or cookies to gather personal data from a website user (10.7.1); and unsolicited commercial e-mail or spam (10.7.2). One area of internet law which received much attention as businesses started to use the web to promote their goods and services was that of domain name disputes (10.8). The chapter rounds off with a few key sources of information on the regulation of the internet and electronic commerce (10.10).

10.2 The Distance Selling Regulations

The Distance Selling Regulations[1] cover distance contracts for goods and services made between suppliers and consumers; but they do not cover business-to-business contracts. A distance contract is one where there has been no face-to-face contact between supplier and consumer up to and including the moment that the contract is concluded. Examples of distance contracts are sales made on the internet, mail order, telephone and fax sales.

The Regulations require suppliers to provide clear and understandable information to enable the consumer to decide whether or not they wish to buy. This must include:

- your business name and, if payment is required in advance, your postal address
- a description of the goods or services
- the price of the goods or services, including all taxes
- delivery costs where applicable
- arrangements for payment, delivery or performance
- the right to cancel the order
- the cost of any premium-rate telephone, fax or internet charges
- how long the offer or the price remains valid
- the minimum duration for any long-term contract
- whether substitute goods or services will be supplied if the order is out of stock or unavailable
- that if substitute goods are to be supplied, in the event of cancellation, the supplier must inform the consumer of the cost of returning any substitute goods.

When an order has been made, the supplier must provide the consumer with written confirmation of the prior information (this could be by letter, fax or e-mail).

Regulation 8 stipulates that, when a supplier provides the order confirmation, this should also include:

- when and how the consumer can exercise the right to cancel
- details of whether the consumer is required to return the goods in the event of cancellation
- information as to whether the supplier or the consumer would be responsible for the costs of returning or recovering the goods
- the geographical address of the place of business where the consumer can contact the supplier

- information about any after-sales services and guarantees.

The supplier must deliver goods or provide services within 30 days, beginning with the day after the consumer sent an order, unless otherwise agreed with the consumer. If the supplier is unable to meet this deadline, the consumer must be informed before the deadline expires and, unless a revised date is agreed, the consumer must be refunded within a further period of 30 days. The consumer is not obliged to agree to a revised date; and if he or she does not, then the contract is thereby cancelled and any money paid must be returned within 30 days.

The Regulations give consumers an unconditional right to cancel an order. If a customer wishes to cancel, he must do so in writing – by letter, fax or e-mail. If payment has already been collected, the refund must be made within 30 days. It is a criminal offence not to repay the consumer within 30 days. Certain contracts cannot be cancelled (unless the parties agree otherwise). This includes the supply of computer software if it is 'unsealed' by the consumer; the supply of newspapers, periodicals and magazines; and the supply of personalized goods or goods made to a consumer's specification. Where the supplier has met his obligations relating to the provision of prior information, the consumer has seven working days to cancel the contract without penalty (the 'cooling off period') starting from the date of receipt of the goods (or the date of conclusion of the contract in the case of services). Where the supplier has failed to meet his obligations to give the consumer the required prior information, the cooling off period is extended to three months. The consumer can cancel the order in this period without penalty and without having to give any reason.

The regulations amend the Unsolicited Goods and Services Act 1971 and the Unsolicited Goods and Services (Northern Ireland) Order 1976 to remove any rights of the supplier in respect of unsolicited goods and services and any obligations on the consumer. As such, consumers can retain unsolicited goods or dispose of them as they wish. They are under no obligation to keep them safe or to return them. It is an offence for a supplier to demand payment from consumers for unsolicited goods or services.

Under the Regulations, if a customer's credit card has been used fraudulently in connection with a distance contract, the customer may cancel the payment, and the card issuer must refund the money to the card account. This removes the previous potential liability of the debtor for the first £50 lost. Customers paying by debit card are not afforded the same protection.

The Distance Selling Regulations are enforced by the Office of Fair Trading, local authority trading standards departments in England, Scotland and Wales, and the Department of Trade, Enterprise and Investment in Northern Ireland. These bodies are under a duty to consider any complaint received and have powers to apply to the courts for an injunction against any person who is considered responsible for a breach of the regulations.

A term contained in a contract will be void if it is inconsistent with a provision for the protection of the consumer contained in the Regulations. The Director General of Fair Trading has a duty to consider genuine complaints received by consumers concerning a breach of the Regulations, and has the power to apply for an injunction against any person responsible for a breach in order to secure compliance with the Regulations.

Some distance contracts are not covered by the Regulations. These include disposals of interest in land, internet auctions and contracts relating to financial services. The European Community has now passed a Directive on Distance Marketing of Financial Services,[2] which will come into force two years after its publication in the Official Journal in 2004.

The Department of Trade and Industry's website (www.dti.gov.uk) is a useful source of information on distance selling.

10.3   The Electronic Commerce (EC Directive) Regulations 2002[3]

The Regulations implement EU directive 2000/31/EC.[4] The purpose of the directive was to ensure the free movement of 'information society services' across the European Community. The definition of an information society service already existed in Community law in directive 98/34/EC.[5] The definition covers any service normally provided for remuneration, at a distance, by means of electronic equipment for the processing (including digital compression) and storage of data, and at the individual request of a recipient of a service, both business-to-business and business-to-consumer, including services provided free of charge to the recipient. The Regulations will cover a range of services, including online newspapers, online databases and online professional services (such as those provided by lawyers and accountants).

The Regulations may apply to you if you provide an information society service such as:

* selling goods or services to businesses or consumers on the internet or by e-mail
* advertising on the internet or by e-mail
* conveying or storing electronic content for your customers or providing access to a communication network.

Online selling and advertising is subject to the laws of the UK if the trader is established here. Establishment in the UK is decided, amongst other things, by pursuance of an economic activity using a permanent place of business for an unlimited period in the UK. The presence of technical equipment to provide services does not of itself constitute establishment. Online services provided from other member states may not be restricted. The effect of this is to allow businesses to operate in any member state they wish as long as they follow the requirements of that jurisdiction. There are exceptions, however, particularly for contracts with consumers, the freedom of parties to choose the applicable law and copyright restrictions.

The Regulations give enforcement authorities the responsibility of ensuring that the provision of an information society service by a service provider established in the UK complies with the legislative requirements, irrespective of whether that service is provided in the UK or in another member state, and that any power, remedy or procedure for taking enforcement action shall be available to secure compliance. Examples of enforcement authorities include trading standards departments, the Office of Fair Trading and the Independent Committee for the Supervision of Standards of Telephone Information Services (ICSTIS).

The Director General of Fair Trading and Trading Standards Departments can also apply for a 'stop now' order if there is a contravention of the Regulations which 'harms the collective interests of consumers'. The courts also have the power to order suppliers to publish corrective statements with a view to eliminating the continuing effects of past infringements. If a supplier fails to comply with a 'stop now' order, then they may be held to be in contempt of court and could face a fine and/or imprisonment. Those to whom

General Information (Regulation 6) – this applies to anyone providing an information society service:

- full geographical and e-mail contact details of the business
- details of any relevant trade organizations to which the service provider belongs
- details on any authorization scheme relevant to the online business
- VAT number, if the online activities are subject to VAT
- clear indications of prices, and whether these are inclusive of tax and delivery costs.

Commercial communications (Regulation 7) – this applies to anyone who actively promotes their goods or services over the internet or by e-mail:

- clear identification that the e-mail is a commercial communication
- clear identification of the person on whose behalf it is sent
- clear identification of any promotional offers that are advertised such as any discounts, premium gifts, competitions, games
- clear explanation of any qualifying conditions for such offers
- clear indication in the header that the communication is unsolicited.

Contracts concluded by electronic means (Regulation 9) – information is to be provided prior to an order being placed:

- the different technical steps to follow to conclude the contract
- the technical means to enable end users to correct any inputting errors prior to the placing of the order
- the languages offered for the conclusion of the contract.

Fig. 10.1   *Information to be provided by information society services*

the Regulations apply must provide certain information in their electronic services (see Figure 10.1).

Regulations 17–19 say that service providers are not liable for damages or criminal sanctions for transmitting unlawful material provided by third parties (such as libellous, obscene or copyright-infringing material) where the intermediary:

- is a mere conduit (i.e. they do not initiate the transaction, select the recipient or modify the information)
- just caches the information as part of automatic, intermediate and temporary storage, without modifying it (the service provider is required to remove or disable access if they obtain actual knowledge that the source of the transmission has done likewise)

- hosts the information provided that the intermediary:
  - does not have actual knowledge of unlawful activity or information and in a claim for damages is not aware of the facts or circumstances from which it would have been apparent that it was unlawful
  - upon obtaining such knowledge or awareness, acts expeditiously to remove or to disable access to the information.

Intermediaries are not required to monitor third party content, but as soon as they are given notice of the unlawful nature of any content, they must act promptly to take down the offending material in order to be able to use the innocent disseminator defence.

In the UK's implementation of the electronic commerce directive, the person accused does not have to prove that they are innocent. The burden of proof lies with the accuser, who has to prove that the accused is guilty.

10.4   Electronic signatures

English law has traditionally taken a liberal view of what satisfies a legislative requirement for a signature, although there are a few key areas where only a hand-written signature on paper will suffice. These include transactions for the sale of land, and also the assignment of copyright and other intellectual property rights.

In Scotland the Requirements of Writing (Scotland) Act 1995 sets out the rules for formalities of signature and contracts generally.

Digital signatures are computer-based personal identities. The signature is a device that uniquely identifies the sender of an electronic message or document, based on public key cryptography. The purpose of the digital signature is to provide a verifiable means of guaranteeing that the sender of the message is the particular individual that they claim to be. Without such signatures it is hard to be sure that an e-mail is not forged or that a web-based vendor of goods and services is trustworthy. Digital signatures are issued by certificate authorities and typically contain the user's name, a serial number, expiry dates and a copy of the certificate holder's public key.

The European Union created a statutory basis for the recognition of electronic signatures throughout its member states with the adoption of directive 1999/93/EC.[6] A key purpose of the directive is to ensure that an electronic signature is not discriminated against purely on the grounds that it is electronic. So long as the signature system, service provider and certificate meet the requirements laid down in the directive, the electronic signature is held to be legally valid.

Section 7 of the Electronic Communications Act 2000 on electronic signatures and related certificates implements the provisions in directive 1999/93/EC on the admission of electronic signatures as evidence in legal proceedings; while the Electronic Signatures Regulations 2002[7] implement the provisions in the directive on the supervision of certification-service providers, their liability in certain circumstances and data protection requirements concerning them.

Librarians have for some time been asking about whether electronic signatures can be used on copyright declaration forms. The Library Regulations[8] require the forms to be signed by the requester. The statutory instrument states that the signature of the person requiring the copyright item must be in 'writing'. Section 178 of the Copyright, Designs and Patents Act 1988 defines 'writing' as including any form of notation or code, whether by hand or otherwise.

A key requirement is that the signature should be personal. It must clearly identify the individual, and needs to be secured in a way that means it could not easily be used by other people. The Electronic Signatures Directive speaks of a personal signature as being 'uniquely linked to and capable of identifying the signatory'.

Fully fledged electronic signature systems which meet the requirements of the Act may not be within the budgetary reach of library and information services. Unless the requirements of the Electronic Communications Act 2000 are met, libraries would therefore be taking a risk if they were to use electronic signatures based, for example, merely on password protection; and ultimately it would be a matter for the courts to decide.

10.5   Jurisdiction

Questions of jurisdiction in the era of global communications are not as straightforward as one might wish. The European Union aims to achieve free movement of goods and services between its member states. Differences between national rules governing jurisdiction and recognition of judgments would hamper the operation of the single market. For this reason, the EU passed council regulation 44/2001 of 22 December 2000 on jurisdiction and the recognition and enforcement of judgments in civil and commercial matters.[9] The Regulation supersedes the Brussels Convention in most of the European Union. It applies to all member states apart from Denmark; so the Brussels Convention on jurisdiction and enforcement of judgments in civil and commercial matters still applies for questions of jurisdiction between Denmark and other member states.

Article 68 says:

> This regulation shall, as between the member states, supersede the Brussels Convention, except as regards the territories of the Member States which fall within the territorial scope of that convention and which are excluded from this regulation pursuant to article 299 of the treaty.

Where a written contract exists between two parties, there will normally be a clause on applicable law which will stipulate the jurisdiction, and this will prevail; but if there isn't a contract, the matter will be decided according to regulation 44/2001, which outlines what will happen. To remove the element of doubt, contracts should therefore contain a clause which says where the contract is to be performed – in other words, where the goods are to be delivered or where the services are to be provided.

Recital 13 says:

> In relation to insurance, consumer contracts and employment, the weaker party should be protected by rules of jurisdiction more favourable to his interests than the general rules provide for.

Article 16 of the Regulation says that 'A consumer may bring proceedings against the other party to a contract either in the courts of the Member State in which that party is domiciled or in the courts for the place where the consumer is domiciled' whereas it goes on to say that 'proceedings may be brought against a consumer by the other party to the contract only in the courts of the Member State in which the consumer is domiciled.'

EU council regulation 44/2001 helps to clarify the situation regarding jurisdiction where both parties are member states of the European Union. However, the internet is global, and in order to reflect this, effective regulation requires international legislation. It is therefore to be hoped that at some stage an international treaty can be negotiated, to be administered by an international organization.

10.6   Advertising law

All advertisements in the UK must be legal, decent, honest and truthful in order to comply with the British Code of Advertising, Sales Promotion and Direct Marketing.[10] The code is administered by the Advertising Standards Authority. It applies to non-broadcast advertisements, sales promotions and direct marketing communications. This includes advertisements in e-mails, online advertisements in paid-for space (such as banner and pop-up advertisements) and marketing databases containing consumers' personal information. They do not apply to broadcast commercials, which are the responsibility of the Independent Television Commission or the Radio Authority. According to the code, companies sending advertisements in the form of text messages or e-mails will have to get the permission of users before they do so. Unsolicited e-mails must also make it clear that they are selling something, without the recipients having to open them. The code reflects EU and UK regulation of distance selling and data privacy, including the EU privacy and electronic communications directive (2002/58/EC). The code acts as the first line of control in protecting consumers. It says that there are over 200 statutes, orders and regulations which affect marketing, of which the Control of Misleading Advertisements Regulations 1988[11] as amended[12] is key. This is a complex area, so if there is any doubt about whether or not an advertisement contains any potential breaches of the law, it would be sensible to get professional legal advice.

The Direct Selling Association (DSA) has completed stage one approval for its consumer code of practice from the Office of Fair Trading.[13] This means that the code of practice in principle meets the core criteria set out by the OFT. The next stage will involve the DSA demonstrating that the promises made at that stage have been fulfilled in practice. The tests include compliance audits, evidence of effective dispute resolution, mystery shopping and complaint handling. Codes that go on to achieve approval carry an OFT logo and receive official promotion.

10.7   The Privacy and Electronic Communications (EC Directive) Regulations 2003

The Regulations implement the directive on privacy and electronic communications,[14] and they revoke the Telecommunications (Data Protection and Privacy) Regulations 1999[15] and the Telecommunications (Data Protection and Privacy) (Amendment) Regulations 2000.[16]

The aim of directive 2002/58/EC is to make the laws regulating use of personal data in the e-commerce sector 'technology neutral', and to extend the law to cover not only voice telephony but also data services, including e-mail and SMS. The directive also specifically covers the use of location-based data and cookies.

Key features of the regulations are:

* that value-added services based on location and traffic data are permitted subject to the consent of subscribers
* that public directories are subject to strict controls
  — all public directories must give subscribers the right – free of charge – to be removed from the directory
  — subscribers must be given information on all the usage possibilities available with the directory, such as, for example, whether reverse searching is enabled
* that there are stricter regulations governing the use of tracking devices such as cookies
* that the use of unsolicited commercial e-mail (spam) and SMS, or text messaging, to mobile phones for direct marketing purposes is regulated.

The directive does not prevent member states from introducing provisions on the retention of traffic and location data for law enforcement purposes. In the UK the Home Office undertook a consultation process on a voluntary code of practice for the retention of communications data during the Spring of 2003.[17]

10.7.1   Cookies

Cookies are text files which are left by a website on a user's hard disk. They can be used to track the online movements of an individual and consequently they help a website operator to build up a profile of that individual. Cookies can be used for a wide range of purposes such as to store user preferences, but the data gathered by a cookie could also be used to initiate targeted advertising (see also 3.11.)

The Privacy and Electronic Communications Directive[18] recognizes that invisible tracking devices such as cookies can be put to good uses – such as storing login and password information – as well as being able to collect information which can then intrude on someone's privacy. The directive seeks to regulate the potential use of cookies to intrude upon the privacy of internet users, which is why it gives internet users a chance to refuse cookies. Cookie-free access does not have to be provided where the cookie is essential to an online service that has been requested, or is being used for 'a legitimate purpose' on a website.

The Privacy and Electronic Communications (EC Directive) Regulations 2003 implement the transparency requirement in the directive, whereby the use of cookies and other invisible tracking devices such as web bugs must be explained clearly by website operators to internet users, and those users must also be given a right to refuse cookies at any time. The internet user is therefore given sufficient information to make an informed choice about which sites they wish to frequent.

10.7.2   Spam

With the introduction of the Privacy and Electronic Communications (EC Directive) Regulations, it is only possible to send e-mails for marketing purposes to people who have previously indicated their consent to receive such messages, unless they are existing customers who have given you their details as part of a request for information about your products or services. In theory this outlaws most spam within the EU, but it remains to be seen just how effective this change in the law will be. Unfortunately, the vast bulk of spam emanating from the USA is unaffected by these laws. Where the obligations are breached, the recipient of the e-mail could take out an action for damages for breach of statutory duty. Reputable companies will want to be seen to be complying with the law, not least because of the potential PR damage or the perceived damage to their brand value in the eyes of their customers.

Industry bodies like the Direct Marketing Association and the Advertising Standards Authority promote their own rules on e-mail marketing through their codes of practice, and these take account of legislative developments. Figure 10.2 provides a checklist of issues to address in order to ensure compliance with these.

1	Make sure that all marketing communications identify you clearly.
2	Ensure that e-mail/SMS marketing communications are identified as such in the subject header.
3	Do not send unsolicited commercial e-mails to people without their prior consent, except in the context of an existing customer relationship, where you may continue to e-mail on an 'opt-out' basis.
4	Give recipients the ability to opt out of receiving future communications.
5	Don't give your customer list to anyone else – even within your own group of companies – unless everyone on the list has consented to this.
6	Where you buy in a list for e-mail marketing purposes, before you go ahead and purchase the list, get written confirmation from the supplier to the effect that everyone on the list has consented to their data being passed on.

Fig. 10.2   *E-mail marketing checklist*

10.8   Domain name disputes

It is important for anyone choosing a domain name to ensure that they do not breach someone else's trade mark rights. In choosing a domain name, first of all people should check to see if that name is still available. There are many services on the web that do this such as Checkdomain[19] or Register.[20] Once you have found a domain name which is available, then as part of the due diligence process it is advisable to conduct a trade mark search at the Patent Office to see if the domain name has been registered as a trade mark under the Trade Marks Act 1994. This can be done online at www.patent.gov.uk. It is also advisable to check whether the name has been registered as a limited company at Companies House. This can be done online at www. companieshouse.gov.uk. Indeed, in view of the international nature of domain names, it is best to do a company/registered trade mark search world-wide. This is because a registered company could have built up good will in that name, and even if they have not registered the name as a trade mark, they could still potentially take action against you under the common law tort of 'passing off'. Once these steps have been taken and you are sure that the domain name is neither a registered trademark nor the name of a registered company, it is worth considering whether to register the name as a UK trade mark and/or as an EU community trade mark. Even if someone registers a trade mark, there is still potential for legal disputes over internet domain names, because trade marks are only registered for particular classes of goods or services; and so several companies from different countries using the same name may each feel that they have a valid claim to a particular domain name.

Where someone owns a domain name, it is often the case that they do not use the domain and have bought it purely for the purpose of selling it. It is possible to contact www.whois.com or www.whoami.com in order to check who owns the domain name, and you can contact them to negotiate your purchase of the domain if it is the name that you are looking for. If you are interested in obtaining a domain name but your chosen name is already being legitimately used, it is also worth looking beyond the common options of .com and .co.uk to the newer domain names .biz, .info, etc.

British Telecommunications v. One in a Million 1998 EWCA Civ 1272

One in a Million registered a number of domain names which contained the trademarks of well known British companies such as Virgin and Marks & Spencer. They then tried to sell these to the companies concerned for many thousands of pounds. The High Court banned them from dealing in domain names; and the Court of Appeal subsequently threw out One in a Million's appeal against the ruling, dismissed their right to appeal to the House of Lords and ordered them to surrender the collection of domain names which they had amassed. In effect the court said that the registered trade mark will usually prevail over the registered domain name.

One in a Million had been ordered by the High Court to pay £65,000 legal costs; and the Court of Appeal subsequently ordered them to pay further legal costs.

The One in a Million case involved cybersquatters who registered the domain names of a number of well known companies, intending to cash in on that name by trying to extract money from the true owner. In the case of Burger King, for example, they offered the company the domain name burgerking.co.uk for £25,000 + VAT.[21]

Court cases can prove to be an extremely expensive way of resolving matters, so domain name disputes are often resolved using alternative dispute-resolution methods such as those available from ICANN, which has a Uniform Dispute Resolution Policy.[22]

10.9   Summary

This chapter has looked at legislation which regulates contracts concluded electronically such as the Distance Selling Regulations and the Electronic Commerce (EC Directive) Regulations; as well as the law relating to electronic signatures. The problems of establishing under which jurisdiction a dispute would be heard are outlined. The chapter has also looked at the data protection and privacy issues involved in electronic communications, as well as how advertising law applies in an electronic environment.

The next chapter deals with computer misuse such as hacking, viruses, fraud and other areas of cybercrime. It deals specifically with how the Computer Misuse Act 1990 is used to combat computer misuse crimes and considers how well it is suited to that task.

10.10   Sources of information

Baker McKenzie available at www.bakernet.com – including the global e-law alert and the pages on global e-commerce law.

Department of Trade and Industry Communications and Information Industries Directorate available at www.dti.gov.uk/cii.

eLexPortal.com, available at www.elexportal.com.

European Commission ecommerce, available at http://europa.eu.int/ information_society/topics/ebusiness/ecommerce/index_en.htm.

ICANN (Internet Corporation for Assigned Names and Numbers), available at www.icann.org, including pages on the Uniform Domain Name Dispute Resolution Policy, available at www.icann.org/udrp.

UK Online for Business, available at www.ukonlineforbusiness.gov.uk.

UNCITRAL (United Nations Commission on International Trade Law), available at www.uncitral.org/english/texts/electcom/ml-elecsig-e.pdf.

United Nations Conference on Trade and Development, Electronic Communications Branch, available at www.unctad.org/ecommerce.

WIPO (World Intellectual Property Organization), available at www.wipo.org, including pages on ecommerce (http://ecommerce.wipo.int/index.html) and domain names (http://ecommerce.wipo.int/domains).

Notes and references

1   Consumer Protection (Distance Selling) Regulations 2000: SI 2000/2334 implementing directive 97/7/EC.

2   Directive 2002/65/EC of the European Parliament and of the Council concerning the distance marketing of consumer financial services and amending Council Directives 90/619/EEC, 97/7/EC and 98/27/EC (17 June 2002) OJL 271/16, 23 September 2002.

3   SI 2002/2013.

4   The E-Commerce Directive (on certain legal aspects of information society serv-

ices, in particular electronic commerce, in the internal market) was adopted on 8 June 2000 and published in the Official Journal of the European Communities on 17 July 2000.

5   Directive 98/34/EC laying down a procedure for the provision of information in the field of technical standards and regulations OJL 204, 21 July 1998, as amended by directive 98/48/EC.

6   Directive 1999/93/EC of the European Parliament and of the Council of 13 December 1999 on a community framework for electronic signatures L13/12, 19 January 2000.

7   SI 2002/318.

8   SI 1989/1212.

9   2001 OJ L12/1, 16 January 2001.

10   11th edn, March 2003.

11   Control of Misleading Advertisements Regulations 1988: SI 1988/915.

12   Control of Misleading Advertisements (Amendment) Regulations 2000: SI 2000/914.

13   *DSA approaches OFT code approval*, Office of Fair Trading press notice 84/02, 3 December 2002.

14   2002/58/EC in OJL 201/37, 31 July 2002.

15   SI 1999/2093.

16   SI 2000/157.

17   *Consultation paper on a code of practice for voluntary retention of communications data*, Home Office, March 2003.

18   The Privacy and Electronic Communications Directive (2002/58/EC).

19   Available at www.checkdomain.com.

20   Available at www.register.com.

21   Banned – domain name dealing, *BBC News Online*, 28 November 1997, available at http://news.bbc.co.uk/1/hi/sci/tech/35458.stm.

22   ICANN maintains a database of all UDRP panel discussions on its website at www.icann.org.

11   Computer misuse

11.1   Introduction

Computer misuse covers activities such as hacking, viruses, fraud, theft and copyright abuse. This chapter looks at the Computer Misuse Act 1990 (CMA) (11.3), and the three offences created by that statute. It then looks at hacking (11.4), and viruses, worms and trojans (11.5). In the case of denial of service attacks (11.6), there are those who feel that the CMA as presently constituted is inadequate. There are likely to be a number of changes to the CMA in order for the UK to be fully compliant with the Council of Europe's Cybercrime Convention. Finally, there is a brief look at the role of the Telecommunications Act 1984 in relation to computer misuse (11.7).

11.2   Background

The phrase 'computer misuse' could be used to refer to a wide range of activities such as accessing inappropriate material on the internet such as pornographic material; inappropriate use of e-mail; hacking; spreading viruses; fraud; theft; copyright abuse; or the use of a computer to harass others, whether that be sexual harassment, racial harassment, or some other form of harassment.

The CBI's Cybercrime Survey[1] ranked the main threats from cybercrime as being:

- viruses
- hacking
- illegal access to databases
- adverse comments on the internet
- intellectual property infringements.

The survey found that most attacks on corporate computer networks are from outside, contrary to the conventional view that most computer security problems are due to insiders. It also found that technological crimes such as viruses and hacking dominate, rather than financial crimes such as credit card fraud; and that loss of reputation, through adverse publicity and loss of trust, is a greater fear than financial loss for most organizations.

According to the Information Security Breaches Survey,[2] 44% of businesses surveyed had suffered at least one malicious security breach. The average cost of a serious security breach was put at £30,000. 56% of the businesses questioned are either not covered by insurance for such security incidents or unsure as to whether or not they are covered.

11.3   General principles of the Computer Misuse Act 1990

The CMA was published in the wake of a Law Commission report[3] in order to create specific offences to secure computers against unauthorized access or modification.

The CMA pre-dates the dramatic growth in the internet, and some people consider it to be not very well suited to certain types of computer misuse, most notably denial of service attacks (see section 11.6). Whilst the Act was originally intended mainly to address the problems caused by computer hacking, it is also being used effectively to deal with the deliberate release of computer viruses.

The CMA creates three offences:

* unauthorized access to computer material (s1)
* unauthorized access with intent to commit or facilitate commission of further offences (s2)
* unauthorized modification of computer material (s3).

Under section 1 of the CMA, it is an offence to cause a computer to perform any function with intent to gain unauthorized access to any program or data held in any computer, knowing at the time that it is unauthorized.

The section specifically provides that the intent of the person need not be directed at any particular program or data, a program or data of any particular kind, or a program or data held in any particular computer. This renders the Act peculiarly suitable for use against activities carried out across networks.

Under section 17(5) a person's access is unauthorized if the person is not himself entitled to control access of the kind in question to the program or data, and he does not have consent to access by him of the kind in question to the program or data from any person who is so entitled.

Under section 2 of the CMA, it is an offence to commit an offence under s1 with intent to commit or facilitate a further offence, whether or not both offences occur on the same occasion.

Under section 3 of the CMA, it is an offence to do anything intentionally and knowingly to cause an unauthorized modification of the contents of any computer which will impair its operation, prevent or hinder access to any program or data, or which will impair the operation of the program or the reliability of the data.

The requisite knowledge is knowledge that any modification he intends to cause is unauthorized. The section provides that intent need not be directed to any particular computer, any particular program or data, or a program or data of any particular kind, or any particular modification or modification of any particular kind.

Computer Misuse Act 1990 – section 3 offence

In a legal case from 2002, a manufacturing business decided to update its computer system. They employed an IT contractor to do the work for them. Unfortunately, they felt that he had not done a very good job and went to a second contractor to get the job completed. When it came to payment, they clearly had to pay for the services of the new contractor and decided that they would not pay the original contractor.

Access to the IT system had been set up for the original contractor to work from home, and this access was still available at the time of the dispute. When the company refused to pay the original contractor, he was upset about this and decided to take matters into his own hands. He accessed the system and deleted all of the files on it. These files included three years' worth of fairly complicated design drawings. The company assessed the amount of damage it had suffered as a result at around £50,000.

It is a criminal offence under section 3 of the Computer Misuse Act 1990 to carry out an unauthorized modification of material held on computer when your intention is to prevent or hinder access to the data or impair its operational reliability. The contractor was prosecuted and convicted, and was jailed for 18 months.

There are a number of lessons from this case, even if some of them may seem rather obvious:

1   Take regular backups.
2   Keep the backups in a separate place.
3   Be careful about who can access the computer system.
4   Be prompt at disabling access for employees and contractors as soon as they cease working for you.
5   Be very careful about who you give remote access to.
6   For contractors – don't damage or disable a computer system, no matter what the provocation might be, as it is surely not worth a prison sentence.

The penalty for the first offence could be up to six months in prison or a fine (up to level 5 on the standard scale) or both; whereas the second and third offences are considered to be much more serious and carry a maximum penalty of up to five years in prison or an unlimited fine or both.

According to section 17 of the Act, a person secures access to any computer program or data held in a computer if by causing a computer to perform any function he:

- alters or erases the program or data
- copies or moves it to any storage medium other than that in which it is held or to a different location in the storage medium in which it is held
- uses it
- has it output from the computer in which it is held (whether by having it displayed or in any other manner).

Computer crime can raise a number of issues relating to jurisdiction, since it is obviously possible for someone anywhere in the world to access a computer located in the UK. Sections 4–9 of the Act deal with the whole question of jurisdiction and, in short, ensure that, so long as either the accused or the computer was within the jurisdiction at the time of the offence, then a prosecution is permitted.

Prison sentence for offences under the Act

Simon Vallor, a web designer, created viruses on his home computer in Llandudno, which he then distributed over the internet in September and October 2001. The viruses were designed to e-mail themselves to everyone in the recipient's address book. One virus was designed to delete all the data on a hard drive on 11 November. At least 29,000 computers were infected in 42 countries, while another 300,000 copies of the virus were stopped by anti-virus software. The cost of the episode ran to millions of pounds for businesses and computer users. Mr Vallor was sentenced to two years' imprisonment for offences under the Computer Misuse Act 1990. It is the harshest sentence so far for this type of offence.

11.4   Hacking

Hacking is the act of deliberately gaining unauthorized access to an information system. Many instances of hacking might be classed as nuisance attacks, but far more serious are instances where the hacker had malicious intent.

Section 1 of the CMA 1990 makes hacking per se a criminal offence, regardless of whether or not any harm is intended. If, for example, a hacker broke into a computer simply out of curiosity, he or she would have committed an offence so long as he or she was aware that his/her access was unauthorized.

Hackers can be deterred through well configured firewall protection, intrusion detection software and filtering software.

11.5 Viruses, worms and trojans

Computer viruses, in the same way as biological viruses, make copies of themselves and cannot exist without a host. They may infect program files, programs in disk sectors, or files that use a macro. There are also computer worms and trojans. Worms are similar to viruses. Like viruses, they make copies of themselves, but do so without the need to modify a host. By repeatedly making copies of itself, a worm tries to drain system resources. Trojans are named after the Trojan Horse – a giant wooden horse that concealed Greek soldiers who used it in order to invade the ancient city of Troy – because trojan horse programs conceal hidden programming which can cause significant damage to your computer.

It is no longer the case that a computer user has to click on a file attachment in order to trigger a virus infection. It may be sufficient merely for the user simply to read an infected e-mail in order for the virus to be launched.

The CMA clearly applies to those who release damaging viruses into the wild, even if the person doing so does not have an intent to damage a particular computer. Some e-mails may not be specifically intended to destroy data or prevent programs from operating, but might simply use e-mail directories to propagate themselves around e-mail systems. Nevertheless, there could still be the possibility of a criminal conviction. Under section 1 of the Act, the use of the recipient's e-mail program to cause the incoming e-mail virus to propagate onwards by means of the e-mail system could be said to be access of an unauthorized nature and would therefore be liable to prosecution under section 1.

Section 3 of the CMA can be used to prosecute people who introduce viruses, worms or trojans to computer systems. Under s3(6), an offence under the Criminal Damage Act 1971 occurs if damage to a computer impairs its physical condition; but it specifically excludes damage which is non-tangible. The wording of s3(6) states that 'a modification of the contents of a computer shall not be regarded as damaging any computer or computer storage medium unless its effect on that computer or computer storage medium impairs its physical condition.'

11.6   Denial of service attacks

Are there occasions where accessing a website could be said to be an offence under the CMA? Accessing a publicly available website is not an offence in itself, as there is an implied authorizatison for people to access the website. Where it gets more tricky is in those instances when that access is abused. Is, for instance, a denial of service attack an offence? Such an attack consists of sending massive quantities of otherwise normal messages or page requests to an internet host, with the result that the server is overloaded, is unable to deal with legitimate requests and in effect becomes unavailable.

The perpetrator of a denial of service attack might wish to use the space on your hard drive and your CPU, combined with the power on many thousands of other machines, in order to take control of those PCs and to have them direct traffic on the web to one well known internet site. This then overloads the web server making the site unavailable.

If the access could be regarded as unauthorized, then there is potentially a section 1 offence and possibly a section 3 offence. However, denial of service attacks are difficult to regulate because they do not necessarily require a breach of security. This would mean that in some instances it would be difficult to initiate a prosecution for a denial of service attack under the current CMA. For this reason, the Earl of Northesk introduced a Computer Misuse (Amendment) Bill,[4] which sought to extend the powers of the CMA to 'denial of service' attacks. The bill reached its second reading on 20 June 2002, but did not progress any further.

Earl Northesk has continued to pursue this issue in Parliament. For example, on 17 March 2003 he asked Lord Falconer whether the government intended to update the CMA in the light of the decision of the European Union justice ministers to approve new laws for dealing with computer hackers and spreaders of computer viruses and worms. Lord Falconer replied by confirming that, on 28 February 2003, approval of the general approach to the European Union framework decision on attacks against information systems was given by the Justice and Home Affairs Council of Ministers. He went on to say that the Government were considering the extent to which the CMA and wider legislation deals with the requirements of the framework decision, and the related provisions contained in the Council of Europe Cybercrime Convention.

Lord Falconer's parliamentary reply also stated that, while existing UK legislation already covered the majority of the requirements of these texts as they relate to offences against computer and information systems, there would need to be some amendments to legislation in order to be fully compliant and that these changes would be brought forward when parliamentary time allowed.

The European Commission issued a consultation document in April 2002 on attacks against information systems.[5] This has in part been prompted by the Council of Europe's cybercrime convention.[6]

The Convention is the first international treaty on crimes committed via the internet and other computer networks, dealing particularly with infringements of copyright, computer-related fraud, child pornography and violations of network security. It also contains a series of powers and procedures such as the search of computer networks and interception.

Its main objective, set out in the preamble, is to pursue a common criminal policy aimed at the protection of society against cybercrime, especially by adopting appropriate legislation and fostering international co-operation.

The Convention is the product of four years of work by Council of Europe experts, but also by the United States, Canada, Japan and other countries which are not members of the organization. It will be supplemented by an additional protocol making any publication of racist and xenophobic propaganda via computer networks a criminal offence.

Companies should set policies for employees to abide by, in order that they know what is expected of them. This can be in the form of a written policy statement on reasonable use of the internet, e-mail and the company intranet. All employees should be given a copy, and this should include new members of staff when they join the firm. It could, for example, be covered as part of the induction process. Well drafted policy statements are of no use if they are not sent to all employees, or some employees are unaware that the policy exists.

It is also important that the principles enshrined in these policies are policed adequately and any breaches are dealt with through the company's disciplinary policy. If companies fail to enforce these policies adequately, they cannot seek to rely on them indiscriminately when dealing with any breaches, as employees would be able to challenge the enforceability of the policy if it were not adequately policed and implemented. There has to be a consistency in their approach.

Examples of unacceptable content should be outlined. For example, in the case of publishing content to the company's intranet, you might want the list of unacceptable content to cover:

- offensive material (such as pornographic, abusive, indecent or profane items)
- items which insult or intimidate someone
- lewd comments, jokes or banter
- swearwords and offensive language
- chain letters
- disclosing personal data without consent of the data controller, contrary to the Data Protection Act 1998
- any purpose which is illegal or contrary to the employer's interest.

Deliberately obtaining unauthorized access to a computer system is not the only way in which a computer system can be damaged. Many disputes arise where software has been written with a time lock or a similar device is built into it so that it disables itself after a certain period of time or unless new passwords are regularly put into it. Where people develop or supply software to clients for their use and the use of such devices has not been agreed with them, then when the device activates and damages or disables the software, it is possible that they will be committing an offence under the CMA.

11.7 Telecommunications Act 1984

It is also necessary to take account of section 43 of the Telecommunications Act 1984 in relation to computer misuse, and not merely the CMA, because section 43 makes it a criminal offence to use a public telecommunications network to send grossly offensive, threatening or obscene material, and a 'public telecommunications network' is defined widely enough for it to be able to cover internet traffic which goes through telephone lines or other cables.

11.8   Summary

This chapter has considered computer misuse, and how the CMA and the Telecommunications Act 1984 are used to deal with various aspects of computer misuse. The forms of computer misuse considered include viruses, worms and trojans; computer hacking; and denial of service attacks. The chapter has also looked ahead to changes likely to take place to ensure that the UK is fully compliant with the Council of Europe's cybercrime convention.

The next chapter looks at the legal implications of discrimination on the grounds of disability, including visual impairment.

Notes and references

1   *Cybercrime Survey 2001: making the information superhighway safe for business*, CBI, 2001 (for the full list of main threats from cybercrime see exhibit 12 in the survey).

2   *Information Security Breaches Survey 2002*, Department of Trade and Industry, 2002, available at www.security-survey.gov.uk.

3   *Criminal Law: computer misuse*, Law Commission Working Paper no. 186, Cm 819, October 1989.

4   HL Bill 79 session 2001/2, The Stationery Office, 2002.

5   European Commission proposal for a council framework decision on attacks against information systems, COM (2002) 0173, 19 April 2002, available at http://europa.eu.int/eur-lex/en/com/pdf/2002/com2002_0173en01.pdf.

6   *Convention on Cybercrime*, Council of Europe, 2001, available at http://conventions.coe.int/Treaty/EN/projets/FinalCybercrime.htm.

12 Disability discrimination

12.1 Introduction

This chapter looks at the legal implications of discrimination on the grounds of disability. It considers the general principles involved (12.2) and how these apply to information services. There are also a number of checklists provided. Key pieces of legislation relating to disability are the Disability Discrimination Act 1995 (DDA) and the Special Educational Needs and Disability Act 2001 (SENDA). We also have to take account of the Copyright (Visually Impaired Persons) Act 2002 (12.3), which was passed in November 2002; and this is considered along with the joint industry guidelines which were produced by the Publishers Licensing Society. The chapter rounds off with a listing of sources of information on disability (12.5) and how it applies in the context of library and information services.

12.2 General principles

Disabled people are among the most excluded in society. They encounter many barriers to accessing the services of archives and libraries, including physical, sensory, attitudinal, cultural and intellectual ones. Library and information services need to ensure that they do not discriminate against those who are disabled. This is not solely a moral issue, it is also a legal issue where organizations need to ensure that they stay within the law. The DDA makes it illegal to discriminate against disabled people in employment, provision of goods, facilities and services, and access to buildings and premises.[1] It was extended to education from September 2002 following amendments introduced by SENDA.

Discrimination against disabled people can take place in either of two ways:

- by treating them less favourably than other people (DDA s20)
- by failing to make a reasonable adjustment (DDA s21) when they are placed at a 'substantial disadvantage' compared to other people for a reason relating to their disability.

A reasonable adjustment might be any action that helps to alleviate a substantial disadvantage. This could involve changing the organization's standard procedures; providing materials in Braille as an additional service; providing appropriate adjustments to the physical environment; or training staff to work with disabled people. The DDA requires institutions to anticipate the needs of people with disabilities and make reasonable adjustments to ensure an appropriate, non-discriminatory environment.

People with disability can include those with physical or mobility impairments; hearing impairments; dyslexia; medical conditions; mental health difficulties; visual impairment; or people with learning difficulties. In section 19 (3) (c) of the DDA, 'access to and use of information services' is given as an example of the type of service to which the DDA applies. So it is quite clear that the DDA applies to those who provide library and information services to the public. In order to ensure that they do not discriminate on the grounds of disability, library services therefore need to take account of disability issues when considering matters of service planning, delivery and quality; they need to be able to provide equality of physical access to their services; and they also need to assess, deliver and evaluate disability training.

Managers of library and information services can make use of a number of toolkits, checklists and best practice standards (12.5) to help them identify and assess whether or not their existing policies and procedures result in disabled people receiving a level of service which is inferior to the one available to everyone else. They should think about the accessibility of their service to people with disabilities; both in terms of physical access and in terms of intellectual access.

Libraries can invest in a number of adaptations for people with disabilities. Adjustments made to the physical access can include:

- ramps
- colour-contrasting handrails
- swing-resistant automatic doors
- ensuring the appropriate widths needed for wheelchairs
- checking the rise of steps and the height of lift-call buttons
- signage and guiding, including international access symbols
- appropriate shelf heights
- access to catalogues and terminals

- access to library publications and websites
- fully adjustable tables and chairs.

If the library is planning a refurbishment, staff should take account of best practice guidance and any relevant British Standards. For example, there is a British Standard covering the slip-resistance of different floor surfaces. Access requirements are often equated with wheelchair access when only around 5% of disabled people are wheelchair users. This lack of understanding can be a barrier to serving the majority of people with disabilities.

There are many adaptations to technology which can greatly assist people with disabilities. These include:

- different-sized keyboards
- mouse alternatives
- lap trays
- wrist rests
- screen magnifiers
- dyslexia and literacy software
- document readers
- voice-recognition technology.

It is also important to ensure that staff are equipped with the knowledge that they need in order to serve disabled users effectively – for example, by being able to adjust a computer to an individual user's needs. Library and information services need to have appropriate policies, procedures and plans in place to serve the needs of their disabled users effectively; and staff training is a key part of ensuring that this isn't just a theoretical aim, but that the policies and procedures are put into practice.

Library and information services need to be mindful about the needs of their disabled users when they prepare promotional literature about their services, and the literature must be accessible to those users.

1 Is the information about library facilities accessible to disabled people?
2 Is promotional literature available in alternative formats such as Braille, audio tape or large print?
3 Is web-based material accessible to those using assistive technology, such

as screen-reading software, or those not using a mouse?

4 Does information about services and facilities make clear the adjustments that are already in place? And does it also point out that additional adjustments can be made on an individual basis?

Institutions are expected to make 'anticipatory' adjustments, and not simply to wait until a disabled person requires a particular adaptation. In considering what anticipatory adjustments should be made, it is important to ask a number of key questions. For example:

1 Are the library buildings accessible?
2 Do they have accessible toilets?
3 Are the fire and emergency procedures appropriate for the library's disabled users?
4 Are the catalogue and instructions on its use available in accessible formats?
5 Are aisles wide enough for wheelchairs?
6 Are there sufficient staff to fetch books for those who cannot reach or see them?
7 Does the library provide materials in large print or online in order to cater for those who cannot use standard print?
8 Are longer loans periods available for those who need them?
9 Have staff been given the appropriate training? For example, could they support someone having an epileptic seizure?

It will ultimately be for the courts to decide what anticipatory adjustments it is reasonable to expect organizations to make in order to ensure that they are not discriminating against people with disabilities. Library and information centres need to be ready to make adjustments on behalf of individuals as necessary. Such adjustments could include:

- allowing extended loan periods to dyslexic or other users
- setting aside books in advance for those who find it difficult to get in to the library because of their disability
- assisting disabled people in using the catalogue, finding resources or using equipment
- fetching books from high or inaccessible shelves.

Libraries need to take reasonable steps to find out if a person is disabled in order that adjustments can be made, and this information needs to be kept confidential. Ignorance of someone's disability is not an adequate defence if an adjustment could have been anticipated.

It is essential to review services periodically in order to take into account any changes in good practice or advances in technology. Figure 12.1 provides a checklist of areas to address in order to ensure compliance with current disability discrimination legislation.

1	Do you have an equal opportunities policy that makes specific reference to disabled people?
2	Has your organization carried out a disability access audit?
3	Does your organization carry out staff training to increase awareness of disability access?
4	How does your organization consult with its disabled users and non-users?
5	In what ways are your services accessible to disabled people?
6	How is technology used in order to improve access for disabled people?
7	How is publicity and promotion targeted towards disabled people?
8	How does your organization keep abreast of the growing body of best practice on access issues for disabled people?

Fig. 12.1   *Compliance checklist*

12.3   Copyright (Visually Impaired Persons) Act 2002

Visually impaired people are those who are blind or partially sighted, and people who are physically unable to hold or manipulate a book, focus or move their eyes or are otherwise physically unable to use a standard print book. The Copyright (Visually Impaired Persons) Act 2002 is intended to give people with sight loss easier access to alternative formats of copyright material, such as large print, Braille and audio. It was originally planned that the Act would be brought into force by Easter 2003, but this didn't happen, and at the time of writing [June 2003] the Act was not yet in force. The Act introduces two exceptions to copyright to overcome problems of access to material by people with visual impairment.

1 **Part I: The 'one-for-one' exception.** This entitles a visually impaired person to make a single accessible copy of a copyright work for their personal use, subject to a number of conditions. In order to be able to make

an accessible copy under this exemption, you must be visually impaired, have or have access to a 'master copy' which is inaccessible because of your visual impairment and know that an accessible copy is not commercially available.

2 **Part II: The 'multiple copy' exception.** Educational establishments or not-for-profit organizations can make multiple accessible copies of a copyright work and supply them to visually impaired people for their personal use, subject to a number of conditions. For example, accessible copies cannot be supplied to anyone who can access a commercially available copy. Within a reasonable time from making accessible copies, copyright owners must be notified of activity under the exception. Where copyright owners have established a licensing scheme covering the activity that would otherwise be permitted under the exception, licences under that scheme must be taken out.

Salient points for libraries are:

1 Only not-for-profit institutions can participate.
2 Most libraries will just be making one-to-one copies based on the user's legal access to the inaccessible copy. Probably only organizations such as the RNIB and National Library for the Blind are likely to want to make multiple copies.
3 The exception applies to non-print materials, including the internet.
4 No institution has to implement this exception if they do not wish to.
5 No institution has to be a repository if it does not wish to.
6 Institutions can charge but only marginal costs.

In 2001 the Publishers Licensing Society issued a set of joint industry guidelines on access to books, journals and magazines for people with a visual impairment. The guidelines are the result of a wide-ranging consultation among rights holders and organizations helping visually impaired people in an effort to strike a balance between the requirements of visually impaired people and the special problems surrounding uncontrolled copying, transcription and distribution.

It may be that the Joint Industry Guidelines on Copyright and Visual Impairment will permit people to make accessible copies in more situations than permitted by the exceptions in the Copyright (Visually Impaired Persons) Act 2002 – for example, the guidelines are not limited with regard to databases – and so long as the Joint Industry Guidelines remain in force, visually impaired people may rely on the guidelines.

12.4   Summary

This chapter has considered the requirement for library and information services to take proper account of the needs of disabled users in the light of the Disability Discrimination Act, the Special Educational Needs Act and the Copyright (Visually Impaired Persons) Act. The word 'disability' covers a wide range of different types of disability, and there is a legal requirement to ensure that people with disabilities are not discriminated against by treating them less favourably than other people or by failing to make reasonable adjustments when they are placed at a 'substantial disadvantage' because of their disability.

12.5   Sources of information

AbilityNet, Accessible IT kits, available at www.abilitynet.org.uk.

Bobby, available at http://bobby.watchfire.com.

Burrington Partnership (2002) Access audit toolkit, available on CD-ROM.

Hopkins, L. (ed.) (2000) Library Service Provision for Blind and Visually-impaired People: a manual of best practice, *Library and Information Commission Research Report 76*, Resource.

National Library for the Blind (2002) *Library Services for Visually Impaired People: a manual of best practice*, available at http://bpm.nlb-online.org/contents.html.

Publishers Licensing Society (2001) *Copyright and Visual Impairment: access to books, magazines and journals by visually impaired people*, Joint industry guidelines.

Publishers Licensing Society (2001) *Permission Requests for Visually Impaired Persons: guidelines for publisher rights owners*.

Resource (2002) *Resource Disability Action Plan: achieving equality of opportunity for disabled people in museums, archives and libraries*.

Resource (2002) *Access to Museums, Archives and Libraries for Disabled Users*, toolkit to help libraries measure how accessible they are to disabled users and identify areas where improvements can be made.

SCONUL (no date) *Access for Users with Disabilities*, SCONUL briefing on the implications of the DDA for libraries.

World Wide Web Consortium (1999) *Web Content Accessibility Guidelines*, available at www.w3.org/TR/WCAG10/.

Notes and references

1   Adjustments requiring alterations to physical features are not required until September 2004.

Bibliography

Armstrong, C. and Bebbington, L. (eds) (2003) *Staying Legal: a guide to issues and practices affecting the library, information and publishing sectors*, 2nd edn, Facet Publishing.

Birkinshaw, P. (2001) *Freedom of Information: the law, the practice and the ideal*, 3rd edn, Butterworths.

Branscomb, A. W. (1995) *Who owns Information: from privacy to public access?* Basic Books.

British Standards Institution, Data Protection Update Service. The service includes the following publications: *Guide to the Practical Implementation of the Data Protection Act 1998*; *Guide to Developing an Email Policy*; *Guide to Developing an Electronic Commerce Policy*; *Guide to Managing Your Database*; *Pre-audit Workbook*; *Guide to Data Controller and Data Processor Contracts*; *Guide to Managing Subject Access Requests*.

Cabinet Office (1997) *Code of Practice on Access to Government Information*, 2nd edn.

Carey, P. (1999) *Media Law*, 2nd edn, Sweet & Maxwell.

Carey, P. (2000) *Data Protection in the UK*, Blackstone Press.

CILIP (2003) *Code of Professional Ethics: draft for consultation*, CILIP.

Clark, C. (1990) *Photocopying from Books and Journals: a guide for all users of copyright and literary works*, British Copyright Council.

Collins, M. (2001) *The Law of Defamation and the Internet*, Oxford University Press.

Consumers International (2001) *Privacy@net: international comparative study of consumer privacy on the internet*.

Cornish, G. (2001) *Copyright: interpreting the law for libraries, archives and information services*, 3rd rev. edn, Library Association Publishing.

EIRENE (European Information Researchers Network) (1993), *Code of Practice for Information Brokers*.

European Commission (2000) *Data Protection in the European Union* [PF-39-99-008-EN-V-C].

Experian (no date) *A Simplified Guide to the Data Protection Act 1998: to assist businesses holding personal information on customers, suppliers, directors, shareholders and others.*

Law Commission (2001) *Electronic Commerce: formal requirements in commercial transactions.*

Law Commission (2002) *Defamation and the Internet: a preliminary investigation, Scoping study no. 2.*

Library Association (1995) *The Library Association Code of Professional Conduct and Guidance Notes*, 2nd edn.

Lloyd, I. (2000) *Legal Aspects of the Information Society*, Butterworths.

Lloyd, I. J. and Simpson, M. (1995) *Law on the Electronic Frontier, Hume papers on public policy Volume 2 No. 4*, available at www.strath.ac.uk/Departments/Law/dept/diglib/book/bookcon.html.

Lowenstein, J. (2002) *The Author's Due: printing and the prehistory of copyright*, University of Chicago Press.

Marett, P. (1996) *Intellectual Property Law*, 2nd edn, Sweet & Maxwell.

Marett, P. (2002) *Information Law in Practice*, Ashgate.

McLeod, T. and Cooling, P. (1990) *Law for Librarians: a handbook for librarians in England and Wales*, London, Library Association Publishing.

McNae, L. and Welsh, T. (2003), *McNae's Essential Law for Journalists*, 17th edn, Butterworths.

Norman, S. (1999a) *Copyright in Further and Higher Education Libraries*, 4th edn, Library Association Publishing.

Norman, S. (1999b) *Copyright in Health Libraries*, 3rd edn, Library Association Publishing.

Norman, S. (1999c) *Copyright in Industrial and Commercial Libraries*, 4th edn, Library Association Publishing.

Norman, S. (1999d) *Copyright in Public Libraries*, 4th edn, Library Association Publishing.

Norman, S. (1999e) *Copyright in School Libraries*, 4th edn, Library Association Publishing.

Norman, S. (1999f) *Copyright in Voluntary Sector Libraries*, 3rd edn, Library Association Publishing.

Norman, S. (2003) *Practical Copyright for Information Professionals*, Facet Publishing.

Office of the Information Commissioner (2000) *Using the Law to Protect Your Information.*

Open University (no date) *Intellectual Property Rights,* Open University B823.

Oppenheim, C. (2001), *The Legal and Regulatory Environment for Electronic Information*, 4th edn, Infonortics.

Oppenheim, C., Davies, E. and Warwood, A. (2000) *Data Protection: guide to the practical implementation of the Data Protection Act 1998*, 2nd edn, British Standards Institution [DISC PD 0012-1: 2000].

Oppenheim, C. and Muir, A. (2001) *Report on Developments World-Wide on National Information Policy Prepared for Re:Source and The Library Association*, available at www.la-hq.org.uk/directory/prof_issues/nip/title.htm.

Padfield, T. (2001) *Copyright for Archivists and Users of Archives*, Public Records Office.

Pedley, P. (2000), *Copyright for Library and Information Services Professionals*, 2nd edn, Aslib.

Schulz, C. and Baumgartner, J. (2001) *Don't Panic! Do E-commerce: a beginner's guide to European law affecting e-commerce*, European Commission Electronic Commerce Team.

Sherman, B. and Bently, L. (2001) *Intellectual Property Law*, Oxford University Press (reissue).

Singleton, S. (2003) *eCommerce: a practical guide to the law*, rev. edn.

Smith, G. (2002) *Internet Law and Regulation*, 3rd edn, Sweet & Maxwell.

Society of Authors (1997) *Copyright in Artistic Works, including Photographs.*

Society of Authors (1999) *Your Copyrights After Your Death.*

Society of Authors (2000) *Libel.*

Society of Authors (2002a) *Copyright and Moral Rights.*

Society of Authors (2002b) *Permissions.*

Tambini, D. (2002) *Ruled by Recluses?: privacy, journalism and the media after the Human Rights Act*, Institute for Public Policy Research.

Ticher, P. (2001) *Data Protection for Library and Information Services*, Aslib.

Index